Microsoft®

Exploring

Word 2002

Volume I

Microsoft®

Exploring

Word 2002

Volume I

Robert T. Grauer

University of Miami

Maryann Barber

University of Miami

PRENTICE HALL   *Upper Saddle River, New Jersey 07458*

Senior Acquisitions Editor: David Alexander
VP/Publisher: Natalie Anderson
Managing Editor: Melissa Whitaker
Assistant Editor: Kerri Limpert
Editorial Assistant: Maryann Broadnax
Technical Editor: Cecil Yarbrough
Media Project Manager: Cathleen Profitko
Marketing Assistant: Jason Smith
Production Manager: Gail Steier deAcevedo
Project Manager: Lynne Breitfeller
Production Editor: Greg Hubit
Associate Director, Manufacturing: Vincent Scelta
Manufacturing Buyer: Lynne Breitfeller
Design Manager: Pat Smythe
Interior Design: Jill Yutkowitz
Cover Design: Blair Brown
Cover Illustration: Marjorie Dressler
Composition: GTS
Printer/Binder: Banta Menasha

APPROVED COURSEWARE

What does this logo mean?

It means this courseware has been approved by the Microsoft® Office User Specialist Program to be among the finest available for learning **Word 2002**. It also means that upon completion of this courseware, you may be prepared to become a Microsoft Office User Specialist.

What is a Microsoft Office User Specialist?

A Microsoft Office User Specialist is an individual who has certified his or her skills in one or more of the Microsoft Office desktop applications of Microsoft Word, Microsoft Excel, Microsoft PowerPoint®, Microsoft Outlook® or Microsoft Access, or in Microsoft Project. The Microsoft Office User Specialist Program typically offers certification exams at the "Core" and "Expert" skill levels.* The Microsoft Office User Specialist Program is the only Microsoft approved program in the world for certifying proficiency in Microsoft Office desktop applications and Microsoft Project. This certification can be a valuable asset in any job search or career advancement.

More Information:

To learn more about becoming a Microsoft Office User Specialist, visit www.mous.net

To purchase a Microsoft Office User Specialist certification exam, visit www.DesktopIQ.com

To learn about other Microsoft Office User Specialist approved courseware from Prentice Hall, visit http://www.prenhall.com/phit/mous_frame.html

---

*The availability of Microsoft Office User Specialist certification exams varies by application, application version and language. Visit www.mous.net for exam availability.

CONTENTS

2

GAINING PROFICIENCY: EDITING AND FORMATTING   49

3

ENHANCING A DOCUMENT: THE WEB AND OTHER RESOURCES   103

4

ADVANCED FEATURES: OUTLINES, TABLES, STYLES, AND SELECTIONS 153

ESSENTIALS OF MICROSOFT® WINDOWS®

PREFACE

Continuing a tradition of excellence, Prentice Hall is proud to announce the latest update in Microsoft Office texts: the new Exploring Microsoft Office XP series by Robert T. Grauer and Maryann Barber.

The hands-on approach and conceptual framework of this comprehensive series helps students master all aspects of the Microsoft Office XP software, while providing the background necessary to transfer and use these skills in their personal and professional lives.

WHAT'S NEW IN THE EXPLORING OFFICE SERIES FOR XP

The entire Exploring Office series has been revised to include the new features found in the Office XP Suite, which contains Word 2002, Excel 2002, Access 2002, PowerPoint 2002, Publisher 2000, FrontPage 2002, and Outlook 2002.

In addition, this revision includes fully revised end-of-chapter material that provides an extensive review of concepts and techniques discussed in the chapter. Many of these exercises feature the World Wide Web and application integration.

Building on the success of the Web site provided for previous editions of this series, Exploring Office XP will introduce the MyPHLIP Companion Web site, a site customized for each instructor that includes on-line, interactive study guides, data file downloads, current news feeds, additional case studies and exercises, and other helpful information. Start out at www.prenhall.com/grauer to explore these resources!

Organization of the Exploring Office Series for XP

The new Exploring Microsoft Office XP series includes four combined Office XP texts from which to choose:

- ■ *Volume I* is MOUS certified in each of the major applications in the Office suite (Word, Excel, Access, and PowerPoint). Three additional modules (Essential Computer Concepts, Essentials of Windows, and Essentials of the Internet) are also included.

- ■ *Volume II* picks up where Volume I left off, covering the advanced topics for the individual applications. A VBA primer has been added.

- ■ The *Brief Microsoft Office XP* edition provides less coverage of the individual applications than Volume I (a total of 8 chapters as opposed to 14). The supplementary modules (Windows, Internet, and Concepts) are not included.

- ■ A new volume, *Getting Started with Office XP*, contains the first chapter from each application (Word, Excel, Access, and PowerPoint), plus three additional modules: Essentials of Windows, Essentials of the Internet, and Essential Computer Concepts.

Individual texts for Word 2002, Excel 2002, Access 2002, and PowerPoint 2002 provide complete coverage of the application and are MOUS certified. For shorter courses, we have created brief versions of the Exploring texts that give students a four-chapter introduction to each application. Each of these volumes is MOUS certified at the Core level.

To complete the full coverage of this series, custom modules on Microsoft Outlook 2002, Microsoft FrontPage 2002, Microsoft Publisher 2002, and a generic introduction to Microsoft Windows are also available.

APPROVED COURSEWARE

This book has been approved by Microsoft to be used in preparation for Microsoft Office User Specialist exams.

The Microsoft Office User Specialist (MOUS) program is globally recognized as the standard for demonstrating desktop skills with the Microsoft Office suite of business productivity applications (Microsoft Word, Microsoft Excel, Microsoft PowerPoint, Microsoft Access, and Microsoft Outlook). With a MOUS certification, thousands of people have demonstrated increased productivity and have proved their ability to utilize the advanced functionality of these Microsoft applications.

By encouraging individuals to develop advanced skills with Microsoft's leading business desktop software, the MOUS program helps fill the demand for qualified, knowledgeable people in the modern workplace. At the same time, MOUS helps satisfy an organization's need for a qualitative assessment of employee skills.

Customize the Exploring Office Series with Prentice Hall's Right PHit Binding Program

The Exploring Office XP series is part of the Right PHit Custom Binding Program, enabling instructors to create their own texts by selecting modules from Office XP Volume I, Volume II, Outlook, FrontPage, and Publisher to suit the needs of a specific course. An instructor could, for example, create a custom text consisting of the core modules in Word and Excel, coupled with the brief modules for Access and PowerPoint, and a brief introduction to computer concepts.

Instructors can also take advantage of Prentice Hall's Value Pack program to shrinkwrap multiple texts together at substantial savings to the student. A value pack is ideal in courses that require complete coverage of multiple applications.

The **Instructor's CD** that accompanies the Exploring Office series contains:

- Student data disks
- Solutions to all exercises and problems
- PowerPoint lectures
- Instructor's manuals in Word format enable the instructor to annotate portions of the instructor manual for distribution to the class
- A Windows-based test manager and the associated test bank in Word format

Prentice Hall's New MyPHLIP Companion Web site at www.prenhall.com/grauer offers current events, exercises, and downloadable supplements. This site also includes an on-line study guide containing true/false, multiple-choice, and essay questions.

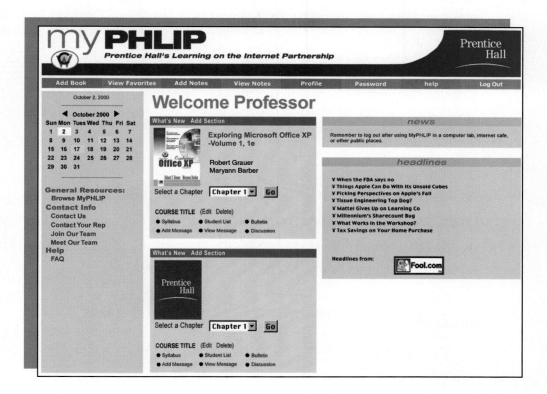

WebCT www.prenhall.com/webct

GOLD LEVEL CUSTOMER SUPPORT available exclusively to adopters of Prentice Hall courses is provided free-of-charge upon adoption and provides you with priority assistance, training discounts, and dedicated technical support.

Blackboard www.prenhall.com/blackboard

Prentice Hall's abundant on-line content, combined with Blackboard's popular tools and interface, result in robust Web-based courses that are easy to implement, manage, and use—taking your courses to new heights in student interaction and learning.

CourseCompass www.coursecompass.com

CourseCompass is a dynamic, interactive on-line course management tool powered by Blackboard. This exciting product allows you to teach with marketing-leading Pearson Education content in an easy-to-use customizable format.

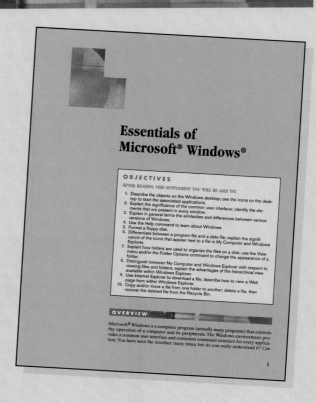

Exploring Microsoft Office XP assumes no prior knowledge of the operating system. A 64-page section introduces the reader to the Essentials of Windows and provides an overview of the operating system. Students are shown the necessary file-management operations to use Microsoft Office successfully.

In-depth tutorials throughout all the Office XP applications enhance the conceptual introduction to each task and guide the student at the computer. Every step in every exercise has a full-color screen shot to illustrate the specific commands. Boxed tips provide alternative techniques and shortcuts and/or anticipate errors that students may make.

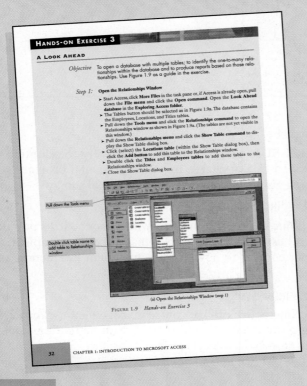

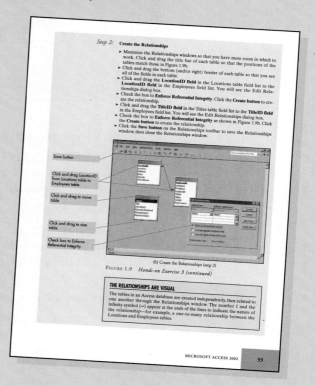

The authors have created an entirely new set of end-of-chapter exercises for every chapter in all of the applications. These new exercises have been written to provide the utmost in flexibility, variety, and difficulty.

Web-based Practice exercises and On Your Own exercises are marked by an icon in the margin and allow further exploration and practice via the World Wide Web.

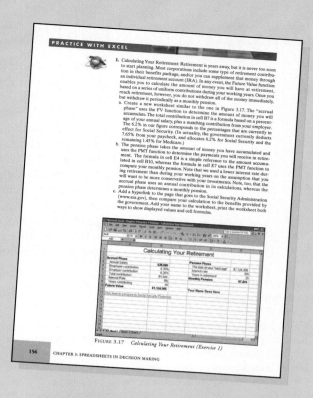

FIGURE 3.17   *Calculating Your Retirement (Exercise 1)*

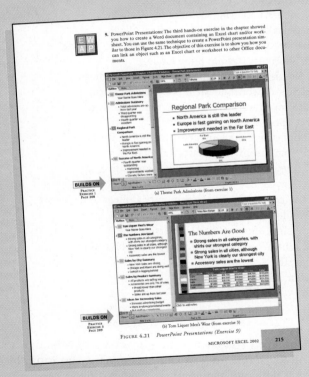

FIGURE 4.21   *PowerPoint Presentations (Exercise 9)*

Integration Exercises are marked by an icon in the margin. These exercises take advantage of the Microsoft Office Suite's power to use multiple applications in one document, spreadsheet, or presentation.

Builds On Exercises require students to use selected application files as the starting point in later exercises, thereby introducing new information to students only as needed.

The end-of-chapter material includes multiple-choice questions for self-evaluation plus additional "on your own" exercises to encourage the reader to further explore the application.

We want to thank the many individuals who have helped to bring this project to fruition. David Alexander, senior editor at Prentice Hall, has provided new leadership in extending the series to Office XP. Cathi Profitko did an absolutely incredible job on our Web site. Melissa Whitaker coordinated the myriad details of production and the certification process. Greg Christofferson was instrumental in the acquisition of supporting software. Lynne Breitfeller was the project manager and manufacturing buyer. Greg Hubit has been masterful as the external production editor for every book in the series. Cecil Yarbrough did an outstanding job in checking the manuscript for technical accuracy. Chuck Cox did his usual fine work as copyeditor. Kerri Limpert was the supplements editor. Cindy Stevens, Tom McKenzie, and Michael Olmstead wrote the instructor manuals. Patricia Smythe developed the innovative and attractive design. We also want to acknowledge our reviewers who, through their comments and constructive criticism, greatly improved the series.

Lynne Band, Middlesex Community College
Don Belle, Central Piedmont Community College
Stuart P. Brian, Holy Family College
Carl M. Briggs, Indiana University School of Business
Kimberly Chambers, Scottsdale Community College
Alok Charturvedi, Purdue University
Jerry Chin, Southwest Missouri State University
Dean Combellick, Scottsdale Community College
Cody Copeland, Johnson County Community College
Larry S. Corman, Fort Lewis College
Janis Cox, Tri-County Technical College
Martin Crossland, Southwest Missouri State University
Paul E. Daurelle, Western Piedmont Community College
Carolyn DiLeo, Westchester Community College
Judy Dolan, Palomar College
David Douglas, University of Arkansas
Carlotta Eaton, Radford University
Judith M. Fitspatrick, Gulf Coast Community College
James Franck, College of St. Scholastica
Raymond Frost, Central Connecticut State University
Midge Gerber, Southwestern Oklahoma State University
James Gips, Boston College
Vernon Griffin, Austin Community College
Ranette Halverson, Midwestern State University
Michael Hassett, Fort Hays State University
Mike Hearn, Community College of Philadelphia
Wanda D. Heller, Seminole Community College
Bonnie Homan, San Francisco State University
Ernie Ivey, Polk Community College
Mike Kelly, Community College of Rhode Island
Jane King, Everett Community College

Rose M. Laird, Northern Virginia Community College
John Lesson, University of Central Florida
David B. Meinert, Southwest Missouri State University
Alan Moltz, Naugatuck Valley Technical Community College
Kim Montney, Kellogg Community College
Bill Morse, DeVry Institute of Technology
Kevin Pauli, University of Nebraska
Mary McKenry Percival, University of Miami
Delores Pusins, Hillsborough Community College
Gale E. Rand, College Misericordia
Judith Rice, Santa Fe Community College
David Rinehard, Lansing Community College
Marilyn Salas, Scottsdale Community College
John Shepherd, Duquesne University
Barbara Sherman, Buffalo State College
Robert Spear, Prince George's Community College
Michael Stewardson, San Jacinto College—North
Helen Stoloff, Hudson Valley Community College
Margaret Thomas, Ohio University
Mike Thomas, Indiana University School of Business
Suzanne Tomlinson, Iowa State University
Karen Tracey, Central Connecticut State University
Antonio Vargas, El Paso Community College
Sally Visci, Lorain County Community College
David Weiner, University of San Francisco
Connie Wells, Georgia State University
Wallace John Whistance-Smith, Ryerson Polytechnic University
Jack Zeller, Kirkwood Community College

A final word of thanks to the unnamed students at the University of Miami, who make it all worthwhile. Most of all, thanks to you, our readers, for choosing this book. Please feel free to contact us with any comments and suggestions.

Robert T. Grauer
rgrauer@miami.edu
www.bus.miami.edu/~rgrauer
www.prenhall.com/grauer

Maryann Barber
mbarber@miami.edu
www.bus.miami.edu/~mbarber

CHAPTER 1

Microsoft® Word 2002: What Will Word Processing Do for Me?

OBJECTIVES

AFTER READING THIS CHAPTER YOU WILL BE ABLE TO:

1. Define word wrap; differentiate between a hard and a soft return.
2. Distinguish between the insert and overtype modes.
3. Describe the elements on the Microsoft Word screen.
4. Create, save, retrieve, edit, and print a simple document.
5. Check a document for spelling; describe the function of the custom dictionary.
6. Describe the AutoCorrect and AutoText features; explain how either feature can be used to create a personal shorthand.
7. Use the thesaurus to look up synonyms and antonyms.
8. Explain the objectives and limitations of the grammar check; customize the grammar check for business or casual writing.
9. Differentiate between the Save and Save As commands; describe various backup options that can be selected.

OVERVIEW

Have you ever produced what you thought was the perfect term paper only to discover that you omitted a sentence or misspelled a word, or that the paper was three pages too short or one page too long? Wouldn't it be nice to make the necessary changes, and then be able to reprint the entire paper with the touch of a key? Welcome to the world of word processing, where you are no longer stuck with having to retype anything. Instead, you retrieve your work from disk, display it on the monitor and revise it as necessary, then print it at any time, in draft or final form.

1

This chapter provides a broad-based introduction to word processing in general and Microsoft Word in particular. We begin by presenting (or perhaps reviewing) the essential concepts of a word processor, then show you how these concepts are implemented in Word. We show you how to create a document, how to save it on disk, then retrieve the document you just created. We introduce you to the spell check and thesaurus, two essential tools in any word processor. We also present the grammar check as a convenient way of finding a variety of errors but remind you there is no substitute for carefully proofreading the final document.

THE BASICS OF WORD PROCESSING

All word processors adhere to certain basic concepts that must be understood if you are to use the programs effectively. The next several pages introduce ideas that are applicable to any word processor (and which you may already know). We follow the conceptual material with a hands-on exercise that enables you to apply what you have learned.

The Insertion Point

The *insertion point* is a flashing vertical line that marks the place where text will be entered. The insertion point is always at the beginning of a new document, but it can be moved anywhere within an existing document. If, for example, you wanted to add text to the end of a document, you would move the insertion point to the end of the document, then begin typing.

Word Wrap

A newcomer to word processing has one major transition to make from a typewriter, and it is an absolutely critical adjustment. Whereas a typist returns the carriage at the end of every line, just the opposite is true of a word processor. One types continually *without* pressing the enter key at the end of a line because the word processor automatically wraps text from one line to the next. This concept is known as *word wrap* and is illustrated in Figure 1.1.

The word *primitive* does not fit on the current line in Figure 1.1a, and is automatically shifted to the next line, *without* the user having to press the enter key. The user continues to enter the document, with additional words being wrapped to subsequent lines as necessary. The only time you use the enter key is at the end of a paragraph, or when you want the insertion point to move to the next line and the end of the current line doesn't reach the right margin.

Word wrap is closely associated with another concept, that of hard and soft returns. A *hard return* is created by the user when he or she presses the enter key at the end of a paragraph; a *soft return* is created by the word processor as it wraps text from one line to the next. The locations of the soft returns change automatically as a document is edited (e.g., as text is inserted or deleted, or as margins or fonts are changed). The locations of the hard returns can be changed only by the user, who must intentionally insert or delete each hard return.

There are two hard returns in Figure 1.1b, one at the end of each paragraph. There are also six soft returns in the first paragraph (one at the end of every line except the last) and three soft returns in the second paragraph. Now suppose the margins in the document are made smaller (that is, the line is made longer) as shown in Figure 1.1c. The number of soft returns drops to four and two (in the first and second paragraphs, respectively) as more text fits on a line and fewer lines are needed. The revised document still contains the two original hard returns, one at the end of each paragraph.

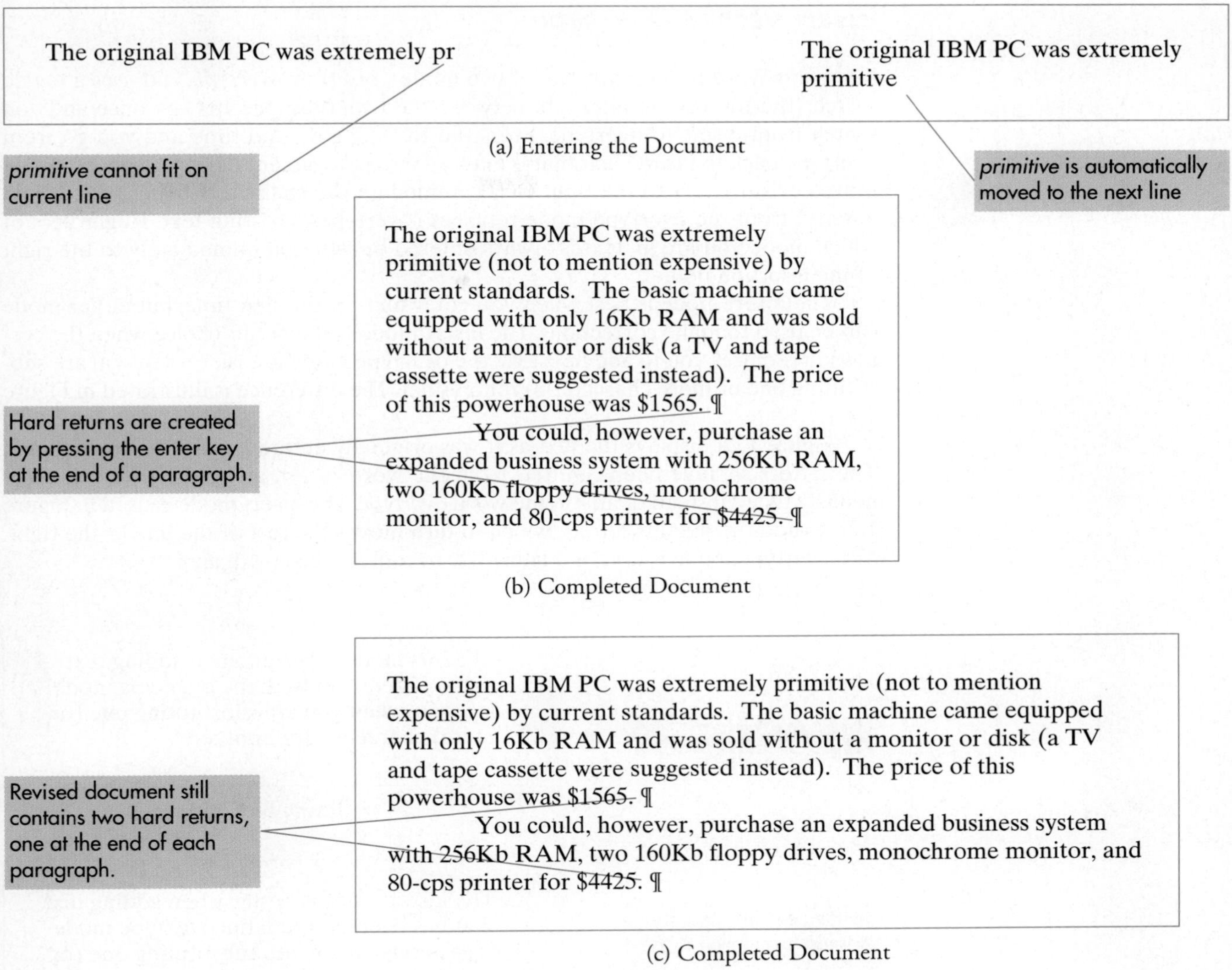

The original IBM PC was extremely pr

The original IBM PC was extremely primitive

(a) Entering the Document

primitive cannot fit on current line

primitive is automatically moved to the next line

The original IBM PC was extremely primitive (not to mention expensive) by current standards. The basic machine came equipped with only 16Kb RAM and was sold without a monitor or disk (a TV and tape cassette were suggested instead). The price of this powerhouse was $1565. ¶
You could, however, purchase an expanded business system with 256Kb RAM, two 160Kb floppy drives, monochrome monitor, and 80-cps printer for $4425. ¶

Hard returns are created by pressing the enter key at the end of a paragraph.

(b) Completed Document

The original IBM PC was extremely primitive (not to mention expensive) by current standards. The basic machine came equipped with only 16Kb RAM and was sold without a monitor or disk (a TV and tape cassette were suggested instead). The price of this powerhouse was $1565. ¶
You could, however, purchase an expanded business system with 256Kb RAM, two 160Kb floppy drives, monochrome monitor, and 80-cps printer for $4425. ¶

Revised document still contains two hard returns, one at the end of each paragraph.

(c) Completed Document

FIGURE 1.1   *Word Wrap*

Toggle Switches

Suppose you sat down at the keyboard and typed an entire sentence without pressing the Shift key; the sentence would be in all lowercase letters. Then you pressed the Caps Lock key and retyped the sentence, again without pressing the Shift key. This time the sentence would be in all uppercase letters. You could repeat the process as often as you like. Each time you pressed the Caps Lock key, the sentence would switch from lowercase to uppercase and vice versa.

The point of this exercise is to introduce the concept of a ***toggle switch***, a device that causes the computer to alternate between two states. The Caps Lock key is an example of a toggle switch. Each time you press it, newly typed text will change from uppercase to lowercase and back again. We will see several other examples of toggle switches as we proceed in our discussion of word processing.

Insert versus Overtype

Microsoft Word is always in one of two modes, **insert** or **overtype**, and uses a toggle switch (the Ins key) to alternate between the two. Press the Ins key once and you switch from insert to overtype. Press the Ins key a second time and you go from overtype back to insert. Text that is entered into a document during the insert mode moves existing text to the right to accommodate the characters being added. Text entered from the overtype mode replaces (overtypes) existing text. Regardless of which mode you are in, text is always entered or replaced immediately to the right of the insertion point.

The insert mode is best when you enter text for the first time, but either mode can be used to make corrections. The insert mode is the better choice when the correction requires you to add new text; the overtype mode is easier when you are substituting one or more character(s) for another. The difference is illustrated in Figure 1.2.

Figure 1.2a displays the text as it was originally entered, with two misspellings. The letters *se* have been omitted from the word *insert,* and an *x* has been erroneously typed instead of an *r* in the word *overtype.* The insert mode is used in Figure 1.2b to add the missing letters, which in turn moves the rest of the line to the right. The overtype mode is used in Figure 1.2c to replace the *x* with an *r.*

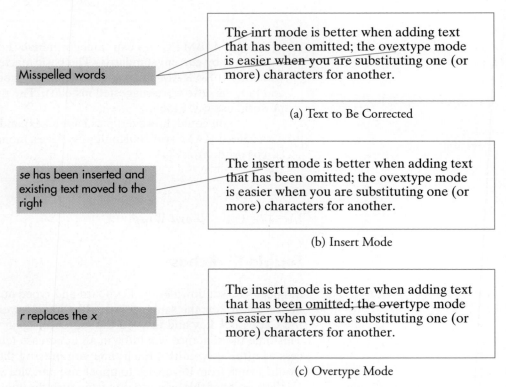

(a) Text to Be Corrected

(b) Insert Mode

(c) Overtype Mode

FIGURE 1.2   *Insert and Overtype Modes*

Deleting Text

The Backspace and Del keys delete one character immediately to the left or right of the insertion point, respectively. The choice between them depends on when you need to erase a character(s). The Backspace key is easier if you want to delete a character immediately after typing it. The Del key is preferable during subsequent editing.

You can delete several characters at one time by selecting (dragging the mouse over) the characters to be deleted, then pressing the Del key. And finally, you can delete and replace text in one operation by selecting the text to be replaced and then typing the new text in its place.

LEARN TO TYPE

The ultimate limitation of any word processor is the speed at which you enter data; hence the ability to type quickly is invaluable. Learning how to type is easy, especially with the availability of computer-based typing programs. As little as a half hour a day for a couple of weeks will have you up to speed, and if you do any significant amount of writing at all, the investment will pay off many times.

INTRODUCTION TO MICROSOFT WORD

We used Microsoft Word to write this book, as can be inferred from the screen in Figure 1.3. Your screen will be different from ours in many ways. You will not have the same document nor is it likely that you will customize Word in exactly the same way. You should, however, be able to recognize the basic elements that are found in the Microsoft Word window that is open on the desktop.

There are actually two open windows in Figure 1.3—an application window for Microsoft Word and a document window for the specific document on which you are working. The application window has its own Minimize, Maximize (or Restore) and Close buttons. The document window has only a Close button. There is, however, only one title bar that appears at the top of the application window and it reflects the application (Microsoft Word) as well as the document name (Word Chapter 1). A menu bar appears immediately below the title bar. Vertical and horizontal scroll bars appear at the right and bottom of the document window. The Windows taskbar appears at the bottom of the screen and shows the open applications.

Microsoft Word is also part of the Microsoft Office suite of applications, and thus shares additional features with Excel, Access, and PowerPoint, that are also part of the Office suite. *Toolbars* provide immediate access to common commands and appear immediately below the menu bar. The toolbars can be displayed or hidden using the Toolbars command in the *View menu*.

The *Standard toolbar* contains buttons corresponding to the most basic commands in Word—for example, opening a file or printing a document. The icon on the button is intended to be indicative of its function (e.g., a printer to indicate the Print command). You can also point to the button to display a *ScreenTip* showing the name of the button. The *Formatting toolbar* appears under the Standard toolbar and provides access to such common formatting operations as boldface, italics, or underlining.

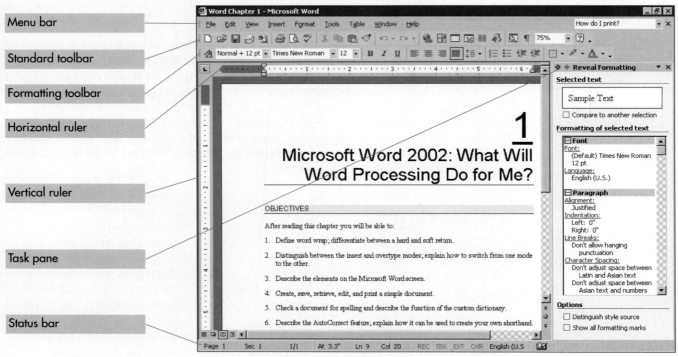

Menu bar

Standard toolbar

Formatting toolbar

Horizontal ruler

Vertical ruler

Task pane

Status bar

FIGURE 1.3 *Microsoft Word*

The toolbars may appear overwhelming at first, but there is absolutely no need to memorize what the individual buttons do. That will come with time. We suggest, however, that you will have a better appreciation for the various buttons if you consider them in groups, according to their general function, as shown in Figure 1.4a. Note, too, that many of the commands in the pull-down menus are displayed with an image that corresponds to a button on a toolbar.

The *horizontal ruler* is displayed underneath the toolbars and enables you to change margins, tabs, and/or indents for all or part of a document. A *vertical ruler* shows the vertical position of text on the page and can be used to change the top or bottom margins.

The *status bar* at the bottom of the document window displays the location of the insertion point (or information about the command being executed). The status bar also shows the status (settings) of various indicators—for example, OVR to show that Word is in the overtype, as opposed to the insert, mode.

THE TASK PANE

All applications in Office XP provide access to a *task pane* that facilitates the execution of subsequent commands. (Microsoft refers to the suite as Office XP, but designates the individual applications as version 2002.) The task pane serves many functions. It can be used to display the formatting properties of selected text, open an existing document, or search for appropriate clip art. The task pane will open automatically in response to certain commands. It can also be toggled open or closed through the Task pane command in the View menu. The task pane is discussed in more detail throughout the chapter.

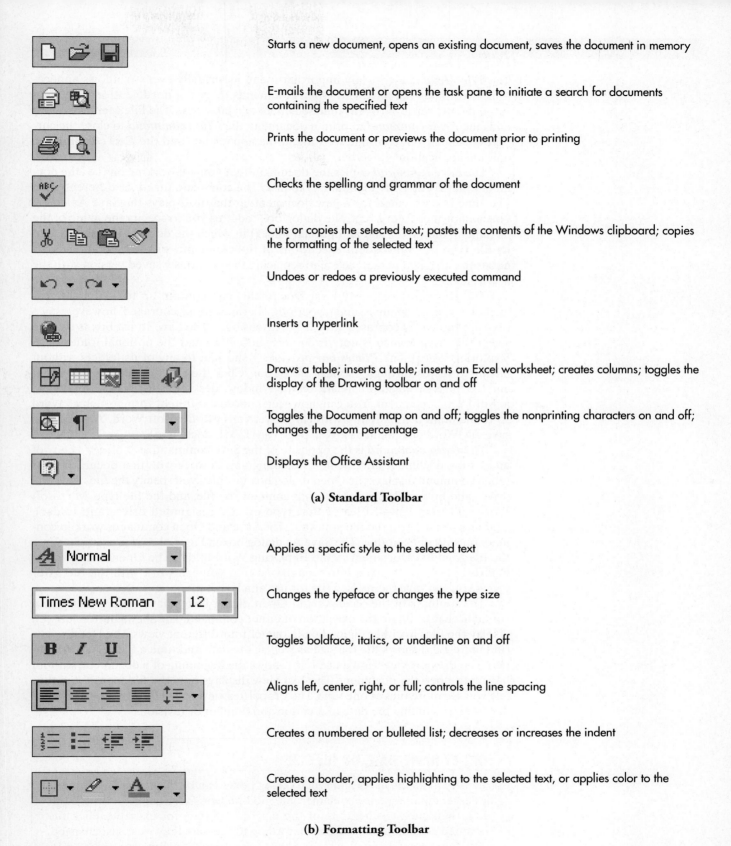

Starts a new document, opens an existing document, saves the document in memory

E-mails the document or opens the task pane to initiate a search for documents containing the specified text

Prints the document or previews the document prior to printing

Checks the spelling and grammar of the document

Cuts or copies the selected text; pastes the contents of the Windows clipboard; copies the formatting of the selected text

Undoes or redoes a previously executed command

Inserts a hyperlink

Draws a table; inserts a table; inserts an Excel worksheet; creates columns; toggles the display of the Drawing toolbar on and off

Toggles the Document map on and off; toggles the nonprinting characters on and off; changes the zoom percentage

Displays the Office Assistant

(a) Standard Toolbar

Applies a specific style to the selected text

Changes the typeface or changes the type size

Toggles boldface, italics, or underline on and off

Aligns left, center, right, or full; controls the line spacing

Creates a numbered or bulleted list; decreases or increases the indent

Creates a border, applies highlighting to the selected text, or applies color to the selected text

(b) Formatting Toolbar

FIGURE 1.4 *Toolbars*

The *File Menu* is a critically important menu in virtually every Windows application. It contains the Save and Open commands to save a document on disk, then subsequently retrieve (open) that document at a later time. The File Menu also contains the *Print command* to print a document, the *Close command* to close the current document but continue working in the application, and the *Exit command* to quit the application altogether.

The *Save command* copies the document that you are working on (i.e., the document that is currently in memory) to disk. The command functions differently the first time it is executed for a new document, in that it displays the Save As dialog box as shown in Figure 1.5a. The dialog box requires you to specify the name of the document, the drive (and an optional folder) in which the document is stored, and its file type. All subsequent executions of the command will save the document under the assigned name, each time replacing the previously saved version with the new version.

The *file name* (e.g., My First Document) can contain up to 255 characters including spaces, commas, and/or periods. (Periods are discouraged, however, since they are too easily confused with DOS extensions.) The Save In list box is used to select the drive (which is not visible in Figure 1.5a) and the optional folder (e.g., Exploring Word). The *Places bar* provides a shortcut to any of its folders without having to search through the Save In list box. Click the Desktop icon, for example, and the file is saved automatically on the Windows desktop. The *file type* defaults to a Word 2002 document. You can, however, choose a different format such as Word 95 to maintain compatibility with earlier versions of Microsoft Word. You can also save any Word document as a Web page (or HTML document).

The *Open command* is the opposite of the Save command as it brings a copy of an existing document into memory, enabling you to work with that document. The Open command displays the Open dialog box in which you specify the file name, the drive (and optionally the folder) that contains the file, and the file type. Microsoft Word will then list all files of that type on the designated drive (and folder), enabling you to open the file you want. The Save and Open commands work in conjunction with one another. The Save As dialog box in Figure 1.5a, for example, saves the file My First Document in the Exploring Word folder. The Open dialog box in Figure 1.5b loads that file into memory so that you can work with the file, after which you can save the revised file for use at a later time.

The toolbars in the Save As and Open dialog boxes have several buttons in common that facilitate the execution of either command. The Views button lets you display the files in either dialog box in one of four different views. The Details view (in Figure 1.5a) shows the file size as well as the date and time a file was last modified. The Preview view (in Figure 1.5b) shows the beginning of a document, without having to open the document. The List view displays only the file names, and thus lets you see more files at one time. The Properties view shows information about the document, including the date of creation and number of revisions.

SORT BY NAME, DATE, OR FILE SIZE

The files in the Save As and Open dialog boxes can be displayed in ascending or descending sequence by name, date modified, or size. Change to the Details view, then click the heading of the desired column; for example, click the Modified column to list the files according to the date they were last changed. Click the column heading a second time to reverse the sequence.

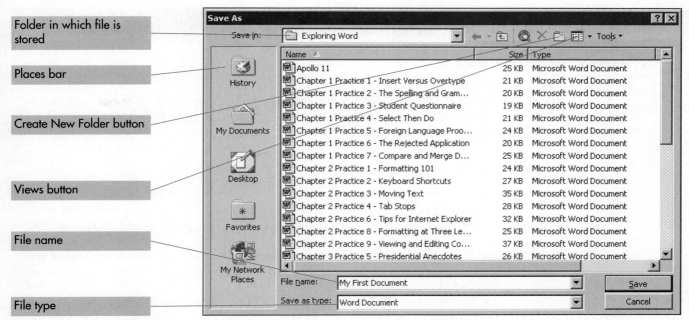

Folder in which file is stored

Places bar

Create New Folder button

Views button

File name

File type

(a) Save As Dialog Box (details view)

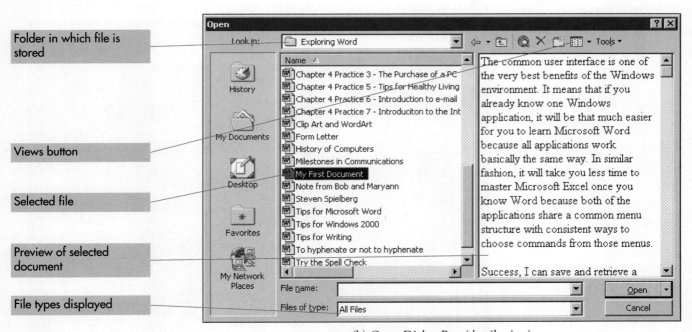

Folder in which file is stored

Views button

Selected file

Preview of selected document

File types displayed

(b) Open Dialog Box (details view)

FIGURE 1.5 *The Save and Open Commands*

LEARNING BY DOING

Every chapter contains a series of hands-on exercises that enable you to apply what you learn at the computer. The exercises in this chapter are linked to one another in that you create a simple document in exercise one, then open and edit that document in exercise two. The ability to save and open a document is critical, and you do not want to spend an inordinate amount of time entering text unless you are confident in your ability to retrieve it later.

MY FIRST DOCUMENT

Objective To start Microsoft Word in order to create, save, and print a simple document; to execute commands via the toolbar or from pull-down menus. Use Figure 1.6 as a guide in doing the exercise.

Step 1: **The Windows Desktop**

> ➤ Turn on the computer and all of its peripherals. The floppy drive should be empty prior to starting your machine. This ensures that the system starts from the hard disk, which contains the Windows files, as opposed to a floppy disk, which does not.
> ➤ Your system will take a minute or so to get started, after which you should see the Windows desktop in Figure 1.6a. Do not be concerned if the appearance of your desktop is different from ours.
> ➤ You may see a Welcome to Windows dialog box with command buttons to take a tour of the operating system. If so, click the appropriate button(s) or close the dialog box.
> ➤ You should be familiar with basic file management and very comfortable moving and copying files from one folder to another. If not, you may want to review this material.

Start button

(a) The Windows Desktop (step 1)

FIGURE 1.6 *Hands-on Exercise 1*

Step 2:   **Obtain the Practice Files**

➤ We have created a series of practice files (also called a "data disk") for you to use throughout the text. Your instructor will make these files available to you in a variety of ways:

• The files may be on a network drive, in which case you use Windows Explorer to copy the files from the network to a floppy disk.

• There may be an actual "data disk" that you are to check out from the lab in order to use the Copy Disk command to duplicate the disk.

➤ You can also download the files from our Web site provided you have an Internet connection. Start Internet Explorer, then go to the Exploring Windows home page at **www.prenhall.com/grauer**.

• Click the book for **Office XP**, which takes you to the Office XP home page. Click the **Student Resources tab** (at the top of the window) to go to the Student Resources page as shown in Figure 1.6b.

• Click the link to **Student Data Disk** (in the left frame), then scroll down the page until you can select Word 2002. Click the link to download the student data disk.

• You will see the File Download dialog box asking what you want to do. The option button to save this program to disk is selected. Click **OK**. The Save As dialog box appears.

• Click the *down arrow* in the Save In list box to enter the drive and folder where you want to save the file. It's best to save the file to the Windows desktop or to a temporary folder on drive C.

• Double click the file after it has been downloaded to your PC, then follow the onscreen instructions.

➤ Check with your instructor for additional information.

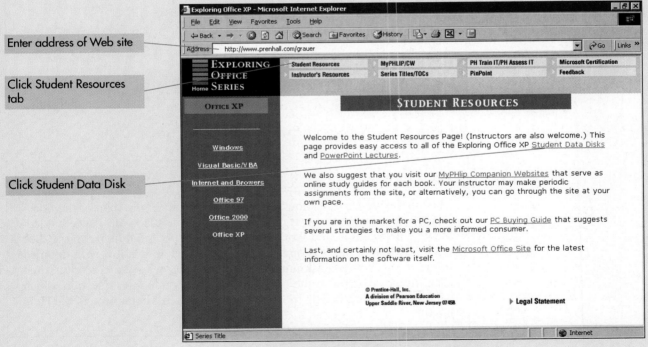

(b) Obtain the Practice Files (step 2)

FIGURE 1.6   *Hands-on Exercise 1 (continued)*

Step 3: **Start Microsoft Word**

➤ Click the **Start button** to display the Start menu. Click (or point to) the Programs menu, then click **Microsoft Word 2002** to start the program.

➤ You should see a blank document within the Word application window. (Click the **New Blank document** button on the Standard toolbar if you do not see a document.) Close the task pane if it is open.

➤ Click and drag the Office Assistant out of the way. (The Assistant is illustrated in step six of this exercise.)

➤ Do not be concerned if your screen is different from ours as we include a troubleshooting section immediately following the exercise.

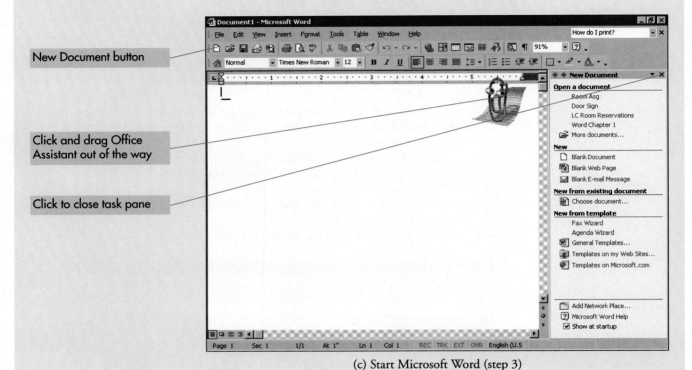

New Document button

Click and drag Office Assistant out of the way

Click to close task pane

(c) Start Microsoft Word (step 3)

FIGURE 1.6 *Hands-on Exercise 1 (continued)*

ASK A QUESTION

Click in the "Ask a Question" list box that appears at the right of the document window, enter the text of a question such as "How do I save a document?", press enter, and Word returns a list of potential help topics. Click any topic that appears promising to open the Help window with detailed information. You can ask multiple questions during a Word session, then click the down arrow in the list box to return to an earlier question, which will return you to the help topics. You can also access help through the Help menu.

Step 4: **Create the Document**

➤ Create the document in Figure 1.6d. Type just as you would on a typewriter with one exception; do *not* press the enter key at the end of a line because Word will automatically wrap text from one line to the next.

➤ Press the **enter key** at the end of the paragraph.

➤ You may see a red or green wavy line to indicate spelling or grammatical errors, respectively. Both features are discussed later in the chapter.

➤ Point to the red wavy line (if any), click the **right mouse button** to display a list of suggested corrections, then click (select) the appropriate substitution.

➤ Ignore the green wavy line (if any).

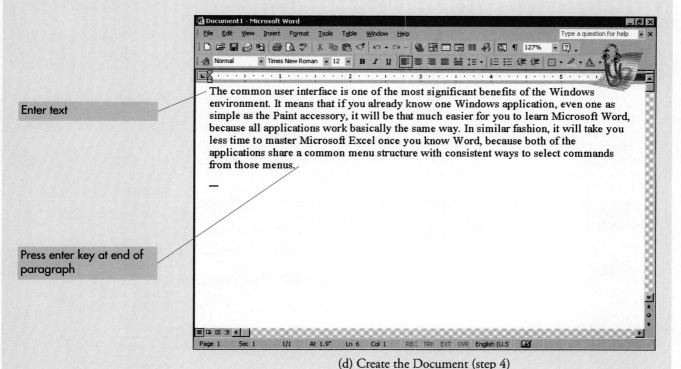

(d) Create the Document (step 4)

FIGURE 1.6   *Hands-on Exercise 1 (continued)*

SEPARATE THE TOOLBARS

You may see the Standard and Formatting toolbars displayed on one row to save space within the application window. If so, we suggest that you separate the toolbars, so that you see all of the buttons on each. Click the Toolbar Options down arrow that appears at the end of any visible toolbar to display toolbar options, then click the option to show the buttons on two rows. Click the down arrow a second time to show the buttons on one row if you want to return to the other configuration.

Step 5: **Save the Document**

➤ Pull down the **File menu** and click **Save** (or click the **Save button** on the Standard toolbar). You should see the Save As dialog box in Figure 1.6e.
➤ If necessary, click the **drop-down arrow** on the View button and select the **Details view**, so that the display on your monitor matches our figure. (The title bar shows Document1 because the file has not yet been saved.)
➤ To save the file:
  • Click the **drop-down arrow** on the Save In list box.
  • Click the appropriate drive, e.g., drive C or drive A, depending on whether or not you installed the data disk on your hard drive.
  • Double click the **Exploring Word folder**, to make it the active folder (the folder in which you will save the document).
  • Click and drag over the default entry in the File name text box. Type **My First Document** as the name of your document. (A DOC extension will be added automatically when the file is saved to indicate that this is a Word document.)
  • Click **Save** or press the **enter key**. The title bar changes to reflect the new document name (My First Document).
➤ Add your name at the end of the document, then click the **Save button** on the Standard toolbar to save the document with the revision.
➤ This time the Save As dialog box does not appear, since Word already knows the name of the document.

Title bar shows Document1

Save button

Click to select drive/folder

Views button

Enter file name

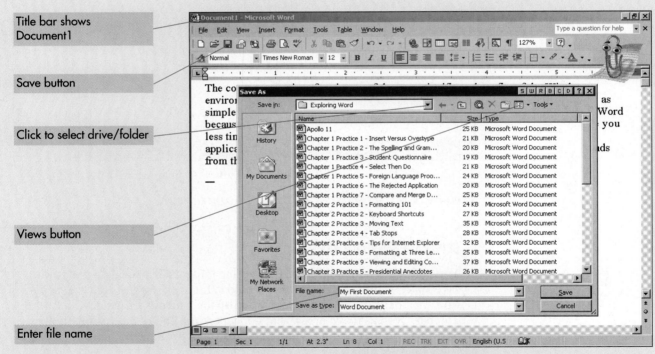

(e) Save the Document (step 5)

FIGURE 1.6 *Hands-on Exercise 1 (continued)*

Step 6: **The Office Assistant**

➤ If necessary, pull down the **Help menu** and click the command to **Show the Office Assistant**. You may see a different character than the one we have selected.
➤ Click the **Assistant**, enter the question, **How do I print?** as shown in Figure 1.6f, then click the **Search button** to look for the answer. The size of the Assistant's balloon expands as the Assistant suggests several topics that may be appropriate.
➤ Click the topic, **Print a document**, which in turn displays a Help window that contains links to various topics, each with detailed information. Click the **Office Assistant** to hide the balloon (or drag the Assistant out of the way).
➤ Click any of the links in the Help window to read the information. You can print the contents of any topic by clicking the **Print button** in the Help window. Close the Help window when you are finished.

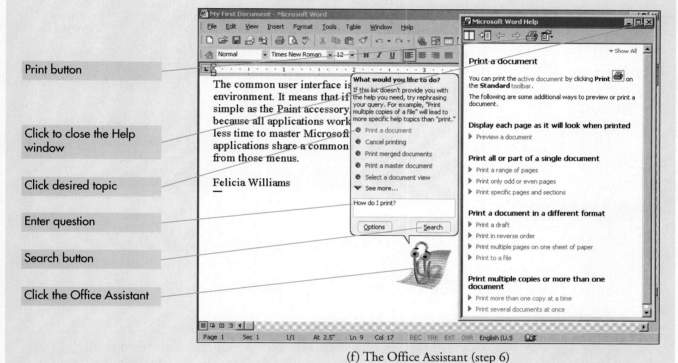

Print button

Click to close the Help window

Click desired topic

Enter question

Search button

Click the Office Assistant

(f) The Office Assistant (step 6)

FIGURE 1.6 *Hands-on Exercise 1 (continued)*

TIP OF THE DAY

You can set the Office Assistant to greet you with a "tip of the day" each time you start Word. Click the Microsoft Word Help button (or press the F1 key) to display the Assistant, then click the Options button to display the Office Assistant dialog box. Click the Options tab, then check the Show the Tip of the Day at Startup box and click OK. The next time you start Microsoft Word, you will be greeted by the Assistant, who will offer you the tip of the day.

Step 7: **Print the Document**

➤ You can print the document in one of two ways:
  • Pull down the **File menu**. Click **Print** to display the dialog box of Figure 1.6g. Click the **OK command button** to print the document.
  • Click the **Print button** on the Standard toolbar to print the document immediately without displaying the Print dialog box.
➤ Submit this document to your instructor.

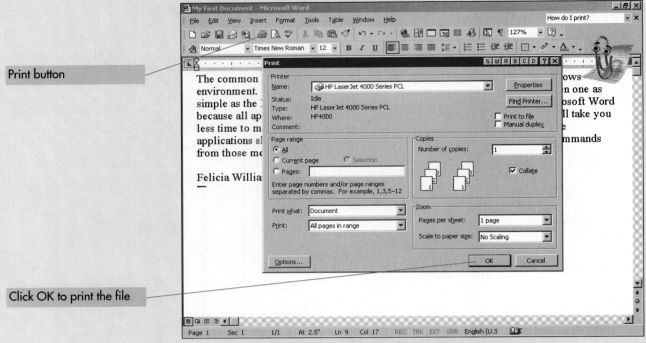

Print button

Click OK to print the file

(g) Print the Document (step 7)

FIGURE 1.6 *Hands-on Exercise 1 (continued)*

ABOUT MICROSOFT WORD

Pull down the Help menu and click About Microsoft Word to display the specific version number and other licensing information, including the product ID. This help screen also contains two very useful command buttons, System Information and Technical Support. The first button displays information about the hardware installed on your system, including the amount of memory and available space on the hard drive. The Technical Support button describes various ways to obtain technical assistance.

Step 8: **Close the Document**

➤ Pull down the **File menu**. Click **Close** to close this document but remain in Word. (If you don't see the Close command, click the **double arrow** at the bottom of the menu.) Click **Yes** if prompted to save the document.
➤ Pull down the **File menu** a second time. Click **Exit** to close Word if you do not want to continue with the next exercise at this time.

MODIFYING AN EXISTING DOCUMENT

Objective   To open an existing document, revise it, and save the revision; to use the Undo, Redo, and Help commands. Use Figure 1.8 as a guide in doing the exercise.

Step 1:   **Open an Existing Document**

> ➤ Start Word. Click and drag the Assistant out of the way if it appears. Close the task pane if it is open because we want you to practice locating a document within the Open dialog box.
> ➤ Pull down the **File menu** and click the **Open command** (or click the **Open button** on the Standard toolbar). You should see an Open dialog box similar to Figure 1.8a.
> ➤ If necessary, click the **drop-down arrow** on the Views button and change to the Details view. Click and drag the vertical border between columns to increase (decrease) the size of a column.
> ➤ Click the **drop-down arrow** on the Look in list box. Select (click) the drive that contains the Exploring Windows folder. Double click the folder to open it.
> ➤ Click the **down arrow** on the vertical scroll bar until you can select **My First Document** from the previous exercise.
> ➤ Double click the document (or click the **Open button** within the dialog box). Your document should appear on the screen.

Open button

Click to select drive/folder

Views button

Click My First Document

Click to scroll through file names

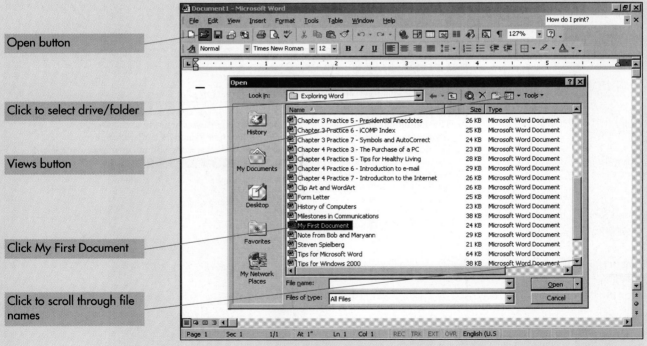

(a) Open an Existing Document (step 1)

FIGURE 1.8   *Hands-on Exercise 2*

Step 2: **Troubleshooting**

➤ Modify the settings within Word so that the document on your screen matches Figure 1.8b.

- To separate the Standard and Formatting toolbars, pull down the **Tools menu**, click **Customize**, click the **Options tab**, then check the box that indicates the Standard and Formatting toolbars should be displayed on two rows. Click the **Close button**.

- To display the complete menus, pull down the **Tools menu**, click **Customize**, click the **Options tab**, then check the box to always show full menus. Click the **Close Button**.

- To change to the Normal view, pull down the **View menu** and click **Normal** (or click the **Normal View button** at the bottom of the window).

- To change the amount of text that is visible on the screen, click the **drop-down arrow** on the **Zoom box** on the Standard toolbar and select **Page Width**.

- To display (hide) the ruler, pull down the **View menu** and toggle the **Ruler command** on or off. End with the ruler on. (If you don't see the Ruler command, click the **double arrow** at the bottom of the menu, or use the **Options command** in the Tools menu to display the complete menus.)

- To show or hide the Office Assistant, pull down the **Help menu** and click the appropriate command.

- Pull down the **View menu** and click the **Toolbars command** to display or hide additional toolbars.

➤ Click the **Show/Hide ¶ button** to display or hide the hard returns as you see fit. The button functions as a toggle switch.

➤ There may still be subtle differences between your screen and ours, depending on the resolution of your monitor. These variations, if any, need not concern you as long as you are able to complete the exercise.

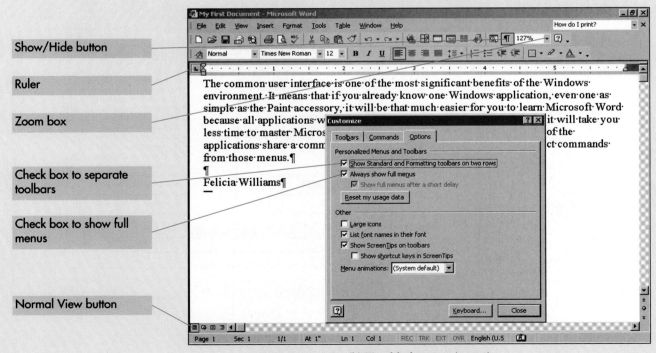

Show/Hide button

Ruler

Zoom box

Check box to separate toolbars

Check box to show full menus

Normal View button

(b) Troubleshooting (step 2)

FIGURE **1.8** *Hands-on Exercise 2 (continued)*

Step 3: **Modify the Document**

➤ Press **Ctrl+End** to move to the end of the document. Press the **up arrow key** once or twice until the insertion point is on a blank line above your name. If necessary, press the **enter key** once (or twice) to add additional blank line(s).

➤ Add the sentence, **Success, I can save and retrieve a document!**, as shown in Figure 1.8c.

➤ Make the following additional modifications to practice editing:
  - Change the phrase *most significant* to **very best**.
  - Change *Paint accessory* to **game of Solitaire**.
  - Change the word *select* to **choose**.

➤ Use the **Ins key** to switch between insert and overtype modes as necessary. (You can also double click the **OVR indicator** on the status bar to toggle between the insert and overtype modes.)

➤ Pull down the **File menu** and click **Save**, or click the **Save button**.

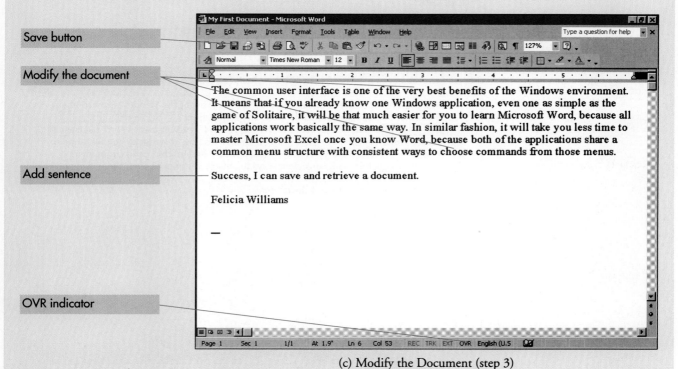

(c) Modify the Document (step 3)

FIGURE 1.8   *Hands-on Exercise 2 (continued)*

MOVING WITHIN A DOCUMENT

Press Ctrl+Home and Ctrl+End to move to the beginning and end of a document, respectively. You can also press the Home or End key to move to the beginning or end of a line. These shortcuts work not just in Word, but in any other Office application, and are worth remembering as they allow your hands to remain on the keyboard as you type.

Step 4: **Deleting Text**

➤ Press and hold the left mouse button as you drag the mouse over the phrase, **even one as simple as the game of Solitaire**, as shown in Figure 1.8d.

➤ Press the **Del** key to delete the selected text from the document. Pull down the **Edit menu** and click the **Undo command** (or click the **Undo button** on the Standard toolbar) to reverse (undo) the last command. The deleted text should be returned to your document.

➤ Pull down the **Edit menu** a second time and click the **Redo command** (or click the **Redo button**) to repeat the Delete command.

➤ Try this simple experiment. Click the **Undo button** repeatedly to undo the commands one at a time, until you have effectively canceled the entire session. Now click the **Redo command** repeatedly, one command at a time, until you have put the entire document back together.

➤ Click the **Save button** on the Standard toolbar to save the revised document a final time.

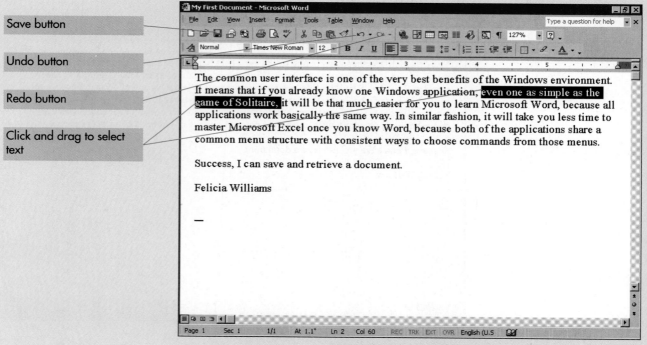

Save button

Undo button

Redo button

Click and drag to select text

(d) Deleting Text (step 4)

FIGURE 1.8 *Hands-on Exercise 2 (continued)*

THE UNDO AND REDO COMMANDS

Click the drop-down arrow next to the Undo button to display a list of your previous actions, then click the action you want to undo, which also undoes all of the preceding commands. Undoing the fifth command in the list, for example, will also undo the preceding four commands. The Redo command works in reverse and cancels the last Undo command.

Step 5: **E-mail Your Document**

➤ You should check with your professor before attempting this step.
➤ Click the **E-mail button** on the Standard toolbar to display a screen similar to Figure 1.8e. The text of your document is entered automatically into the body of the e-mail message.
➤ Enter your professor's e-mail address in the To text box. The document title is automatically entered in the Subject line. Press the **Tab key** to move to the Introduction line. Type a short note above the inserted document to your professor, then click the **Send a Copy button** to mail the message.
➤ The e-mail window closes and you are back in Microsoft Word. The introductory text has been added to the document. Pull down the **File menu**. Click **Close** to close the document (there is no need to save the document).
➤ Pull down the **File menu**. Click **Exit** if you do not want to continue with the next exercise at this time.

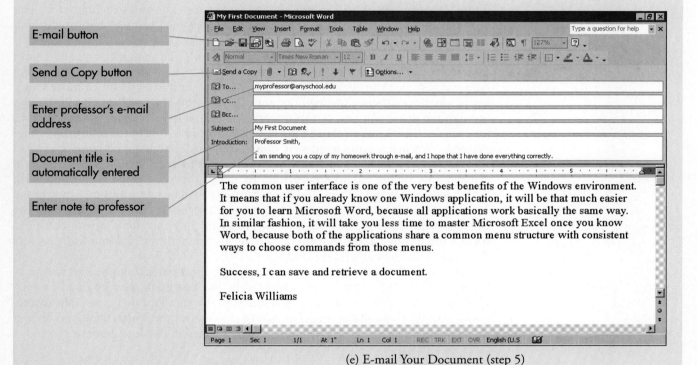

(e) E-mail Your Document (step 5)

FIGURE **1.8**   *Hands-on Exercise 2 (continued)*

DOCUMENT PROPERTIES

Prove to your instructor how hard you've worked by printing various statistics about your document, including the number of revisions and the total editing time. Pull down the File menu, click the Print command to display the Print dialog box, click the drop-down arrow in the Print What list box, select Document properties, then click OK. You can view the information (without printing) by pulling down the File menu, clicking the Properties command, then selecting the Statistics tab.

There is simply no excuse to misspell a word, since the **spell check** is an integral part of Microsoft Word. (The spell check is also available for every other application in the Microsoft Office.) Spelling errors make your work look sloppy and discourage the reader before he or she has read what you had to say. They can cost you a job, a grade, a lucrative contract, or an award you deserve.

The spell check can be set to automatically check a document as text is entered, or it can be called explicitly by clicking the Spelling and Grammar button on the Standard toolbar. The spell check compares each word in a document to the entries in a built-in dictionary, then flags any word that is in the document, but not in the built-in dictionary, as an error.

The dictionary included with Microsoft Office is limited to standard English and does not include many proper names, acronyms, abbreviations, or specialized terms, and hence, the use of any such item is considered a misspelling. You can, however, add such words to a **custom dictionary** so that they will not be flagged in the future. The spell check will inform you of repeated words and irregular capitalization. It cannot, however, flag properly spelled words that are used improperly, and thus cannot tell you that *Two be or knot to be* is not the answer.

The capabilities of the spell check are illustrated in conjunction with Figure 1.9a. Microsoft Word will indicate the errors as you type by underlining them in red. Alternatively, you can click the Spelling and Grammar button on the Standard toolbar at any time to move through the entire document. The spell check will then go through the document and return the errors one at a time, offering several options for each mistake. You can change the misspelled word to one of the alternatives suggested by Word, leave the word as is, or add the word to a custom dictionary.

The first error is the word *embarassing,* with Word's suggestion(s) for correction displayed in the list box in Figure 1.9b. To accept the highlighted suggestion, click the Change command button, and the substitution will be made automatically in the document. To accept an alternative suggestion, click the desired word, then click the Change command button. Alternatively, you can click the AutoCorrect button to correct the mistake in the current document, and, in addition, automatically correct the same mistake in any future document.

The spell check detects both irregular capitalization and duplicated words, as shown in Figures 1.9c and 1.9d, respectively. The last error, *Grauer*, is not a misspelling per se, but a proper noun not found in the standard dictionary. No correction is required, and the appropriate action is to ignore the word (taking no further action)—or better yet, add it to the custom dictionary so that it will not be flagged in future sessions.

A spell check will catch embarassing mistakes, iRregular capitalization, and duplicate words words. It will also flag proper nouns, for example Robert Grauer, but you can add these terms to a custom dictionary. It will not notice properly spelled words that are used incorrectly; for example, too bee or knot to be is not the answer.

(a) The Text

FIGURE 1.9 *The Spell Check*

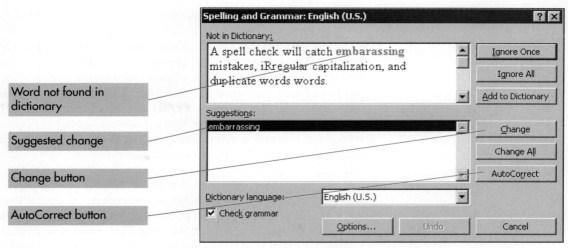

Word not found in dictionary

Suggested change

Change button

AutoCorrect button

(b) Ordinary Misspelling

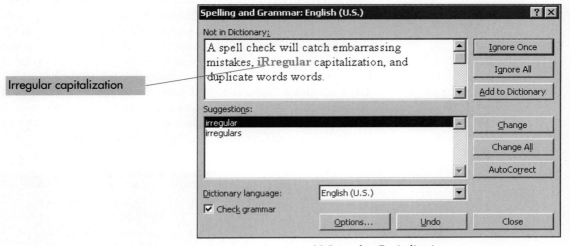

Irregular capitalization

(c) Irregular Capitalization

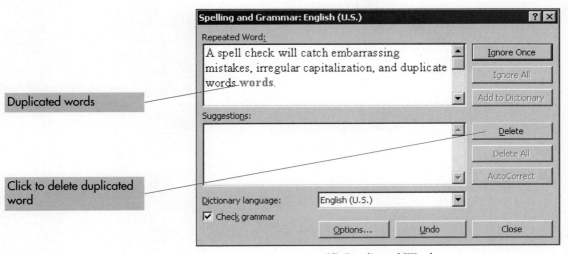

Duplicated words

Click to delete duplicated word

(d) Duplicated Word

FIGURE 1.9   *The Spell Check (continued)*

AutoCorrect and AutoText

The **AutoCorrect** feature corrects mistakes as they are made without any effort on your part. It makes you a better typist. If, for example, you typed *teh* instead of *the,* Word would change the spelling without even telling you. Word will also change *adn* to *and, i* to *I,* and occu*r*ence to occu*rr*ence. All of this is accomplished through a pre-defined table of common mistakes that Word uses to make substitutions whenever it encounters an entry in the table. You can add additional items to the table to include the frequent errors you make. You can also use the feature to define your own short-hand—for example, cis for Computer Information Systems as shown in Figure 1.10a.

The AutoCorrect feature will also correct mistakes in capitalization; for example, it will capitalize the first letter in a sentence, recognize that MIami should be Miami, and capitalize the days of the week. It's even smart enough to correct the accidental use of the Caps Lock key, and it will toggle the key off!

The **AutoText** feature is similar in concept to AutoCorrect in that both substitute a predefined item for a specific character string. The difference is that the substitution occurs automatically with the AutoCorrect entry, whereas you have to take deliberate action for the AutoText substitution to take place. AutoText entries can also include significantly more text, formatting, and even clip art.

Microsoft Word includes a host of predefined AutoText entries. And as with the AutoCorrect feature, you can define additional entries of your own. (You may, how-ever, not be able to do this in a computer lab environment.) The entry in Figure 1.10b is named "signature" and once created, it is available to all Word documents. To insert an AutoText entry into a new document, just type the first several letters in the AutoText name (signature in our example), then press the enter key when Word displays a ScreenTip containing the text of the entry.

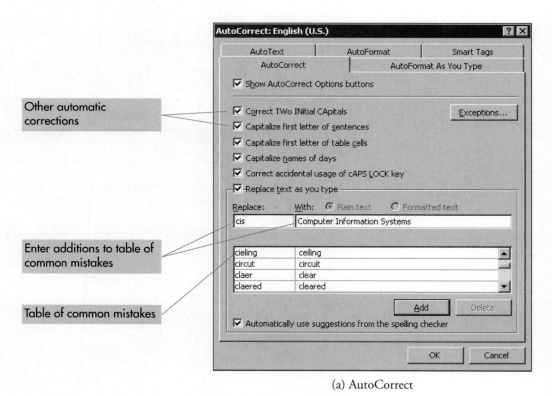

(a) AutoCorrect

FIGURE 1.10   *AutoCorrect and AutoText*

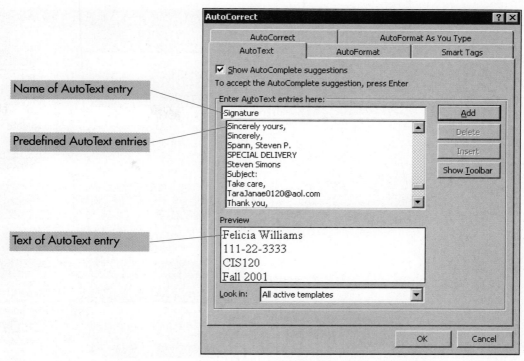

Name of AutoText entry

Predefined AutoText entries

Text of AutoText entry

(b) AutoText

FIGURE 1.10 *AutoCorrect and AutoText (continued)*

THESAURUS

The ***thesaurus*** helps you to avoid repetition and polish your writing. The thesaurus is called from the Language command in the Tools menu. You position the cursor at the appropriate word within the document, then invoke the thesaurus and follow your instincts. The thesaurus recognizes multiple meanings and forms of a word (for example, adjective, noun, and verb) as in Figure 1.11a. Click a meaning, then double click a synonym to produce additional choices as in Figure 1.11b. You can explore further alternatives by selecting a synonym or antonym and clicking the Look Up button. We show antonyms in Figure 1.11c.

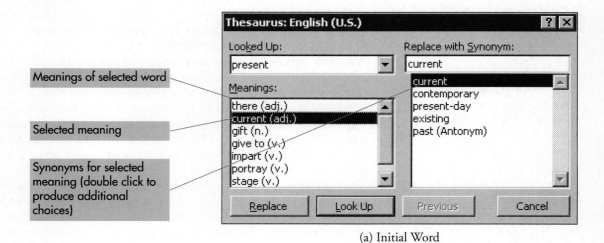

Meanings of selected word

Selected meaning

Synonyms for selected meaning (double click to produce additional choices)

(a) Initial Word

FIGURE 1.11 *The Thesaurus*

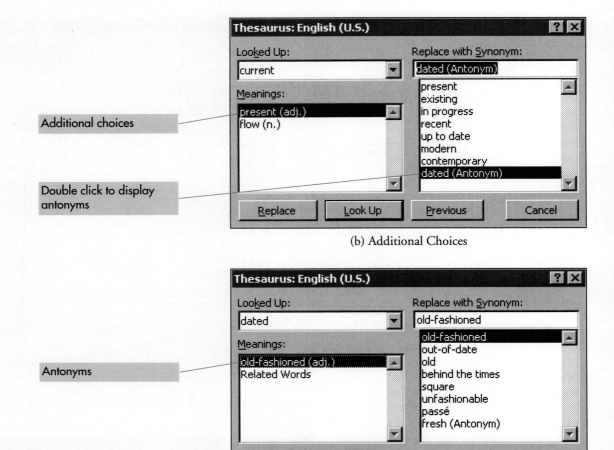

Additional choices

Double click to display antonyms

(b) Additional Choices

Antonyms

(c) Antonyms

FIGURE 1.11 *The Thesaurus (continued)*

GRAMMAR CHECK

The *grammar check* attempts to catch mistakes in punctuation, writing style, and word usage by comparing strings of text within a document to a series of predefined rules. As with the spell check, errors are brought to the screen, where you can accept the suggested correction and make the replacement automatically, or more often, edit the selected text and make your own changes.

You can also ask the grammar check to explain the rule it is attempting to enforce. Unlike the spell check, the grammar check is subjective, and what seems appropriate to you may be objectionable to someone else. Indeed, the grammar check is quite flexible, and can be set to check for different writing styles; that is, you can implement one set of rules to check a business letter and a different set of rules for casual writing. Many times, however, you will find that the English language is just too complex for the grammar check to detect every error, although it will find many errors.

The grammar check caught the inconsistency between subject and verb in Figure 1.12a and suggested the appropriate correction (am instead of are). In Figure 1.12b, it suggested the elimination of the superfluous comma. These examples show the grammar check at its best, but it is often more subjective and less capable. It missed the error "no perfect" in Figure 1.12c (although it did catch "to" instead of "too"). Suffice it to say, that there is no substitute for carefully proofreading every document.

Inconsistency between
subject and verb

Suggested correction

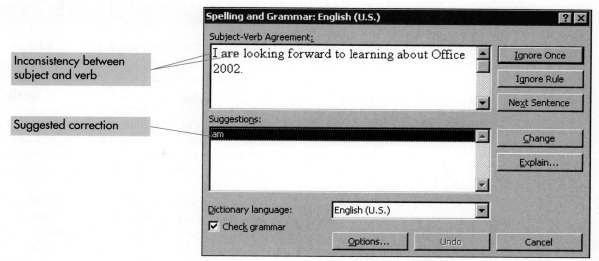

(a) Inconsistent Verb

Two commas are detected

Suggested correction

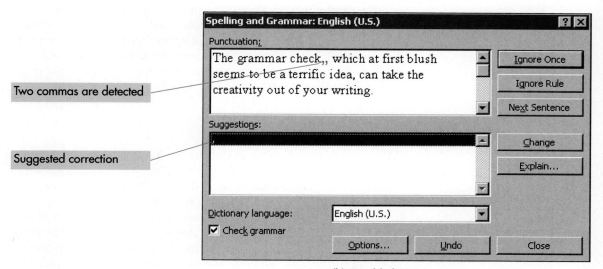

(b) Doubled Punctuation

Missed correction

Detected error

Suggested correction

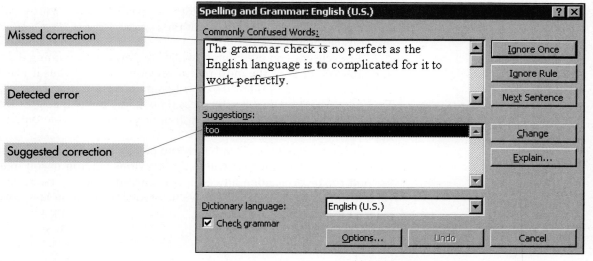

(c) Limitations

FIGURE 1.12   *The Grammar Check*

The Save command was used in the first two exercises. The Save As command will be introduced in the next exercise as a very useful alternative. We also introduce you to different backup options. We believe that now, when you are first starting to learn about word processing, is the time to develop good working habits.

You already know that the Save command copies the document currently being edited (the document in memory) to disk. The initial execution of the command requires you to assign a file name and to specify the drive and folder in which the file is to be stored. All subsequent executions of the Save command save the document under the original name, replacing the previously saved version with the new one.

The **Save As command** saves another copy of a document under a different name (and/or a different file type), and is useful when you want to retain a copy of the original document. The Save As command provides you with two copies of a document. The original document is kept on disk under its original name. A copy of the document is saved on disk under a new name and remains in memory. All subsequent editing is done on the new document.

We cannot overemphasize the importance of periodically saving a document, so that if something does go wrong, you won't lose all of your work. Nothing is more frustrating than to lose two hours of effort, due to an unexpected program crash or to a temporary loss of power. Save your work frequently, at least once every 15 minutes. Pull down the File menu and click Save, or click the Save button on the Standard toolbar. Do it!

Backup Options

Microsoft Word offers several different *backup* options. We believe the two most important options are to create a backup copy in conjunction with every save command, and to periodically (and automatically) save a document. Both options are implemented in step 3 in the next hands-on exercise.

Figure 1.13 illustrates the option to create a backup copy of the document every time a Save command is executed. Assume, for example, that you have created the simple document, *The fox jumped over the fence* and saved it under the name "Fox". Assume further that you edit the document to read, *The quick brown fox jumped over the fence,* and that you saved it a second time. The second save command changes the name of the original document from "Fox" to "Backup of Fox", then saves the current contents of memory as "Fox". In other words, the disk now contains two versions of the document: the current version "Fox" and the most recent previous version "Backup of Fox".

The cycle goes on indefinitely, with "Fox" always containing the current version, and "Backup of Fox" the most recent previous version. Thus if you revise and save the document a third time, "Fox" will contain the latest revision while "Backup of Fox" would contain the previous version alluding to the quick brown fox. The original (first) version of the document disappears entirely since only two versions are kept.

The contents of "Fox" and "Backup of Fox" are different, but the existence of the latter enables you to retrieve the previous version if you inadvertently edit beyond repair or accidentally erase the current "Fox" version. Should this occur (and it will), you can always retrieve its predecessor and at least salvage your work prior to the last save operation.

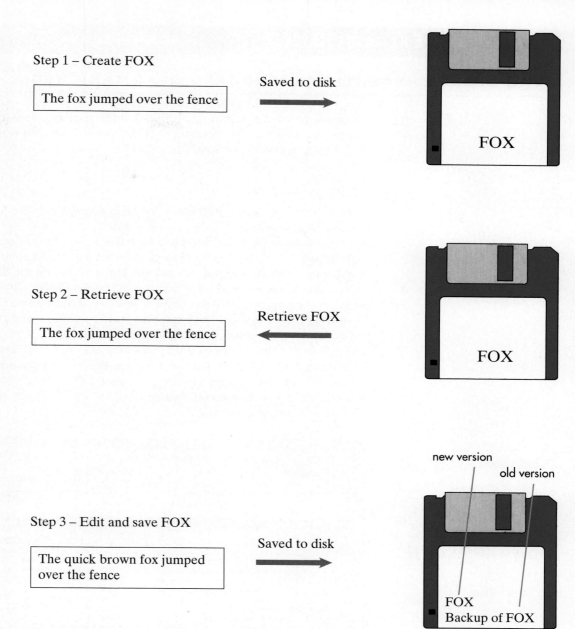

Step 1 – Create FOX

| The fox jumped over the fence |

Saved to disk

FOX

Step 2 – Retrieve FOX

| The fox jumped over the fence |

Retrieve FOX

FOX

Step 3 – Edit and save FOX

| The quick brown fox jumped over the fence |

Saved to disk

new version

old version

FOX
Backup of FOX

FIGURE 1.13 *Backup Procedures*

COMPARE AND MERGE DOCUMENTS

The Compare and Merge Documents command lets you compare the content of two documents to one another in order to see the differences between those documents. It is very useful if you have lost track of different versions of a document and/or if you are working with others. You can also use the command to see how well you did the hands-on exercises. The command highlights the differences in the documents and then it gives you the option to accept or reject changes. See exercise 7 at the end of the chapter.

THE SPELL CHECK, THESAURUS, AND GRAMMAR CHECK

Objective   To open an existing document, check it for spelling, then use the Save As command to save the document under a different file name. Use Figure 1.14 as a guide in the exercise.

Step 1:   **Preview a Document**

➤ Start Microsoft Word. Pull down the **Help menu**. Click the command to **Hide** the **Office Assistant**.

➤ If necessary, pull down the **View menu** and click the command to open the **Task pane**. Click the link to **More documents** in the task pane or pull down the **File menu** and click **Open** (or click the **Open button** on the Standard toolbar). You should see a dialog box similar to the one in Figure 1.14a.

➤ Select the appropriate drive, drive C or drive A, depending on the location of your data. Double click the **Exploring Word folder** to make it the active folder (the folder from which you will open the document).

➤ Scroll in the Name list box until you can select (click) the **Try the Spell Check** document. Click the **drop-down arrow** on the **Views button** and click **Preview** to preview the document as shown in Figure 1.14a.

➤ Click the **Open command button** to open the file. Your document should appear on the screen.

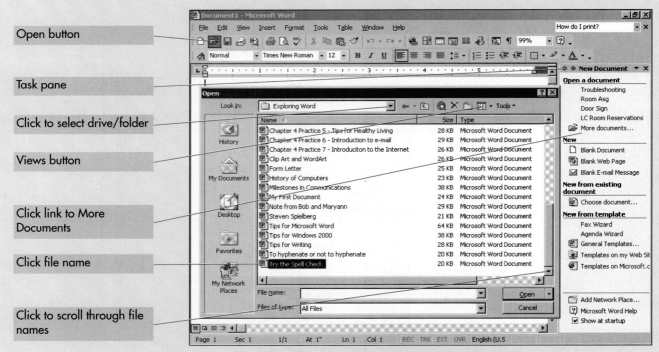

Open button

Task pane

Click to select drive/folder

Views button

Click link to More Documents

Click file name

Click to scroll through file names

(a) Preview a Document (step 1)

FIGURE 1.14   *Hands-on Exercise 3*

Step 2: **The Save As Command**

➤ Pull down the **File menu**. Click **Save As** to produce the dialog box in Figure 1.14b.

➤ Enter **Modified Spell Check** as the name of the new document. (A file name may contain up to 255 characters, and blanks are permitted.) Click the **Save command button**.

➤ There are now two identical copies of the file on disk: Try the Spell Check, which we supplied, and Modified Spell Check, which you just created.

➤ The title bar shows the latter name (Modified Spell Check) as it is the document in memory. All subsequent changes will be made to this document.

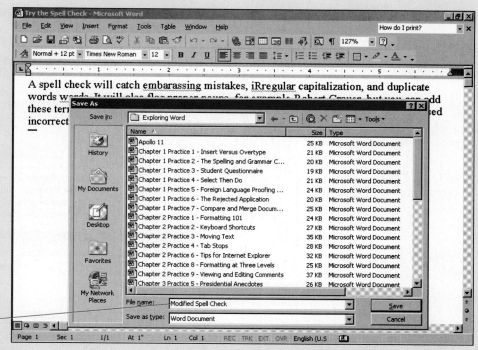

Enter new file name

(b) The Save As Command (step 2)

FIGURE 1.14   *Hands-on Exercise 3 (continued)*

THE WORD COUNT TOOLBAR

How close are you to completing the 500-word paper that your professor assigned? Pull down the Tools menu and click the Word Count command to display a dialog box that shows the number of pages, words, paragraphs, and characters in your document. There is also a command button to display the Word Count toolbar so that it remains on the screen throughout the session. Click the Recount button on the toolbar at any time to see the current statistics for your document.

Step 3: **The Spell Check**

➤ If necessary, press **Ctrl+Home** to move to the beginning of the document. Click the **Spelling and Grammar button** on the Standard toolbar to check the document.

➤ "Embarassing" is flagged as the first misspelling as shown in Figure 1.14c. Click the **Change button** to accept the suggested spelling.

➤ "iRregular" is flagged as an example of irregular capitalization. Click the **Change button** to accept the suggested correction.

➤ Continue checking the document, which displays misspellings and other irregularities one at a time. Click the appropriate command button as each mistake is found.

  • Click the **Delete button** to remove the duplicated word.
  • Click the **Ignore Once button** to accept Grauer (or click the **Add button** to add Grauer to the custom dictionary).

➤ The last sentence is flagged because of a grammatical error and is discussed in the next step.

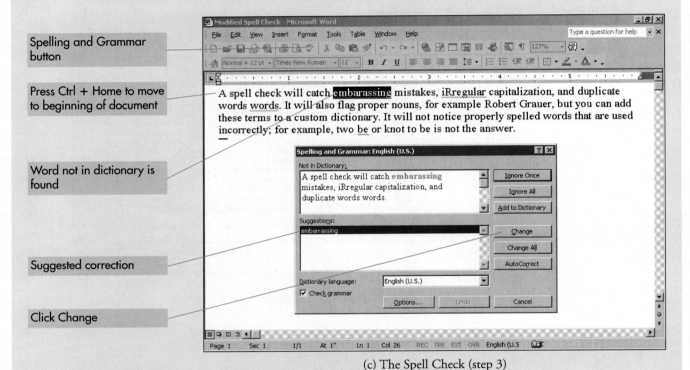

Spelling and Grammar button

Press Ctrl + Home to move to beginning of document

Word not in dictionary is found

Suggested correction

Click Change

(c) The Spell Check (step 3)

FIGURE 1.14 *Hands-on Exercise 3 (continued)*

AUTOMATIC SPELLING AND GRAMMAR CHECKING

Red and green wavy lines may appear throughout a document to indicate spelling and grammatical errors, respectively. Point to any underlined word, then click the right mouse button to display a context-sensitive help menu with suggested corrections. To enable (disable) these options, pull down the Tools menu, click the Options command, click the Spelling and Grammar tab, and check (clear) the options to check spelling (or grammar) as you type.

Step 4: **The Grammar Check**

➤ The last phrase, "Two be or knot to be is not the answer", should be flagged as an error, as shown in Figure 1.14d. If this is not the case:
  • Pull down the **Tools menu**, click **Options**, then click the **Spelling and Grammar tab**.
  • Check the box to **Check Grammar with Spelling**, then click the button to **Recheck document**. Click **Yes** when told that the spelling and grammar check will be reset, then click **OK** to close the Options dialog box.
  • Press **Ctrl+Home** to return to the beginning of the document, then click the **Spelling and Grammar button** to recheck the document.
➤ The Grammar Check suggests substituting "are" for "be", which is not what you want. Click in the preview box and make the necessary corrections. Change "two" to "to" and "knot" to "not". Click **Change**.
➤ Click **OK** when you see the dialog box indicating that the spelling and grammar check is complete. Enter any additional grammatical changes manually. Save the document.

Grammatical error is found

Click and make desired correction

Suggested correction is not what is wanted

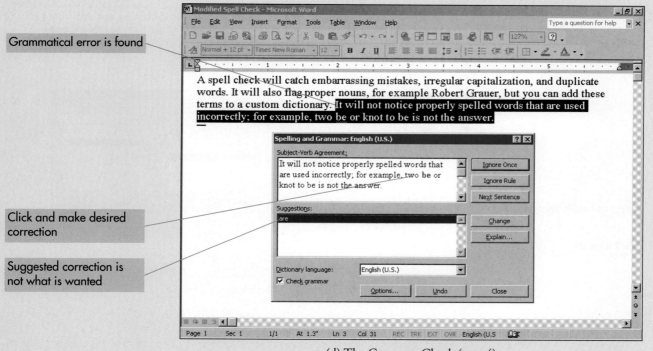

(d) The Grammar Check (step 4)

FIGURE 1.14   *Hands-on Exercise 3 (continued)*

CHECK SPELLING ONLY

The grammar check is invoked by default in conjunction with the spell check. You can, however, check the spelling of a document without checking its grammar. Pull down the Tools menu, click Options to display the Options dialog box, then click the Spelling and Grammar tab. Clear the box to check grammar with spelling, then click OK to accept the change and close the dialog box.

Step 5:   **The Thesaurus**

➤ Select the word **flag**, which appears toward the beginning of your document.
➤ Pull down the **Tools menu**, click **Language**, then click **Thesaurus** to display the associated dialog box as shown in Figure 1.14e.
➤ Choose the proper form of the word; that is, you want to find synonyms for the word "flag" when it is used as a verb as opposed to its use as a noun.
➤ Select **identify** from the list of synonyms, then click the **Replace button** to make the change automatically.
➤ Right click the word **incorrectly** (which appears in the last sentence) to display a context-sensitive menu, click **synonyms**, then choose **inaccurately** to make the substitution into the document.
➤ Save the document.

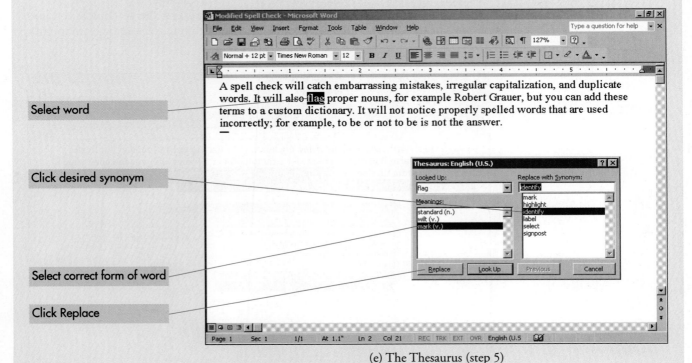

Select word

Click desired synonym

Select correct form of word

Click Replace

(e) The Thesaurus (step 5)

FIGURE 1.14   *Hands-on Exercise 3 (continued)*

FOREIGN LANGUAGE PROOFING TOOLS

The English version of Microsoft Word supports the spelling, grammar, and thesaurus features in more than 80 foreign languages. Support for Spanish and French is built in at no additional cost, whereas you will have to pay an additional fee for other languages. Just pull down the Tools menu and click the Select Language command to change to a different language. You can even check multiple languages within the same document. See practice exercise 5 at the end of the chapter.

Step 6: **AutoCorrect**

> ➤ Press **Ctrl+End** to move to the end of the document. Press the **enter key** twice.
> ➤ Type the *misspelled* phrase, **Teh AutoCorrect feature corrects common spelling mistakes**. Word will automatically change "Teh" to "The".
> ➤ Press the **Home key** to return to the beginning of the line, where you will notice a blue line, under the "T", indicating that an automatic correction has taken place. Point to the blue line, then click the **down arrow** to display the AutoCorrect options.
> ➤ Click the command to **Control AutoCorrect options**, which in turn displays the dialog box in Figure 1.14f. Click the **AutoCorrect tab**, then click the **down arrow** on the scroll bar to view the list of corrections. Close the dialog box.
> ➤ Add the sentence, **The feature also changes special symbols such as :) to ☺ to indicate I understand my work**. (You will have to use the AutoCorrect options to change the first ☺ back to the :) within the sentence.)

Point to blue line

Click down arrow

AutoCorrect tab

Click to view list of automatic corrections

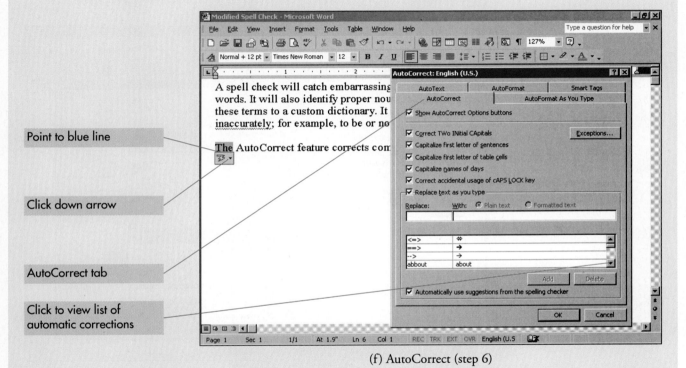

(f) AutoCorrect (step 6)

FIGURE 1.14   *Hands-on Exercise 3 (continued)*

CREATE YOUR OWN SHORTHAND

Use AutoCorrect to expand abbreviations such as "usa" for United States of America. Pull down the Tools menu, click AutoCorrect Options, type the abbreviation in the Replace text box and the expanded entry in the With text box. Click the Add command button, then click OK to exit the dialog box and return to the document. The next time you type usa in a document, it will automatically be expanded to United States of America.

Step 7: **Create an AutoText Entry**

➤ Press **Ctrl+End** to move to the end of the document. Press the **enter key** twice. Enter your name and class.
➤ Click and drag to select the information you just entered. Pull down the **Insert menu**, select the **AutoText command**, then select **AutoText** to display the AutoCorrect dialog box in Figure 1.14g.
➤ Your name (Felicia Williams in our example) is suggested automatically as the name of the AutoText entry. Click the **Add button**.
➤ To test the entry, you can delete your name and other information, then use the AutoText feature. Your name and other information should still be highlighted. Press the **Del key** to delete the information.
➤ Type the first few letters of your name and watch the screen as you do. You should see a ScreenTip containing your name and other information. Press the **enter key** or the **F3 key** when you see the ScreenTip.
➤ Save the document. Print the document for your instructor. Exit Word.

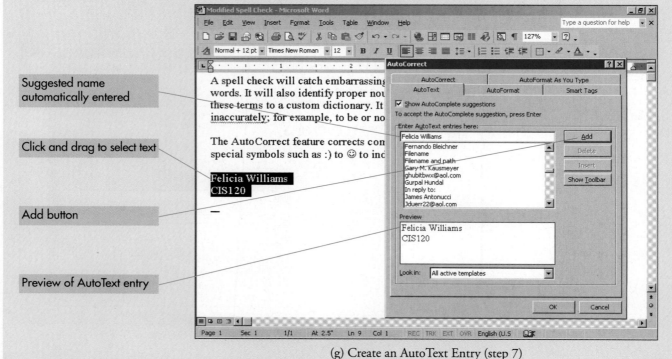

Suggested name automatically entered

Click and drag to select text

Add button

Preview of AutoText entry

(g) Create an AutoText Entry (step 7)

FIGURE 1.14 *Hands-on Exercise 3 (continued)*

THE AUTOTEXT TOOLBAR

Point to any visible toolbar, click the right mouse button to display a context-sensitive menu, then click AutoText to display the AutoText toolbar. The AutoText toolbar groups the various AutoText entries into categories, making it easier to select the proper entry. Click the down arrow on the All Entries button to display the various categories, click a category, then select the entry you want to insert into the document.

The chapter provided a broad-based introduction to word processing in general and to Microsoft Word in particular. Help is available from many sources. You can use the Help menu or the Office Assistant as you can in any Office application. You can also go to the Microsoft Web site to obtain more recent, and often more detailed, information.

Microsoft Word is always in one of two modes, insert or overtype; the choice between the two depends on the desired editing. The insertion point marks the place within a document where text is added or replaced.

The enter key is pressed at the end of a paragraph, but not at the end of a line because Word automatically wraps text from one line to the next. A hard return is created by the user when he or she presses the enter key; a soft return is created by Word as it wraps text and begins a new line.

The Save and Open commands work in conjunction with one another. The Save command copies the document in memory to disk under its existing name. The Open command retrieves a previously saved document. The Save As command saves the document under a different name and is useful when you want to retain a copy of the current document prior to all changes.

A spell check compares the words in a document to those in a standard and/or custom dictionary and offers suggestions to correct the mistakes it finds. It will detect misspellings, duplicated phrases, and/or irregular capitalization, but will not flag properly spelled words that are used incorrectly. Foreign-language proofing tools for French and Spanish are built into the English version of Microsoft Word 2002.

The AutoCorrect feature corrects predefined spelling errors and/or mistakes in capitalization, automatically, as the words are entered. The AutoText feature is similar in concept except that it can contain longer entries that include formatting and clip art. Either feature can be used to create a personal shorthand to expand abbreviations as they are typed.

The thesaurus suggests synonyms and/or antonyms. It can also recognize multiple forms of a word (noun, verb, and adjective) and offer suggestions for each. The grammar check searches for mistakes in punctuation, writing style, and word usage by comparing strings of text within a document to a series of predefined rules.

KEY TERMS

AutoCorrect (p. 26)
AutoText (p. 26)
Backup (p. 30)
Close command (p. 8)
Custom dictionary (p. 24)
Exit command (p. 8)
File menu (p. 8)
File name (p. 8)
File type (p. 8)
Formatting toolbar (p. 5)
Grammar check (p. 28)
Hard return (p. 2)
Horizontal ruler (p. 6)

Insert mode (p. 4)
Insertion point (p. 2)
Normal view (p. 17)
Office Assistant (p. 12)
Open command (p. 8)
Overtype mode (p. 4)
Places Bar (p. 8)
Print command (p. 8)
Print Layout view (p. 17)
Save As command (p. 30)
Save command (p. 8)
ScreenTip (p. 5)
Show/Hide ¶ button (p. 17)

Soft return (p. 2)
Spell check (p. 24)
Standard toolbar (p. 5)
Status bar (p. 6)
Task pane (p. 6)
Thesaurus (p. 27)
Toggle switch (p. 3)
Toolbar (p. 5)
Undo command (p. 22)
Vertical ruler (p. 6)
View menu (p. 20)
Word wrap (p. 2)

1. When entering text within a document, the enter key is normally pressed at the end of every:
   (a) Line
   (b) Sentence
   (c) Paragraph
   (d) All of the above

2. Which menu contains the commands to save the current document, or to open a previously saved document?
   (a) The Tools menu
   (b) The File menu
   (c) The View menu
   (d) The Edit menu

3. How do you execute the Print command?
   (a) Click the Print button on the standard toolbar
   (b) Pull down the File menu, then click the Print command
   (c) Use the appropriate keyboard shortcut
   (d) All of the above

4. The Open command:
   (a) Brings a document from disk into memory
   (b) Brings a document from disk into memory, then erases the document on disk
   (c) Stores the document in memory on disk
   (d) Stores the document in memory on disk, then erases the document from memory

5. The Save command:
   (a) Brings a document from disk into memory
   (b) Brings a document from disk into memory, then erases the document on disk
   (c) Stores the document in memory on disk
   (d) Stores the document in memory on disk, then erases the document from memory

6. What is the easiest way to change the phrase, *revenues, profits, gross margin,* to read *revenues, profits, and gross margin*?
   (a) Use the insert mode, position the cursor before the *g* in *gross,* then type the word *and* followed by a space
   (b) Use the insert mode, position the cursor after the *g* in *gross,* then type the word *and* followed by a space
   (c) Use the overtype mode, position the cursor before the *g* in *gross,* then type the word *and* followed by a space
   (d) Use the overtype mode, position the cursor after the *g* in *gross,* then type the word *and* followed by a space

7. A document has been entered into Word with a given set of margins, which are subsequently changed. What can you say about the number of hard and soft returns before and after the change in margins?
   (a) The number of hard returns is the same, but the number and/or position of the soft returns is different
   (b) The number of soft returns is the same, but the number and/or position of the hard returns is different
   (c) The number and position of both hard and soft returns is unchanged
   (d) The number and position of both hard and soft returns is different

8. Which of the following will be detected by the spell check?
   (a) Duplicate words
   (b) Irregular capitalization
   (c) Both (a) and (b)
   (d) Neither (a) nor (b)

9. Which of the following is likely to be found in a custom dictionary?
   (a) Proper names
   (b) Words related to the user's particular application
   (c) Acronyms created by the user for his or her application
   (d) All of the above

10. Ted and Sally both use Word. Both have written a letter to Dr. Joel Stutz and have run a spell check on their respective documents. Ted's program flags *Stutz* as a misspelling, whereas Sally's accepts it as written. Why?
    (a) The situation is impossible; that is, if they use identical word processing programs they should get identical results
    (b) Ted has added *Stutz* to his custom dictionary
    (c) Sally has added *Stutz* to her custom dictionary
    (d) All of the above reasons are equally likely as a cause of the problem

11. The spell check will do all of the following *except:*
    (a) Flag properly spelled words used incorrectly
    (b) Identify misspelled words
    (c) Accept (as correctly spelled) words found in the custom dictionary
    (d) Suggest alternatives to misspellings it identifies

12. The AutoCorrect feature will:
    (a) Correct errors in capitalization as they occur during typing
    (b) Expand user-defined abbreviations as the entries are typed
    (c) Both (a) and (b)
    (d) Neither (a) nor (b)

13. When does the Save As dialog box appear?
    (a) The first time a file is saved using either the Save or Save As commands
    (b) Every time a file is saved
    (c) Both (a) and (b)
    (d) Neither (a) nor (b)

14. Which of the following is true about the thesaurus?
    (a) It recognizes different forms of a word; for example, a noun and a verb
    (b) It provides antonyms as well as synonyms
    (c) Both (a) and (b)
    (d) Neither (a) nor (b)

15. The grammar check:
    (a) Implements different rules for casual and business writing
    (b) Will detect all subtleties in the English language
    (c) Is always run in conjunction with a spell check
    (d) All of the above

ANSWERS

1. c	6. a	11. a
2. b	7. a	12. c
3. d	8. c	13. a
4. a	9. d	14. c
5. c	10. c	15. a

1. Insert versus Overtype: Open the *Chapter 1 Practice 1* document that is shown in Figure 1.15 and make the following changes.
   a. Enter your instructor's name and your name in the To and From lines, respectively.
   b. Change "better" to "preferable" in the third line of the first paragraph.
   c. Delete the word "then" from the last line in the first paragraph.
   d. Click at the end of the first paragraph, and add the sentence, "The insert mode adds characters at the insertion point while moving existing text to the right in order to make room for the new text."
   e. Delete the last paragraph, which describes how to delete text. Create a new paragraph in its place with the following text: "There are two other keys that function as toggle switches of which you should be aware. The Caps Lock key toggles between upper- and lowercase letters. The Num Lock key alternates between typing numbers and using the arrow keys."
   f. Print the revised document for your instructor.
   g. Create a cover sheet for the assignment with your name, your instructor's name, today's date, and the assignment number.

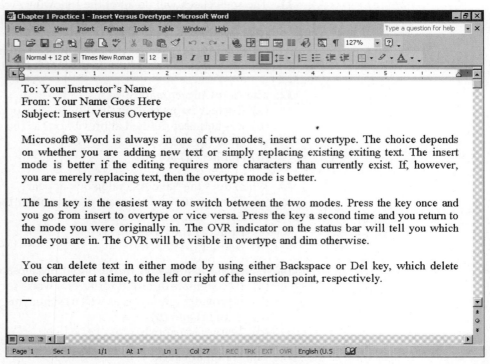

FIGURE 1.15 *Insert versus Overtype (Exercise 1)*

2. The Spelling and Grammar Check: Open the *Chapter 1 Practice* 2 document that is displayed in Figure 1.16, then run the spelling and grammar check to correct the various errors that are contained in the original document. Print this version of the corrected document for your instructor.

   Read the corrected document carefully and make any other necessary corrections. You should find several additional errors because the English language is very complicated and it is virtually impossible to correct every error automatically. Print this version of the document as well. Add a cover page and submit both versions of the corrected document to your instructor.

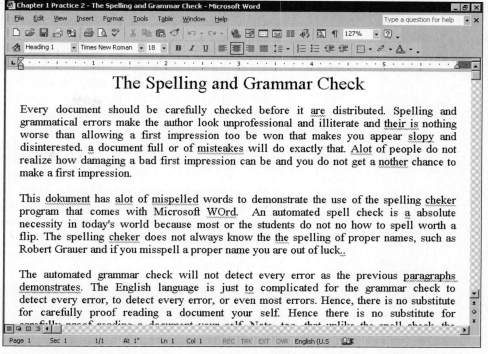

FIGURE 1.16   *The Spelling and Grammar Check (Exercise 2)*

3. Student Questionnaire: Use the partially completed document in *Chapter 1 Practice 3* to describe your background. If there is time in the class, your instructor can have you exchange assignments with another student. There are many variations on this "icebreaker," and the assignment will let you gain practice with Microsoft Word.

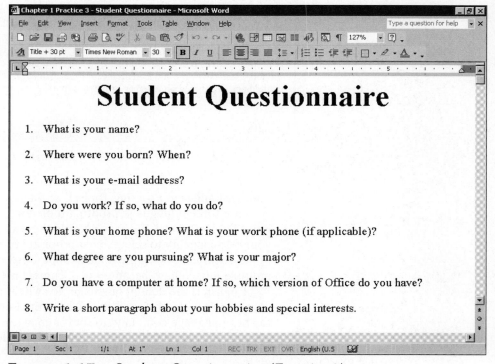

FIGURE 1.17   *Student Questionnaire (Exercise 3)*

4. **Select-Then-Do:** Formatting is not covered in this chapter, but it is very easy to apply basic formatting to a document, especially if you have used another application in Microsoft Office. Many formatting operations are implemented in the context of "select-then-do" as described in the document in Figure 1.18. You select the text that you want to format, then you execute the appropriate formatting command, most easily by clicking the appropriate button on the Formatting toolbar. The function of each button should be apparent from its icon, but you can simply point to a button to display a ScreenTip that is indicative of its function.

   An unformatted version of the document in Figure 1.18 is found in the *Chapter 1 Practice 4* document in the Exploring Word folder. Open the document, then format it to match the completed document in the figure. The title of the document is centered in 22-point Arial, whereas the rest of the document is set in 12-point Times New Roman. Boldface, italicize, and highlight the text as indicated in the actual document. A color font is also indicated, but do not be concerned if you do not have a color printer. Add your name to the bottom of the completed document, then print the document for your instructor.

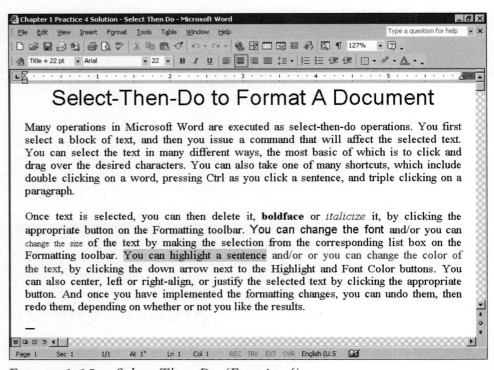

FIGURE 1.18 *Select-Then-Do (Exercise 4)*

5. **Foreign Language Proofing Tools:** Use the document in Figure 1.19 to practice with the foreign language proofing tools for French and Spanish that are built into Microsoft Word. We have entered the text of the document for you, but it is your responsibility to select the appropriate proofing tool for the different parts of the document. Open the document in *Chapter 1 Practice 5*, which will indicate multiple misspellings because the document is using the English spell check.

   English is the default language. To switch to a different language, select the phrase, pull down the Tools menu, click the Language command, and then click the Set Language command to set (or change) the language in effect. Add your name to the completed document and print it for your instructor.

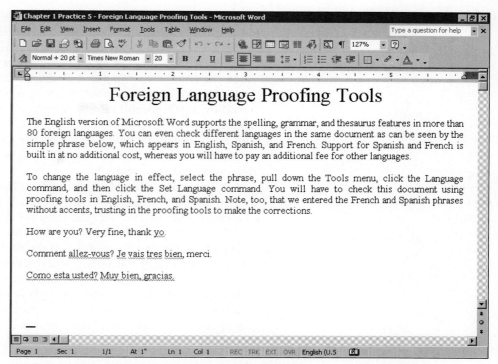

FIGURE 1.19   *Foreign Language Proofing Tools (Exercise 5)*

6. The Rejected Job Applicant: The individual who wrote the letter in Figure 1.20 has been rejected for every job for which he has applied. He is a good friend and you want to help. Open the document in *Chapter 1 Practice 6* and correct the obvious spelling errors. Read the document carefully and make any additional corrections that you think appropriate. Sign your name and print the corrected letter.

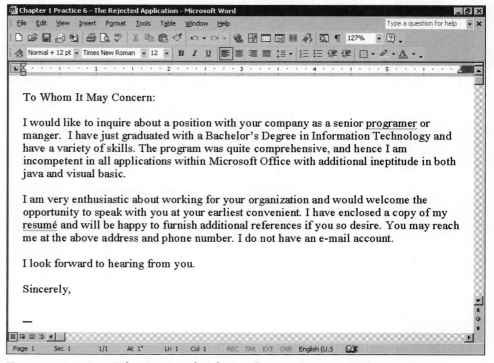

FIGURE 1.20   *The Rejected Job Applicant (Exercise 6)*

BUILDS ON

HANDS-ON
EXERCISE 2,
PAGES 19–23

7. Compare and Merge Documents: The Compare and Merge Documents command lets you compare two documents in order to see the changes between those documents. You can use the command to see how well you completed the first two hands-on exercises. Proceed as follows:

a. Open the completed *Chapter 1 Practice 7* document in the Exploring Word folder. This document contains a paragraph from the hands-on exercise followed by a paragraph that describes the Compare and Merge Documents command.

b. Pull down the Tools menu and click the Compare and Merge Documents command to display the associated dialog box and select *My First Document* (the document you created).

c. Check the box for Legal Blackline (to display a thin black line in the left margin showing where the changes occur), then click the Compare button. The two documents are merged together as shown in Figure 1.21. Click the Print button to print the merged documents for your instructor.

d. Accept or reject the changes as you see fit. Use the Help command to learn more about merging documents and tracking changes.

e. Summarize your thoughts about these commands in a short note to your instructor. Compare your findings to those of your classmates.

f. Learn how to insert comments into a document that contain suggestions for improving the document. What happens if different users insert comments into the same document?

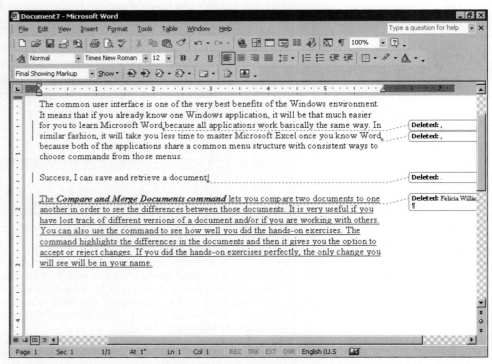

FIGURE 1.21 *Compare and Merge Documents (Exercise 7)*

Acronym Finder

Do you know what the acronym, PCMCIA stands for? Some might say it stands for "People Can't Memorize Computer Industry Acronyms", although the real meaning is "Personal Computer Memory Card International Association", which refers to the PC cards that are used with notebook computers. Use your favorite Internet search engine to locate a site that publishes lists of acronyms. Select five computer-related terms and create a short document with the acronym and its meaning. Select a second list of any five acronyms that appeal to you. Print the document and submit it to your instructor.

The Reference Desk

The Reference Desk, at www.refdesk.com, contains a treasure trove of information for the writer. You will find access to several online dictionaries, encyclopedias, and other references. Go to the site and select five links that you think will be of interest to you as a writer. Create a short document that contains the name of the site, its Web address, and a brief description of the information that is found at the site. Print the document and submit it to your instructor.

Planning for Disaster

Do you have a backup strategy? Do you even know what a backup strategy is? You should learn, because sooner or later you will wish you had one. You will erase a file, be unable to read from a floppy disk, or worse yet suffer a hardware failure in which you are unable to access the hard drive. The problem always seems to occur the night before an assignment is due. The ultimate disaster is the disappearance of your computer, by theft or natural disaster (e.g., Hurricane Andrew). Describe in 250 words or less the backup strategy you plan to implement in conjunction with your work in this class.

A Letter Home

You really like this course and want very much to have your own computer, but you're strapped for cash and have decided to ask your parents for help. Write a one-page letter describing the advantages of having your own system and how it will help you in school. Tell your parents what the system will cost, and that you can save money by buying through the mail. Describe the configuration you intend to buy (don't forget to include the price of software) and then provide prices from at least three different companies. Cut out the advertisements and include them in your letter. Bring your material to class and compare your research with that of your classmates.

Computer Magazines

A subscription to a computer magazine should be given serious consideration if you intend to stay abreast in a rapidly changing field. The reviews on new products are especially helpful, and you will appreciate the advertisements should you need to buy. Go to the library or a newsstand and obtain a magazine that appeals to you, then write a brief review of the magazine for class. Devote at least one paragraph to an article or other item you found useful.

A Junior Year Abroad

How lucky can you get? You are spending the second half of your junior year in Paris. The problem is you will have to submit your work in French, and the English version of Microsoft Word won't do. Is there a foreign-language version available? What about the dictionary and thesaurus? How do you enter the accented characters, which occur so frequently? You are leaving in two months, so you'd better get busy. What are your options? *Bon voyage!*

Changing Menus and Toolbars

Office XP enables you to display a series of short menus that contain only basic commands. The additional commands are made visible by clicking the double arrow that appears at the bottom of the menu. New commands are added to the menu as they are used, and conversely, other commands are removed if they are not used. A similar strategy is followed for the Standard and Formatting toolbars that are displayed on a single row, and thus do not show all of the buttons at one time. The intent is to simplify Office XP for the new user by limiting the number of commands that are visible. The consequence, however, is that the individual is not exposed to new commands, and hence may not use Office to its full potential. Which set of menus do you prefer? How do you switch from one set to the other?

CHAPTER 2

Gaining Proficiency:
Editing and Formatting

OBJECTIVES

AFTER READING THIS CHAPTER YOU WILL BE ABLE TO:

1. Define the select-then-do methodology; describe several shortcuts with the mouse and/or the keyboard to select text.
2. Move and copy text within a document; distinguish between the Windows clipboard and the Office clipboard.
3. Use the Find, Replace, and Go To commands to substitute one character string for another.
4. Define scrolling; scroll to the beginning and end of a document.
5. Distinguish between the Normal and Print Layout views; state how to change the view and/or magnification of a document.
6. Define typography; distinguish between a serif and a sans serif typeface; use the Format Font command to change the font and/or type size.
7. Use the Format Paragraph command to change line spacing, alignment, tabs, and indents, and to control pagination.
8. Use the Borders and Shading command to box and shade text.
9. Describe the Undo and Redo commands and how they are related to one another.
10. Use the Page Setup command to change the margins and/or orientation; differentiate between a soft and a hard page break.
11. Enter and edit text in columns; change the column structure of a document through section formatting.

OVERVIEW

The previous chapter taught you the basics of Microsoft Word and enabled you to create and print a simple document. The present chapter significantly extends your capabilities, by presenting a variety of commands to change the contents and appearance of a document. These operations are known as editing and formatting, respectively.

49

You will learn how to move and copy text within a document and how to find and replace one character string with another. You will also learn the basics of typography and how to switch between different fonts. You will be able to change alignment, indentation, line spacing, margins, and page orientation. All of these commands are used in three hands-on exercises, which require your participation at the computer, and which are the very essence of the chapter.

SELECT-THEN-DO

Many operations in Word take place within the context of a *select-then-do* methodology; that is, you select a block of text, then you execute the command to operate on that text. The most basic way to select text is by dragging the mouse; that is, click at the beginning of the selection, press and hold the left mouse button as you move to the end of the selection, then release the mouse.

Selected text is affected by any subsequent operation; for example, clicking the Bold or Italic button changes the selected text to boldface or italics, respectively. You can also drag the selected text to a new location, press the Del key to erase the selected text, or execute any other editing or formatting command. The text continues to be selected until you click elsewhere in the document.

MOVING AND COPYING TEXT

The ability to move and/or copy text is essential in order to develop any degree of proficiency in editing. A move operation removes the text from its current location and places it elsewhere in the same (or even a different) document; a copy operation retains the text in its present location and places a duplicate elsewhere. Either operation can be accomplished using the Windows clipboard and a combination of the *Cut*, *Copy*, and *Paste commands*.

The *Windows clipboard* is a temporary storage area available to any Windows application. Selected text is cut or copied from a document and placed onto the clipboard from where it can be pasted to a new location(s). A move requires that you select the text and execute a Cut command to remove the text from the document and place it on the clipboard. You then move the insertion point to the new location and paste the text from the clipboard into that location. A copy operation necessitates the same steps except that a Copy command is executed rather than a cut, leaving the selected text in its original location as well as placing a copy on the clipboard. (The *Paste Special command* can be used instead of the Paste command to paste the text without the associated formatting.)

The Cut, Copy, and Paste commands are found in the Edit menu, or alternatively, can be executed by clicking the appropriate buttons on the Standard toolbar. The contents of the Windows clipboard are replaced by each subsequent Cut or Copy command, but are unaffected by the Paste command. The contents of the clipboard can be pasted into multiple locations in the same or different documents.

Microsoft Office has its own clipboard that enables you to collect and paste multiple items. The *Office clipboard* differs from the Windows clipboard in that the contents of each successive Copy command are added to the clipboard. Thus, you could copy the first paragraph of a document to the Office clipboard, then copy (add) a bulleted list in the middle of the document to the Office clipboard, and finally copy (add) the last paragraph (three items in all) to the Office clipboard. You could then go to another place in the document or to a different document altogether, and paste the contents of the Office clipboard (three separate items) with a single command.

Selected text is copied automatically to the Office clipboard regardless of whether you use the Copy command in the Edit menu, the Copy button on the Standard toolbar, or the Ctrl+C shortcut. The Office clipboard is accessed through the Edit menu and/or the task pane.

The Find, Replace, and Go To commands share a common dialog box with different tabs for each command as shown in Figure 2.1. The ***Find command*** locates one or more occurrences of specific text (e.g., a word or phrase). The ***Replace command*** goes one step further in that it locates the text, and then enables you to optionally replace (one or more occurrences of) that text with different text. The ***Go To command*** goes directly to a specific place (e.g., a specific page) in the document.

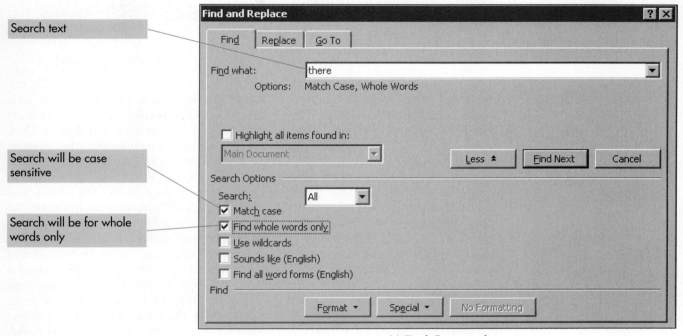

(a) Find Command

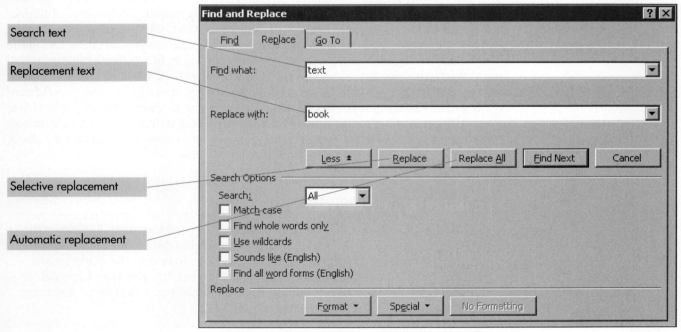

(b) Replace Command

FIGURE 2.1 *The Find, Replace, and Go To Commands*

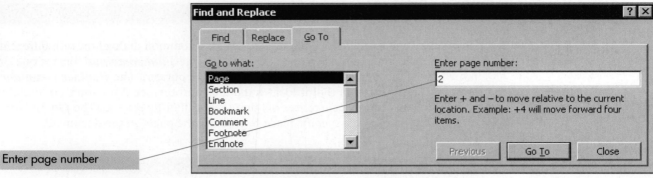

Enter page number

(c) Go To Command

FIGURE 2.1 *The Find, Replace, and Go To Commands (continued)*

The search in both the Find and Replace commands is case sensitive or case insensitive. A ***case-sensitive search*** (where Match Case is selected as in Figure 2.1a) matches not only the text, but also the use of upper- and lowercase letters. Thus, *There* is different from *there,* and a search on one will not identify the other. A ***case-insensitive search*** (where Match Case is *not* selected as in Figure 2.1b) is just the opposite and finds both *There* and *there.* A search may also specify ***whole words only*** to identify *there,* but not *therefore* or *thereby.* And finally, the search and replacement text can also specify different numbers of characters; for example, you could replace *16* with *sixteen.*

The Replace command in Figure 2.1b implements either ***selective replacement***, which lets you examine each occurrence of the character string in context and decide whether to replace it, or ***automatic replacement***, where the substitution is made automatically. Selective replacement is implemented by clicking the Find Next command button, then clicking (or not clicking) the Replace button to make the substitution. Automatic replacement (through the entire document) is implemented by clicking the Replace All button. This often produces unintended consequences and is not recommended; for example, if you substitute the word *text* for *book,* the word *textbook* would become *texttext,* which is not what you had in mind.

The Find and Replace commands can include formatting and/or special characters. You can, for example, change all italicized text to boldface, or you can change five consecutive spaces to a tab character. You can also use special characters in the character string such as the "any character" (consisting of ^?). For example, to find all four-letter words that begin with "f" and end with "l" (such as *fall, fill,* or *fail*), search for f^?^?l. (The question mark stands for any character, just like a ***wild card*** in a card game.) You can also search for all forms of a word; for example, if you specify *am,* it will also find *is* and *are.* You can even search for a word based on how it sounds. When searching for *Marion,* for example, check the Sounds Like check box, and the search will find both *Marion* and *Marian.*

INSERT THE DATE AND TIME

Most documents include the date and time they were created. Pull down the Insert menu, select the Date and Time command to display the Date and Time dialog box, then choose a format. Check the box to update the date automatically if you want your document to reflect the date on which it is opened, or clear the box to retain the date on which the document was created. See practice exercise 5 at the end of the chapter.

Scrolling occurs when a document is too large to be seen in its entirety. Figure 2.2a displays a large printed document, only part of which is visible on the screen as illustrated in Figure 2.2b. In order to see a different portion of the document, you need to scroll, whereby new lines will be brought into view as the old lines disappear.

To: Our Students
From: Robert Grauer and Mary Ann Barber

Welcome to the wonderful world of word processing. Over the next several chapters we will build a foundation in the basics of Microsoft Word, and then teach you to format specialized documents, create professional looking tables and charts, publish well-designed newsletters, and create Web pages. Before you know it, you will be a word processing and desktop publishing wizard!

The first chapter presented the basics of word processing and showed you how to create a simple document. You learned how to insert, replace, and/or delete text. This chapter will teach you about fonts and special effects (such as **boldfacing** and *italicizing*) and how to use them effectively — how too little is better than too much.

You will go on to experiment with margins, tab stops, line spacing, and justification, learning first to format simple documents and then going on to longer, more complex ones. It is with the latter that we explore headers and footers, page numbering, widows and orphans (yes, we really did mean widows and orphans). It is here that we bring in graphics, working with newspaper-type columns, and the elements of a good page design. And without question, we will introduce the tools that make life so much easier (and your writing so much more impressive) — the Spell Check, Grammar Check, Thesaurus, and Styles.

If you are wondering what all these things are, read on in the text and proceed with the hands-on exercises. We will show you how to create a simple newsletter, and then improve it by adding graphics, fonts, and WordArt. You will create a simple calendar using the Tables feature, and then create more intricate forms that will rival anything you have seen. You will learn how to create a résumé with your beginner's skills, and then make it look like so much more with your intermediate (even advanced) skills. You will learn how to download resources from the Internet and how to create your own Web page. Last, but not least, run a mail merge to produce the cover letters that will accompany your résumé as it is mailed to companies across the United States (and even the world).

It is up to you to practice, for it is only through working at the computer, that you will learn what you need to know. Experiment and don't be afraid to make mistakes. Practice and practice some more.

Our goal is for you to learn and to enjoy what you are learning. We have great confidence in you, and in our ability to help you discover what you can do. Visit the home page for the <u>Exploring Windows series</u>. You can also send us e-mail. Bob's address is <u>rgrauer@miami.edu</u>. Mary Ann's address is <u>mbarber@miami.edu</u>. As you read the last sentence, notice that Microsoft Word is Web-enabled and that the Internet and e-mail references appear as hyperlinks in this document. Thus, you can click the address of our home page from within this document and then you can view the page immediately, provided you have an Internet connection. You can also click the e-mail address to open your mail program, provided it has been configured correctly.

We look forward to hearing from you and hope that you will like our textbook. You are about to embark on a wonderful journey toward computer literacy. Be patient and inquisitive.

(a) Printed Document

FIGURE 2.2 *Scrolling*

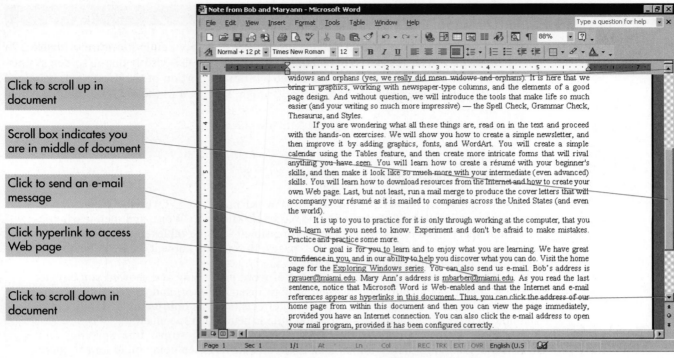

Click to scroll up in document

Scroll box indicates you are in middle of document

Click to send an e-mail message

Click hyperlink to access Web page

Click to scroll down in document

(b) Screen Display

FIGURE 2.2 *Scrolling (continued)*

Scrolling comes about automatically as you reach the bottom of the screen. Entering a new line of text, clicking on the down arrow within the scroll bar, or pressing the down arrow key brings a new line into view at the bottom of the screen and simultaneously removes a line at the top. (The process is reversed at the top of the screen.)

Scrolling can be done with either the mouse or the keyboard. Scrolling with the mouse (e.g., clicking the down arrow in the scroll bar) changes what is displayed on the screen, but does not move the insertion point, so that you must click the mouse after scrolling prior to entering the text at the new location. Scrolling with the keyboard, however (e.g., pressing Ctrl+Home or Ctrl+End to move to the beginning or end of a document, respectively), changes what is displayed on the screen as well as the location of the insertion point, and you can begin typing immediately.

Scrolling occurs most often in a vertical direction as shown in Figure 2.2. It can also occur horizontally, when the length of a line in a document exceeds the number of characters that can be displayed horizontally on the screen.

WRITE NOW, EDIT LATER

You write a sentence, then change it, and change it again, and one hour later you've produced a single paragraph. It happens to every writer—you stare at a blank screen and flashing cursor and are unable to write. The best solution is to brainstorm and write down anything that pops into your head, and to keep on writing. Don't worry about typos or spelling errors because you can fix them later. Above all, resist the temptation to continually edit the few words you've written because overediting will drain the life out of what you are writing. The important thing is to get your ideas on paper.

The *View menu* provides different views of a document. Each view can be displayed at different magnifications, which in turn determine the amount of scrolling necessary to see remote parts of a document.

The *Normal view* is the default view and it provides the fastest way to enter text. The *Print Layout view* more closely resembles the printed document and displays the top and bottom margins, headers and footers, page numbers, graphics, and other features that do not appear in the Normal view. The Normal view tends to be faster because Word spends less time formatting the display.

The *Zoom command* displays the document on the screen at different magnifications; for example, 75%, 100%, or 200%. (The Zoom command does not affect the size of the text on the printed page.) A Zoom percentage (magnification) of 100% displays the document in the approximate size of the text on the printed page. You can increase the percentage to 200% to make the characters appear larger. You can also decrease the magnification to 75% to see more of the document at one time.

Word will automatically determine the magnification if you select one of four additional Zoom options—Page Width, Text Width, Whole Page, or Many Pages (Whole Page and Many Pages are available only in the Print Layout view). Figure 2.3, for example, displays a two-page document in Print Layout view. The 40% magnification is determined automatically once you specify the number of pages.

The View menu also provides access to two additional views—the Outline view and the Web Layout view. The Outline view does not display a conventional outline, but rather a structural view of a document that can be collapsed or expanded as necessary. The Web Layout view is used when you are creating a Web page. Both views are discussed in later chapters.

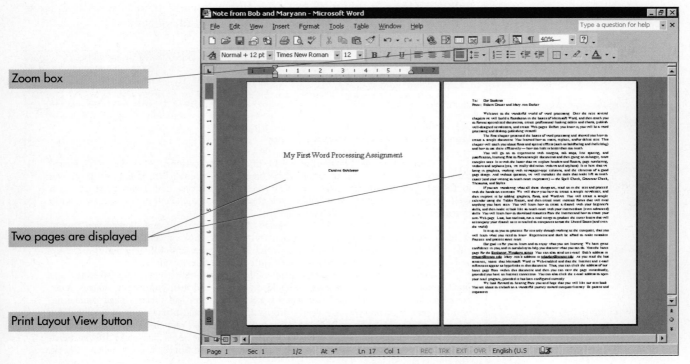

Zoom box

Two pages are displayed

Print Layout View button

FIGURE 2.3   *View Menu and Zoom Command*

EDITING A DOCUMENT

Objective   To edit an existing document; to use the Find and Replace commands; to move and copy text using the clipboard and the drag-and-drop facility. Use Figure 2.4 as a guide in the exercise.

Step 1:   **The View Menu**

➤ Start Word as described in the hands-on exercises from Chapter 1. Pull down the **File menu** and click **Open** (or click the **Open button** on the toolbar).
  • Click the **drop-down arrow** on the Look In list box. Click the appropriate drive, drive C or drive A, depending on the location of your data.
  • Double click the **Exploring Word folder** to make it the active folder (the folder in which you will save the document).
  • Scroll in the Name list box (if necessary) until you can click the **Note from Bob and Maryann** to select this document. Double click the **document icon** or click the **Open command button** to open the file.
➤ The document should appear on the screen as shown in Figure 2.4a.
➤ Change to the Print Layout view at Page Width magnification:
  • Pull down the **View menu** and click **Print Layout** (or click the **Print Layout View button** above the status bar) as shown in Figure 2.4a.
  • Click the **down arrow** in the Zoom box to change to **Page Width**.
➤ Click and drag the mouse to select the phrase **Our Students**, which appears at the beginning of the document. Type your name to replace the selected text.
➤ Pull down the **File menu**, click the **Save As command**, then save the document as **Modified Note**. (This creates a second copy of the document.)

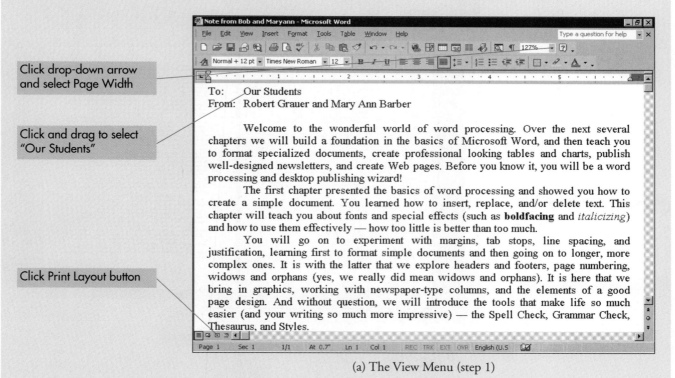

Click drop-down arrow and select Page Width

Click and drag to select "Our Students"

Click Print Layout button

(a) The View Menu (step 1)

FIGURE 2.4   *Hands-on Exercise 1*

Step 2: **Scrolling**

➤ Click and drag the **scroll box** within the vertical scroll bar to scroll to the end of the document as shown in Figure 2.4b. Click immediately before the period at the end of the last sentence.

➤ Type a **comma** and a space, then insert the phrase **but most of all, enjoy**.

➤ Drag the **scroll box** to the top of the scroll bar to get back to the beginning of the document.

➤ Click immediately before the period ending the first sentence, press the **space bar**, then add the phrase **and desktop publishing**.

➤ Use the keyboard to practice scrolling shortcuts. Press **Ctrl+Home** and **Ctrl+End** to move to the beginning and end of a document, respectively. Press **PgUp** or **PgDn** to scroll one screen in the indicated direction.

➤ Save the document.

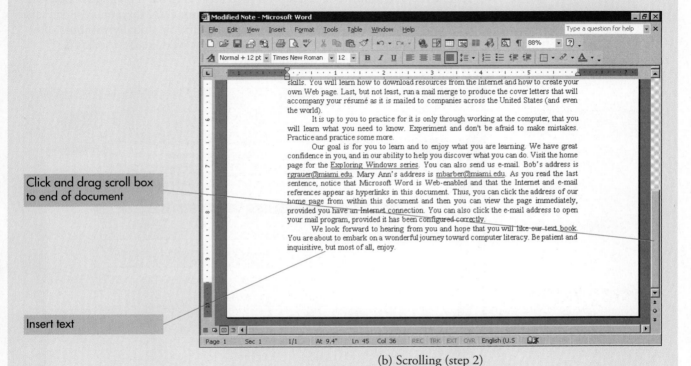

Click and drag scroll box to end of document

Insert text

(b) Scrolling (step 2)

FIGURE 2.4   *Hands-on Exercise 1 (continued)*

THE MOUSE AND THE SCROLL BAR

Scroll quickly through a document by clicking above or below the scroll box to scroll up or down an entire screen. Move to the top, bottom, or an approximate position within a document by dragging the scroll box to the corresponding position in the scroll bar; for example, dragging the scroll box to the middle of the bar moves the mouse pointer to the middle of the document. Scrolling with the mouse does not change the location of the insertion point, however, and thus you must click the mouse at the new location prior to entering text at that location.

Step 3:   **The Replace Command**

➤ Press **Ctrl+Home** to move to the beginning of the document. Pull down the **Edit menu**. Click **Replace** to produce the dialog box of Figure 2.4c. Click the **More button** to display the available options. Clear the check boxes.

➤ Type **text** in the Find what text box. Press the **Tab key**. Type **book** in the Replace with text box.

➤ Click the **Find Next button** to find the first occurrence of the word *text*. The dialog box remains on the screen and the first occurrence of *text* is selected. This is *not* an appropriate substitution.

➤ Click the **Find Next button** to move to the next occurrence without making the replacement. This time the substitution is appropriate.

➤ Click **Replace** to make the change and automatically move to the next occurrence where the substitution is again inappropriate. Click **Find Next** a final time. Word will indicate that it has finished searching the document. Click **OK**.

➤ Change the Find and Replace strings to **Mary Ann** and **Maryann**, respectively. Click the **Replace All button** to make the substitution globally without confirmation. Word will indicate that two replacements were made. Click **OK**.

➤ Close the dialog box. Save the document.

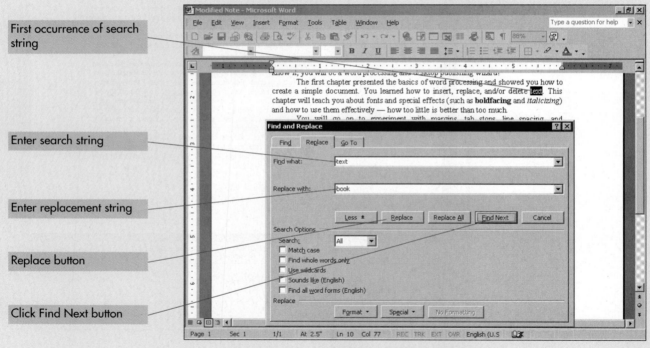

First occurrence of search string

Enter search string

Enter replacement string

Replace button

Click Find Next button

(c) The Replace Command (step 3)

FIGURE 2.4   *Hands-on Exercise 1 (continued)*

SEARCH FOR SPECIAL CHARACTERS

Use the Find and Replace commands to search for special characters such as tabs or paragraph marks. Click the More button in either dialog box, then click the Special command button that appears in the expanded dialog box to search for the additional characters. You could, for example, replace erroneous paragraph marks with a simple space, or replace five consecutive spaces with a Tab character.

Step 4: **The Windows Clipboard**

➤ Press **PgDn** to scroll toward the end of the document until you come to the paragraph beginning **It is up to you**. Select the sentence **Practice and practice some more** by dragging the mouse. (Be sure to include the period.)

➤ Pull down the **Edit menu** and click the **Copy command** or click the **Copy button**.

➤ Press **Ctrl+End** to scroll to the end of the document. Press the **space bar**. Pull down the **Edit menu** and click the **Paste command** (or click the **Paste button**).

➤ Click the **Paste Options button** if it appears as shown in Figure 2.4d to see the available options, then press **Esc** to suppress the context-sensitive menu.

➤ Click and drag to select the sentence asking you to visit our home page, which includes a hyperlink (underlined blue text). Click the **Copy button**.

➤ Press **Ctrl+End** to move to the end of the document. Pull down the **Edit menu**, click the **Paste Special command** to display the Paste Special dialog box. Select **Unformatted text** and click **OK**.

➤ The sentence appears at the end of the document, but without the hyperlink formatting. Click the **Undo button** since we do not want the sentence. You have, however, seen the effect of the Paste Special command.

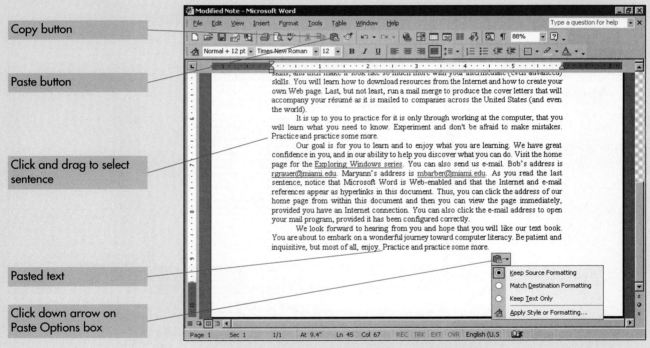

Copy button

Paste button

Click and drag to select sentence

Pasted text

Click down arrow on Paste Options box

(d) The Windows Clipboard (step 4)

FIGURE 2.4   *Hands-on Exercise 1 (continued)*

PASTE OPTIONS

Text can be copied with or without the associated formatting according to the selected option in the Paste Options button. (The button appears automatically whenever the source and destination paragraphs have different formatting.) The default is to keep the source formatting (the formatting of the copied object). The button disappears as soon as you begin typing.

Step 5: **The Office Clipboard**

➤ Pull down the **Edit menu** and click the **Office Clipboard command** to open the task pane as shown in Figure 2.4e. The contents of your clipboard will differ.
➤ Right click the first entry in the task pane that asks you to visit our home page, then click the **Delete command**. Delete all other items except the one urging you to practice what was copied in the last hands-on exercise.
➤ Click and drag to select the three sentences that indicate you can send us e-mail, and that contain our e-mail addresses. Click the **Copy button** to copy these sentences to the Office clipboard, which now contains two icons.
➤ Press **Ctrl+End** to move to the end of the document, press **enter** to begin a new paragraph, and press the **Tab key** to indent the paragraph. Click the **Paste All button** on the Office clipboard to paste both items at the end of the document. (You may have to add a space between the two sentences.)
➤ Close the task pane.

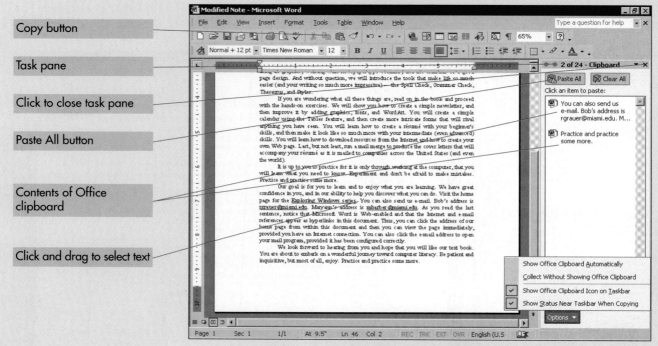

Copy button

Task pane

Click to close task pane

Paste All button

Contents of Office clipboard

Click and drag to select text

(e) The Office Clipboard (step 5)

FIGURE 2.4   *Hands-on Exercise 1 (continued)*

THE OFFICE CLIPBOARD

The Office clipboard is different from the Windows clipboard. Each successive Cut or Copy command (in any Office application) adds an object to the Office clipboard (up to a maximum of 24), whereas it replaces the contents of the Windows clipboard. You may, however, have to set the option to automatically copy to the Office clipboard for this to take place. Pull down the Edit menu, click the Office Clipboard command to open the task pane, and click the Options button at the bottom of the task pane. Check the option to always copy to the Office clipboard.

Step 6: **Undo and Redo Commands**

➤ Click the **drop-down arrow** next to the Undo button to display the previously executed actions as in Figure 2.4f. The list of actions corresponds to the editing commands you have issued since the start of the exercise.

➤ Click **Paste** (the first command on the list) to undo the last editing command; the sentence asking you to send us e-mail disappears from the last paragraph.

➤ Click the **Undo button** a second time and the sentence, Practice and practice some more, disappears from the end of the last paragraph.

➤ Click the remaining steps on the undo list to retrace your steps through the exercise one command at a time. Alternatively, you can scroll to the bottom of the list and click the last command.

➤ Either way, when the undo list is empty, you will have the document as it existed at the start of the exercise. Click the **drop-down arrow** for the Redo command to display the list of commands you have undone.

➤ Click each command in sequence (or click the command at the bottom of the list) and you will restore the document.

➤ Save the document.

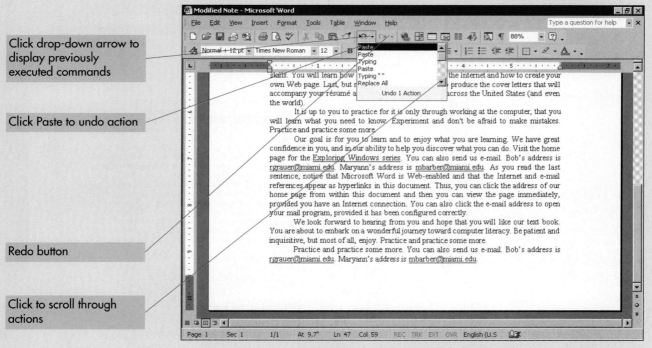

Click drop-down arrow to display previously executed commands

Click Paste to undo action

Redo button

Click to scroll through actions

(f) Undo and Redo Commands (step 6)

FIGURE 2.4 *Hands-on Exercise 1 (continued)*

KEYBOARD SHORTCUTS—CUT, COPY AND PASTE

Ctrl+X, Ctrl+C, and Ctrl+V are keyboard shortcuts to cut, copy, and paste, respectively. The "X" is supposed to remind you of a pair of scissors. The shortcuts are easier to remember when you realize that the operative letters, X, C, and V, are next to each other on the keyboard. The shortcuts work in virtually any Windows application. See practice exercise 2 at the end of the chapter.

Step 7: **Drag and Drop**

➤ Scroll to the top of the document. Click and drag to select the phrase **format specialized documents** (including the comma and space) as shown in Figure 2.4g, then drag the phrase to its new location immediately before the word *and*. (A dotted vertical bar appears as you drag the text, to indicate its new location.)

➤ Release the mouse button to complete the move. Click the **drop-down arrow** for the Undo command; click **Move** to undo the move.

➤ To copy the selected text to the same location (instead of moving it), press and hold the **Ctrl key** as you drag the text to its new location. (A plus sign appears as you drag the text, to indicate it is being copied rather than moved.)

➤ Practice the drag-and-drop procedure several times until you are confident you can move and copy with precision.

➤ Click anywhere in the document to deselect the text. Save the document.

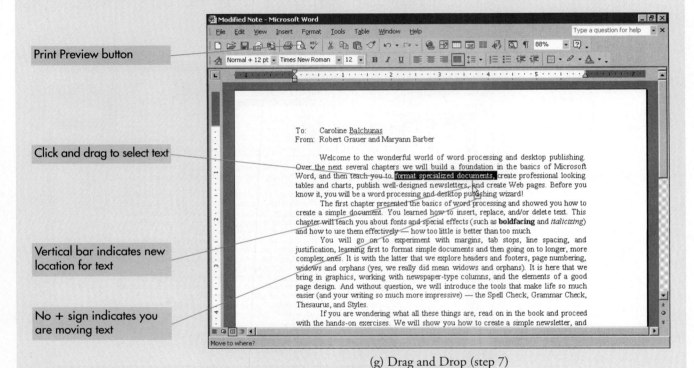

(g) Drag and Drop (step 7)

FIGURE 2.4 *Hands-on Exercise 1 (continued)*

SELECTING TEXT

The selection bar, a blank column at the far left of the document window, makes it easy to select a line, paragraph, or the entire document. To select a line, move the mouse pointer to the selection bar, point to the line and click the left mouse button. To select a paragraph, move the mouse pointer to the selection bar, point to any line in the paragraph, and double click the mouse. To select the entire document, move the mouse pointer to the selection bar and press the Ctrl key while you click the mouse.

Step 8: **The Print Preview Command**

➤ Pull down the **File menu** and click **Print Preview** (or click the **Print Preview button** on the Standard toolbar). You should see your entire document as shown in Figure 2.4h.

➤ Check that the entire document fits on one page—that is, check that you can see the last paragraph. If not, click the **Shrink to Fit button** on the toolbar to automatically change the font size in the document to force it onto one page.

➤ Click the **Print button** to print the document so that you can submit it to your instructor. Click the **Close button** to exit Print Preview and return to your document.

➤ Close the document. Exit Word if you do not want to continue with the next exercise at this time.

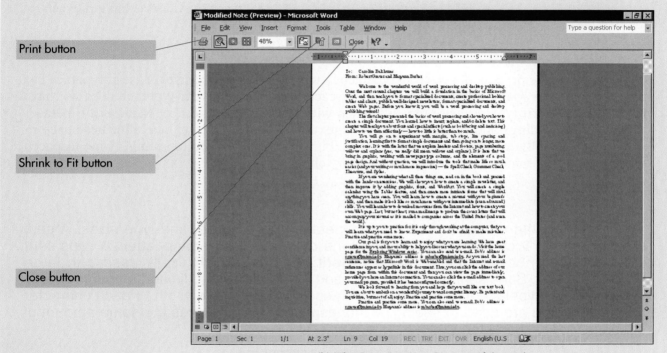

Print button

Shrink to Fit button

Close button

(h) The Print Preview Command (step 8)

FIGURE 2.4 *Hands-on Exercise 1 (continued)*

INSERT COMMENTS INTO A DOCUMENT

Share your thoughts electronically with colleagues and other students by inserting comments into a document. Click in the document where you want the comment to go, pull down the Insert menu, click the Comment command, and enter the text of the comment. All comments appear on the screen in the right margin of the document. The comments can be printed or suppressed according to the option selected in the Print command. See exercise 9 at the end of the chapter.

Typography is the process of selecting typefaces, type styles, and type sizes. The importance of these decisions is obvious, for the ultimate success of any document depends greatly on its appearance. Type should reinforce the message without calling attention to itself and should be consistent with the information you want to convey.

A ***typeface*** or ***font*** is a complete set of characters (upper- and lowercase letters, numbers, punctuation marks, and special symbols). Figure 2.5 illustrates three typefaces—***Times New Roman***, ***Arial***, and ***Courier New***—that are accessible from any Windows application.

A definitive characteristic of any typeface is the presence or absence of tiny cross lines that end the main strokes of each letter. A ***serif typeface*** has these lines. A ***sans serif typeface*** (*sans* from the French for *without*) does not. Times New Roman and Courier New are examples of a serif typeface. Arial is a sans serif typeface.

Typography is the process of selecting typefaces, type styles, and type sizes. A serif typeface has tiny cross strokes that end the main strokes of each letter. A sans serif typeface does not have these strokes. Serif typefaces are typically used with large amounts of text. Sans serif typefaces are used for headings and limited amounts of text. A proportional typeface allocates space in accordance with the width of each character and is what you are used to seeing. A monospaced typeface uses the same amount of space for every character.

(a) Times New Roman (serif and proportional)

Typography is the process of selecting typefaces, type styles, and type sizes. A serif typeface has tiny cross strokes that end the main strokes of each letter. A sans serif typeface does not have these strokes. Serif typefaces are typically used with large amounts of text. Sans serif typefaces are used for headings and limited amounts of text. A proportional typeface allocates space in accordance with the width of each character and is what you are used to seeing. A monospaced typeface uses the same amount of space for every character.

(b) Arial (sans serif and proportional)

```
Typography is the process of selecting typefaces, type styles,
and type sizes. A serif typeface has tiny cross strokes that end
the main strokes of each letter. A sans serif typeface does not
have these strokes. Serif typefaces are typically used with large
amounts of text. Sans serif typefaces are used for headings and
limited amounts of text. A proportional typeface allocates space
in accordance with the width of each character and is what you
are used to seeing. A monospaced typeface uses the same amount of
space for every character.
```

Courier New (serif and monospaced)

FIGURE 2.5   *Typefaces*

Serifs help the eye to connect one letter with the next and are generally used with large amounts of text. This book, for example, is set in a serif typeface. A sans serif typeface is more effective with smaller amounts of text and appears in headlines, corporate logos, airport signs, and so on.

A second characteristic of a typeface is whether it is monospaced or proportional. A ***monospaced typeface*** (e.g., Courier New) uses the same amount of space for every character regardless of its width. A ***proportional typeface*** (e.g., Times New Roman or Arial) allocates space according to the width of the character. Monospaced fonts are used in tables and financial projections where text must be precisely lined up, one character underneath the other. Proportional typefaces create a more professional appearance and are appropriate for most documents. Any typeface can be set in different ***type styles*** (such as regular, **bold**, or *italic*).

Type Size

Type size is a vertical measurement and is specified in points. One ***point*** is equal to $1/72$ of an inch; that is, there are 72 points to the inch. The measurement is made from the top of the tallest letter in a character set (for example, an uppercase T) to the bottom of the lowest letter (for example, a lowercase y). Most documents are set in 10 or 12 point type. Newspaper columns may be set as small as 8 point type, but that is the smallest type size you should consider. Conversely, type sizes of 14 points or higher are ineffective for large amounts of text.

Figure 2.6 shows the same phrase set in varying type sizes. Some typefaces appear larger (smaller) than others even though they may be set in the same point size. The type in Figure 2.6a, for example, looks smaller than the corresponding type in Figure 2.6b even though both are set in the same point size. Note, too, that you can vary the type size of a specific font within a document for emphasis. The eye needs at least two points to distinguish between different type sizes.

Format Font Command

The ***Format Font command*** gives you complete control over the typeface, size, and style of the text in a document. Executing the command before entering text will set the format of the text you type from that point on. You can also use the command to change the font of existing text by selecting the text, then executing the command. Either way, you will see the dialog box in Figure 2.7, in which you specify the font (typeface), style, and point size.

You can choose any of the special effects, such as SMALL CAPS, superscripts, or subscripts. You can also change the underline options (whether or not spaces are to be underlined). You can even change the color of the text on the monitor, but you need a color printer for the printed document. (The Character Spacing and Text Effects tabs produce different sets of options in which you control the spacing and appearance of the characters and are beyond the scope of our discussion.)

TYPOGRAPHY TIP—USE RESTRAINT

More is not better, especially in the case of too many typefaces and styles, which produce cluttered documents that impress no one. Try to limit yourself to a maximum of two typefaces per document, but choose multiple sizes and/or styles within those typefaces. Use boldface or italics for emphasis; but do so in moderation, because if you emphasize too many elements, the effect is lost.

This is Arial 8 point type

This is Arial 10 point type

This is Arial 12 point type

This is Arial 18 point type

This is Arial 24 point type

This is Arial 30 point type

(a) Sans Serif Typeface

This is Times New Roman 8 point type

This is Times New Roman 10 point type

This is Times New Roman 12 point type

This is Times New Roman 18 point type

This is Times New Roman 24 point type

This is Times New Roman 30 point

(b) Serif Typeface

FIGURE 2.6 *Type Size*

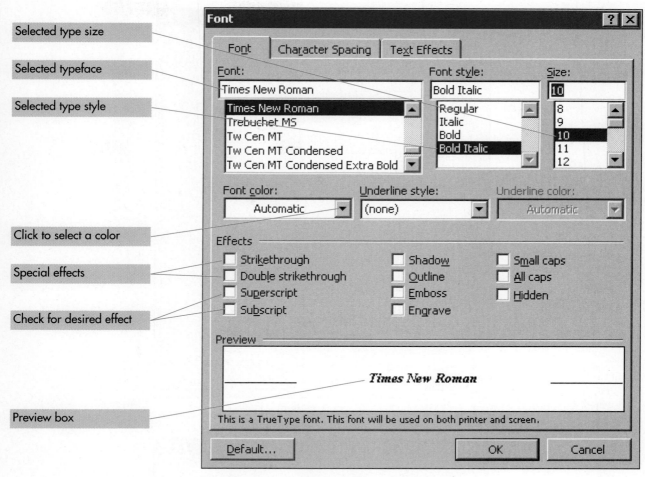

Selected type size

Selected typeface

Selected type style

Click to select a color

Special effects

Check for desired effect

Preview box

FIGURE 2.7 *Format Font Command*

The Preview box shows the text as it will appear in the document. The message at the bottom of the dialog box indicates that Times New Roman is a TrueType font and that the same font will be used on both the screen and the printer. TrueType fonts ensure that your document is truly WYSIWYG (What You See Is What You Get) because the fonts you see on the monitor will be identical to those in the printed document.

PAGE SETUP COMMAND

The *Page Setup command* in the File menu lets you change margins, paper size, orientation, paper source, and/or layout. All parameters are accessed from the dialog box in Figure 2.8 by clicking the appropriate tab within the dialog box.

The default margins are indicated in Figure 2.8a and are one inch on the top and bottom of the page, and one and a quarter inches on the left and right. You can change any (or all) of these settings by entering a new value in the appropriate text box, either by typing it explicitly or clicking the up/down arrow. All of the settings in the Page Setup command apply to the whole document regardless of the position of the insertion point. (Different settings for any option in the Page Setup dialog box can be established for different parts of a document by creating sections. Sections also affect column formatting, as discussed later in the chapter.)

Margins tab

Margin settings

Click box to select page
orientation

Preview box

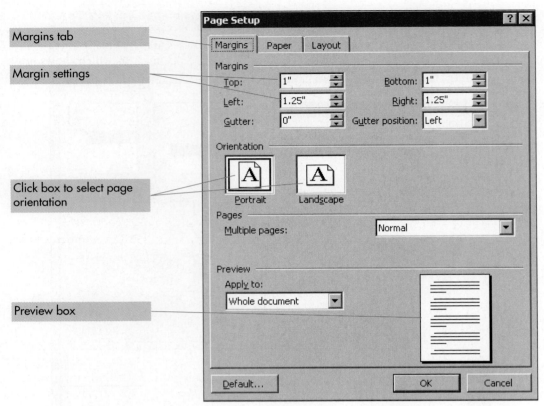

(a) Margins Tab

Layout tab

Settings for
headers/footers

Preview box

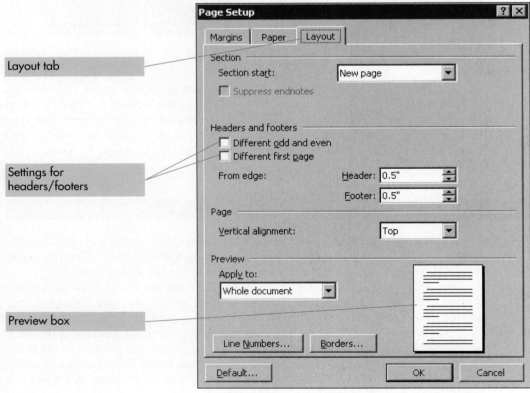

(b) Layout Tab

FIGURE 2.8   Page Setup Command

The *Margins tab* also enables you to change the orientation of a page as shown in Figure 2.8b. *Portrait orientation* is the default. *Landscape orientation* flips the page 90 degrees so that its dimensions are 11 × 8½ rather than the other way around. Note, too, the Preview area in both Figures 2.8a and 2.8b, which shows how the document will appear with the selected parameters.

The Paper tab (not shown in Figure 2.8) is used to specify which tray should be used on printers with multiple trays, and is helpful when you want to load different types of paper simultaneously. The Layout tab in Figure 2.8b is used to specify options for headers and footers (text that appears at the top or bottom of each page in a document), and/or to change the vertical alignment of text on the page.

Page Breaks

One of the first concepts you learned was that of word wrap, whereby Word inserts a soft return at the end of a line in order to begin a new line. The number and/or location of the soft returns change automatically as you add or delete text within a document. Soft returns are very different from the hard returns inserted by the user, whose number and location remain constant.

In much the same way, Word creates a *soft page break* to go to the top of a new page when text no longer fits on the current page. And just as you can insert a hard return to start a new paragraph, you can insert a *hard page break* to force any part of a document to begin on a new page. A hard page break is inserted into a document using the Break command in the Insert menu or more easily through the Ctrl+enter keyboard shortcut. (You can prevent the occurrence of awkward page breaks through the Format Paragraph command as described later in the chapter.)

AN EXERCISE IN DESIGN

The following exercise has you retrieve an existing document from the set of practice files, then experiment with various typefaces, type styles, and point sizes. The original document uses a monospaced (typewriter style) font, without boldface or italics, and you are asked to improve its appearance. The first step directs you to save the document under a new name so that you can always return to the original if necessary.

There is no right and wrong with respect to design, and you are free to choose any combination of fonts that appeals to you. The exercise takes you through various formatting options but lets you make the final decision. It does, however, ask you to print the final document and submit it to your instructor. Experiment freely and print multiple versions with different designs.

IMPOSE A TIME LIMIT

A word processor is supposed to save time and make you more productive. It will do exactly that, provided you use the word processor for its primary purpose—writing and editing. It is all too easy, however, to lose sight of that objective and spend too much time formatting the document. Concentrate on the content of your document rather than its appearance. Impose a time limit on the amount of time you will spend on formatting. End the session when the limit is reached.

Objective   To experiment with character formatting; to change fonts and to use bold-face and italics; to copy formatting with the format painter; to insert a page break and see different views of a document. Use Figure 2.9 as a guide in the exercise.

Step 1:   **Open the Existing Document**

➤ Start Word. Pull down the **File menu** and click **Open** (or click the **Open button** on the toolbar). To open a file:
  • Click the **drop-down arrow** on the Look In list box. Click the appropriate drive, drive C or drive A, depending on the location of your data.
  • Double click the **Exploring Word folder** to make it the active folder (the folder in which you will open and save the document).
  • Scroll in the **Open list box** (if necessary) until you can click **Tips for Writing** to select this document.
➤ Double click the **document icon** or click the **Open command button** to open the document shown in Figure 2.9a.
➤ Pull down the **File menu**. Click the **Save As command** to save the document as **Modified Tips**. The new document name appears on the title bar.
➤ Pull down the **View menu** and click **Normal** (or click the **Normal View button** above the status bar). Set the magnification (zoom) to **Page Width**.

New file name is displayed in title bar

Click drop-down arrow to change magnification

Normal View button

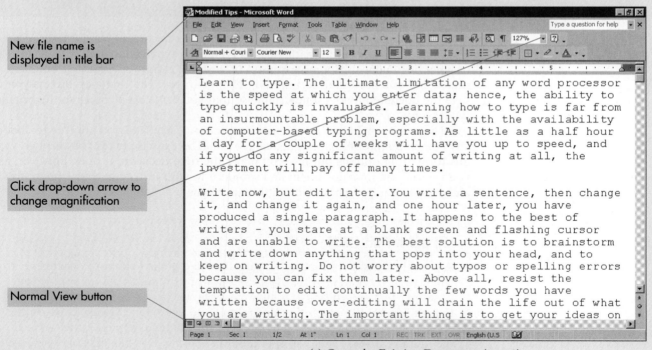

(a) Open the Existing Document (step 1)

FIGURE 2.9   *Hands-on Exercise 2*

Step 2:   **Change the Font**

➤ Pull down the **Edit menu** and click the **Select All command** (or press **Ctrl+A**) to select the entire document as shown in Figure 2.9b.
➤ Click the **down arrow** on the Font List box and choose a different font. We selected **Times New Roman**. Click the **down arrow** on the Font Size list box and choose a different type size.
➤ Pull down the **Format menu** and select the **Font command** to display the Font dialog box, where you can also change the font and/or font size.
➤ Experiment with different fonts and font sizes until you are satisfied. We ended with 12 point Times New Roman.
➤ Save the document.

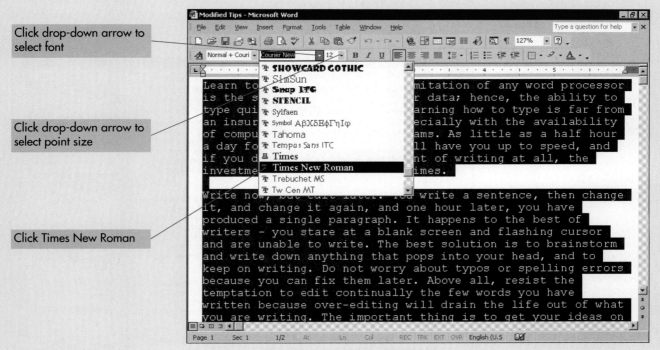

Click drop-down arrow to select font

Click drop-down arrow to select point size

Click Times New Roman

(b) Change the Font (step 2)

FIGURE 2.9   *Hands-on Exercise 2 (continued)*

FIND AND REPLACE FORMATTING

The Replace command enables you to replace formatting as well as text. To replace any text set in bold with the same text in italics, pull down the Edit menu, and click the Replace command. Click the Find what text box, but do *not* enter any text. Click the More button to expand the dialog box. Click the Format command button, click Font, click Bold in the Font Style list, and click OK. Click the Replace with text box and again do *not* enter any text. Click the Format command button, click Font, click Italic in the Font Style list, and click OK. Click the Find Next or Replace All command button to do selective or automatic replacement. Use a similar technique to replace one font with another.

Step 3:   **Boldface and Italics**

➤ Select the sentence **Learn to type** at the beginning of the document.
➤ Click the **Italic button** on the Formatting toolbar to italicize the selected phrase, which will remain selected after the italics take effect.
➤ Click the **Bold button** to boldface the selected text. The text is now in bold italic.
➤ Pull down the **View menu** and open the task pane. Click the **down arrow** in the task pane and select **Reveal Formatting** as shown in Figure 2.9c.
➤ Click anywhere in the heading, **Learn to Type**, to display its formatting properties. This type of information can be invaluable if you are unsure of the formatting in effect. Close the task pane.
➤ Experiment with different styles (bold, italics, underlining, bold italics) until you are satisfied. Each button functions as a toggle switch to turn the selected effect on or off.

Bold button

Select first sentence

Italics button

Click drop-down arrow and select Reveal Formatting

Formatting specifications of selected text

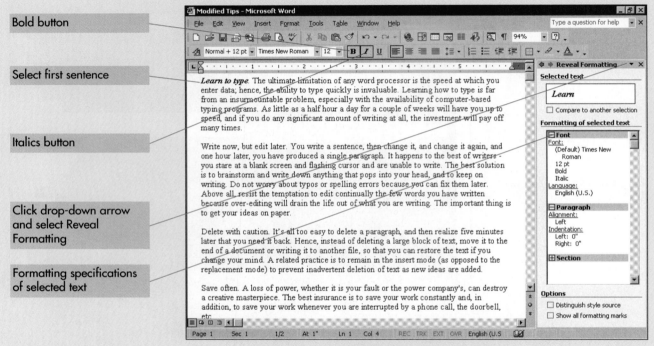

(c) Boldface and Italics (step 3)

FIGURE 2.9   *Hands-on Exercise 2 (continued)*

UNDERLINING TEXT

Underlining is less popular than it was, but Word provides a complete range of underlining options. Select the text to underline, pull down the Format menu, click Font to display the Font dialog box, and click the Font tab if necessary. Click the down arrow on the Underline Style list box to choose the type of underlining you want. You can choose whether to underline the words only (i.e., the underline does not appear in the space between words). You can also choose the type of line you want—solid, dashed, thick, or thin.

Step 4: **The Format Painter**

➤ Click anywhere within the sentence Learn to Type. **Double click** the **Format Painter button** on the Standard toolbar. The mouse pointer changes to a paint-brush as shown in Figure 2.9d.

➤ Drag the mouse pointer over the next title, **Write now**, **but edit later**, and release the mouse. The formatting from the original sentence (bold italic) has been applied to this sentence as well.

➤ Drag the mouse pointer (in the shape of a paintbrush) over the remaining titles (the first sentence in each paragraph) to copy the formatting. You can click the down arrow on the vertical scroll bar to bring more of the document into view.

➤ Click the **Format Painter button** after you have painted the title of the last tip to turn the feature off. (Note that clicking the Format Painter button, rather than double clicking, will paint only one item.)

➤ Save the document.

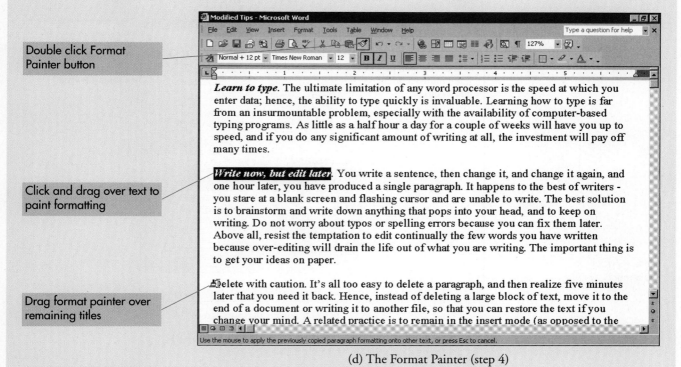

Double click Format Painter button

Click and drag over text to paint formatting

Drag format painter over remaining titles

(d) The Format Painter (step 4)

FIGURE 2.9   *Hands-on Exercise 2 (continued)*

HIGHLIGHTING TEXT

You will love the Highlight tool, especially if you are in the habit of high-lighting text with a pen. Click the down arrow next to the tool to select a color (yellow is the default) to change the mouse pointer to a pen, then click and drag to highlight the desired text. Continue dragging the mouse to highlight as many selections as you like. Click the Highlight tool a second time to turn off the feature. See practice exercise 2 at the end of the chapter.

Step 5:   **Change Margins**

➤ Press **Ctrl+End** to move to the end of the document as shown in Figure 2.9e. You will see a dotted line indicating a soft page break. (If you do not see the page break, it means that your document fits on one page because you used a different font and/or a smaller point size. We used 12 point Times New Roman.)

➤ Pull down the **File menu**. Click **Page Setup**. Click the **Margins tab** if necessary. Change the bottom margin to **.75** inch.

➤ Check that these settings apply to the **Whole Document**. Click **OK**. Save the document.

➤ The page break disappears because more text fits on the page.

Soft page break

Enter bottom margin of .75″

Settings apply to Whole document

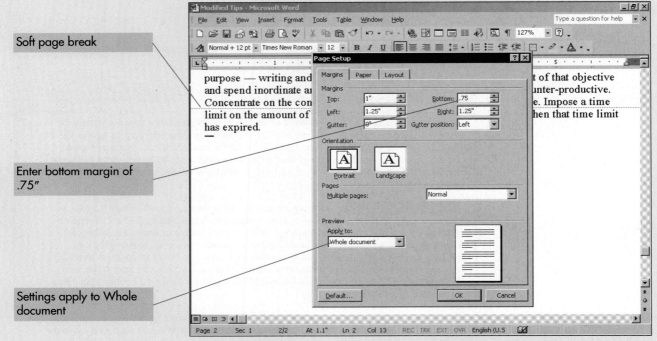

(e) Change Margins (step 5)

FIGURE 2.9   *Hands-on Exercise 2 (continued)*

DIALOG BOX SHORTCUTS

You can use keyboard shortcuts to select options in a dialog box. Press Tab (Shift+Tab) to move forward (backward) from one field or command button to the next. Press Alt plus the underlined letter to move directly to a field or command button. Press enter to activate the selected command button. Press Esc to exit the dialog box without taking action. Press the space bar to toggle check boxes on or off. Press the down arrow to open a drop-down list box once the list has been accessed, then press the up or down arrow to move between options in a list box. These are uniform shortcuts that apply to any Windows application.

Step 6: **Create the Title Page**

➤ Press **Ctrl+Home** to move to the beginning of the document. Press **enter** three or four times to add a few blank lines.
➤ Press **Ctrl+enter** to insert a hard page break. You will see the words "Page Break" in the middle of a dotted line as shown in Figure 2.9f.
➤ Press the **up arrow key** three times. Enter the title **Tips for Writing**. Select the title, and format it in a larger point size, such as 24 points.
➤ Press **enter** to move to a new line. Type your name and format it in a different point size, such as 14 points.
➤ Select both the title and your name as shown in the figure. Click the **Center button** on the Formatting toolbar.
➤ Save the document.

Font button

Font size button

Click and drag to select text

Ctrl+Enter creates a hard page break

Center button

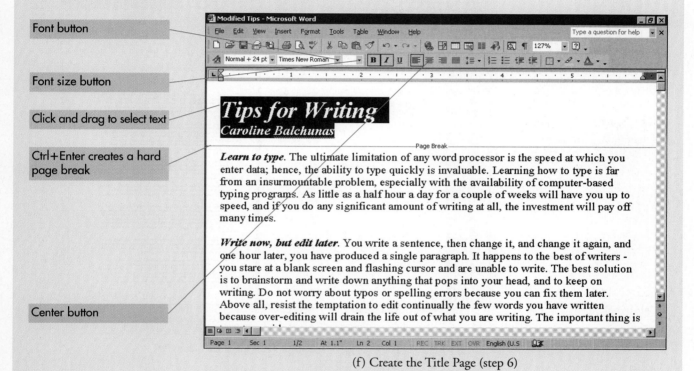

(f) Create the Title Page (step 6)

FIGURE 2.9 *Hands-on Exercise 2 (continued)*

DOUBLE CLICK AND TYPE

Creating a title page is a breeze if you take advantage of the (double) click and type feature. Pull down the View menu and change to the Print Layout view. Double click anywhere on the page and you can begin typing immediately at that location, without having to type several blank lines, or set tabs. The feature does not work in the Normal view or in a document that has columns. To enable (disable) the feature, pull down the Tools menu, click the Options command, click the Edit tab, then check (clear) the Enable Click and Type check box.

Step 7:   **The Completed Document**

➤ Pull down the **View menu** and click **Print Layout** (or click the **Print Layout button** above the status bar).

➤ Click the **Zoom Control arrow** on the Standard toolbar and select **Two Pages**. Release the mouse to view the completed document in Figure 2.9g.

➤ You may want to add additional blank lines at the top of the title page to move the title further down on the page.

➤ Save the document. Be sure that the document fits on two pages (the title page and text), then click the **Print button** on the Standard toolbar to print the document for your instructor.

➤ Exit Word if you do not want to continue with the next exercise at this time.

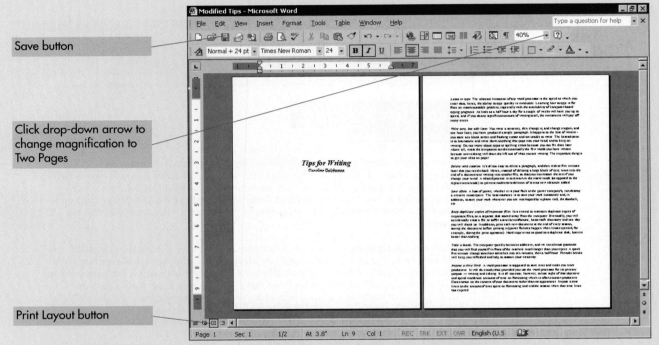

Save button

Click drop-down arrow to change magnification to Two Pages

Print Layout button

(g) The Completed Document (step 7)

FIGURE 2.9   *Hands-on Exercise 2 (continued)*

THE PAGE SETUP COMMAND

The Page Setup command controls the margins of a document, and by extension, it controls the amount of text that fits on a page. Pull down the File menu and click the Page Setup command to display the Page Setup dialog box, click the Margins tab, then adjust the left and right (or top and bottom) margins to fit additional text on a page. Click the down arrow in the Apply to area to select the whole document. Click OK to accept the settings and close the dialog box.

A change in typography is only one way to alter the appearance of a document. You can also change the alignment, indentation, tab stops, or line spacing for any paragraph(s) within the document. You can control the pagination and prevent the occurrence of awkward page breaks by specifying that an entire paragraph has to appear on the same page, or that a one-line paragraph (e.g., a heading) should appear on the same page as the next paragraph. You can include borders or shading for added emphasis around selected paragraphs.

All of these features are implemented at the paragraph level and affect all selected paragraphs. If no paragraphs are selected, the commands affect the entire current paragraph (the paragraph containing the insertion point), regardless of the position of the insertion point when the command is executed.

Alignment

Text can be aligned in four different ways as shown in Figure 2.10. It may be justified (flush left/flush right), left aligned (flush left with a ragged right margin), right aligned (flush right with a ragged left margin), or centered within the margins (ragged left and right).

Left aligned text is perhaps the easiest to read. The first letters of each line align with each other, helping the eye to find the beginning of each line. The lines themselves are of irregular length. There is uniform spacing between words, and the ragged margin on the right adds white space to the text, giving it a lighter and more informal look.

Justified text produces lines of equal length, with the spacing between words adjusted to align at the margins. It may be more difficult to read than text that is left aligned because of the uneven (sometimes excessive) word spacing and/or the greater number of hyphenated words needed to justify the lines.

Type that is centered or right aligned is restricted to limited amounts of text where the effect is more important than the ease of reading. Centered text, for example, appears frequently on wedding invitations, poems, or formal announcements. Right aligned text is used with figure captions and short headlines.

Indents

Individual paragraphs can be indented so that they appear to have different margins from the rest of a document. Indentation is established at the paragraph level; thus different indentation can be in effect for different paragraphs. One paragraph may be indented from the left margin only, another from the right margin only, and a third from both the left and right margins. The first line of any paragraph may be indented differently from the rest of the paragraph. And finally, a paragraph may be set with no indentation at all, so that it aligns on the left and right margins.

The indentation of a paragraph is determined by three settings: the *left indent*, the *right indent*, and a *special indent* (if any). There are two types of special indentation, first line and hanging, as will be explained shortly. The left and right indents are set to zero by default, as is the special indent, and produce a paragraph with no indentation at all as shown in Figure 2.11a. Positive values for the left and right indents offset the paragraph from both margins as shown in Figure 2.11b.

The *first line indent* (Figure 2.11c) affects only the first line in the paragraph and is implemented by pressing the Tab key at the beginning of the paragraph. A *hanging indent* (Figure 2.11d) sets the first line of a paragraph at the left indent and indents the remaining lines according to the amount specified. Hanging indents are often used with bulleted or numbered lists.

We, the people of the United States, in order to form a more perfect Union, establish justice, insure domestic tranquillity, provide for the common defense, promote the general welfare, and secure the blessings of liberty to ourselves and our posterity, do ordain and establish this Constitution for the United States of America.

(a) Justified (flush left/flush right)

We, the people of the United States, in order to form a more perfect Union, establish justice, insure domestic tranquillity, provide for the common defense, promote the general welfare, and secure the blessings of liberty to ourselves and our posterity, do ordain and establish this Constitution for the United States of America.

(b) Left Aligned (flush left/ragged right)

We, the people of the United States, in order to form a more perfect Union, establish justice, insure domestic tranquillity, provide for the common defense, promote the general welfare, and secure the blessings of liberty to ourselves and our posterity, do ordain and establish this Constitution for the United States of America.

(c) Right Aligned (ragged left/flush right)

We, the people of the United States, in order to form a more perfect Union, establish justice, insure domestic tranquillity, provide for the common defense, promote the general welfare, and secure the blessings of liberty to ourselves and our posterity, do ordain and establish this Constitution for the United States of America.

(d) Centered (ragged left/ragged right)

FIGURE 2.10   *Alignment*

The left and right indents are defined as the distance between the text and the left and right margins, respectively. Both parameters are set to zero in this paragraph and so the text aligns on both margins. Different indentation can be applied to different paragraphs in the same document.

(a) No Indents

Positive values for the left and right indents offset a paragraph from the rest of a document and are often used for long quotations. This paragraph has left and right indents of one-half inch each. Different indentation can be applied to different paragraphs in the same document.

(b) Left and Right Indents

A first line indent affects only the first line in the paragraph and is implemented by pressing the Tab key at the beginning of the paragraph. The remainder of the paragraph is aligned at the left margin (or the left indent if it differs from the left margin) as can be seen from this example. Different indentation can be applied to different paragraphs in the same document.

(c) First Line Indent

A hanging indent sets the first line of a paragraph at the left indent and indents the remaining lines according to the amount specified. Hanging indents are often used with bulleted or numbered lists. Different indentation can be applied to different paragraphs in the same document.

(d) Hanging (Special) Indent

FIGURE 2.11   *Indents*

Tabs

Anyone who has used a typewriter is familiar with the function of the Tab key; that is, press Tab and the insertion point moves to the next **tab stop** (a measured position to align text at a specific place). The Tab key is much more powerful in Word as you can choose from four different types of tab stops (left, center, right, and decimal). You can also specify a **leader character**, typically dots or hyphens, to draw the reader's eye across the page. Tabs are often used to create columns of text within a document.

The default tab stops are set every ½ inch and are left aligned, but you can change the alignment and/or position with the Format Tabs command. Figure 2.12 illustrates a dot leader in combination with a right tab to produce a Table of Contents. The default tab stops have been cleared in Figure 2.12a, in favor of a single right tab at 5.5 inches. The option button for a dot leader has also been checked. The resulting document is shown in Figure 2.12b.

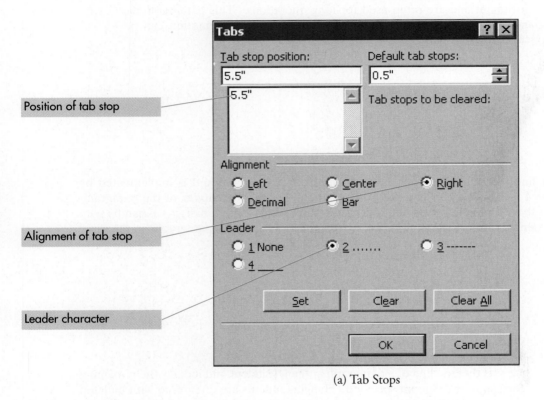

Position of tab stop

Alignment of tab stop

Leader character

(a) Tab Stops

Right tab with dot leader

(b) Table of Contents

FIGURE 2.12 *Tabs*

Hyphenation

Hyphenation gives a document a more professional look by eliminating excessive gaps of white space. It is especially useful in narrow columns and/or justified text. Hyphenation is implemented through the Language command in the Tools menu. You can choose to hyphenate a document automatically, in which case the hyphens are inserted as the document is created. (Microsoft Word will automatically rehyphenate the document to adjust for subsequent changes in editing.)

You can also hyphenate a document manually, to have Word prompt you prior to inserting each hyphen. Manual hyphenation does not, however, adjust for changes that affect the line breaks, and so it should be done only after the document is complete. And finally, you can fine-tune the use of hyphenation by preventing a hyphenated word from breaking if it falls at the end of a line. This is done by inserting a *nonbreaking hyphen* (press Ctrl+Shift+Hyphen) when the word is typed initially.

Line Spacing

Line spacing determines the space between the lines in a paragraph. Word provides complete flexibility and enables you to select any multiple of line spacing (single, double, line and a half, and so on). You can also specify line spacing in terms of points (there are 72 points per inch).

Line spacing is set at the paragraph level through the Format Paragraph command, which sets the spacing within a paragraph. The command also enables you to add extra spacing before the first line in a paragraph or after the last line. (Either technique is preferable to the common practice of single spacing the paragraphs within a document, then adding a blank line between paragraphs.)

FORMAT PARAGRAPH COMMAND

The *Format Paragraph command* is used to specify the alignment, indentation, line spacing, and pagination for the selected paragraph(s). As indicated, all of these features are implemented at the paragraph level and affect all selected paragraphs. If no paragraphs are selected, the command affects the entire current paragraph (the paragraph containing the insertion point).

The Format Paragraph command is illustrated in Figure 2.13. The Indents and Spacing tab in Figure 2.13a calls for a hanging indent, line spacing of 1.5 lines, and justified alignment. The preview area within the dialog box enables you to see how the paragraph will appear within the document.

The Line and Page Breaks tab in Figure 2.13b illustrates an entirely different set of parameters in which you control the pagination within a document. The check boxes in Figure 2.13b enable you to prevent the occurrence of awkward soft page breaks that detract from the appearance of a document.

You might, for example, want to prevent widows and orphans, terms used to describe isolated lines that seem out of place. A *widow* refers to the last line of a paragraph appearing by itself at the top of a page. An *orphan* is the first line of a paragraph appearing by itself at the bottom of a page.

You can also impose additional controls by clicking one or more check boxes. Use the Keep Lines Together option to prevent a soft page break from occurring within a paragraph and ensure that the entire paragraph appears on the same page. (The paragraph is moved to the top of the next page if it doesn't fit on the bottom of the current page.) Use the Keep with Next option to prevent a soft page break between the two paragraphs. This option is typically used to keep a heading (a one-line paragraph) with its associated text in the next paragraph.

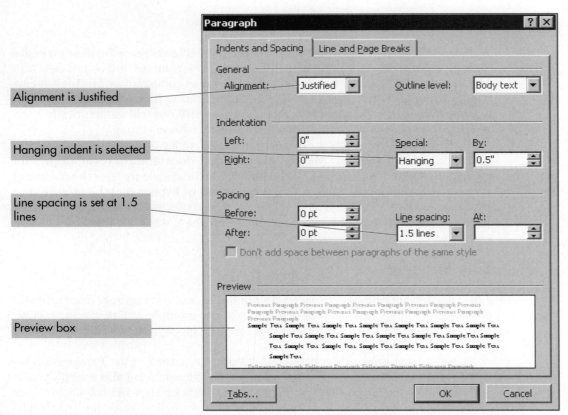

Alignment is Justified

Hanging indent is selected

Line spacing is set at 1.5 lines

Preview box

(a) Indents and Spacing

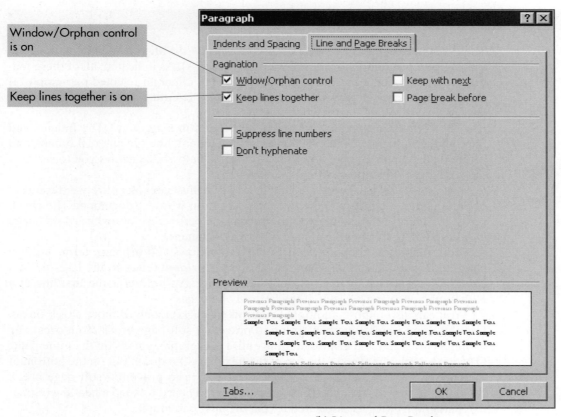

Window/Orphan control is on

Keep lines together is on

(b) Line and Page Breaks

FIGURE 2.13   *Format Paragraph Command*

Borders and Shading

The **Borders and Shading command** puts the finishing touches on a document and is illustrated in Figure 2.14. The command is applied to selected text within a paragraph, to the entire paragraph if no text is selected, or to the entire page if the Page Border tab is selected. Thus, you can create boxed and/or shaded text as well as place horizontal or vertical lines around different quantities of text.

You can choose from several different line styles in any color (assuming you have a color printer). You can place a uniform border around a paragraph (choose Box), or you can choose a shadow effect with thicker lines at the right and bottom. You can also apply lines to selected sides of a paragraph(s) by selecting a line style, then clicking the desired sides as appropriate.

The Page Border tab enables you to place a decorative border around one or more selected pages. As with a paragraph border, you can place the border around the entire page, or you can select one or more sides. The page border also provides an additional option to use preselected clip art instead of ordinary lines.

Shading is implemented independently of the border. Clear (no shading) is the default. Solid (100%) shading creates a solid box where the text is turned white so you can read it. Shading of 10 or 20 percent is generally most effective to add emphasis to the selected paragraph. The Borders and Shading command is implemented on the paragraph level and affects the entire paragraph (unless text has been selected within the paragraph)—either the current or selected paragraph(s).

The two command buttons at the bottom of the dialog box provide additional options. The Show Toolbar button displays the Tables and Borders toolbar that facilitates both borders and shading. The Horizontal Line button provides access to a variety of attractive designs.

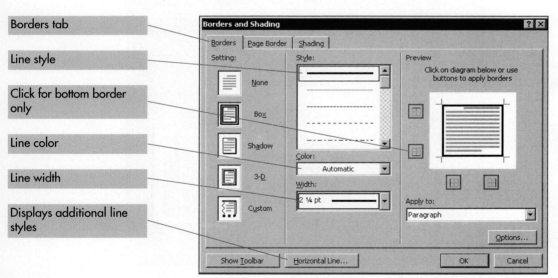

FIGURE 2.14   *Paragraph Borders and Shading*

FORMATTING AND THE PARAGRAPH MARK

The paragraph mark ¶ at the end of a paragraph does more than just indicate the presence of a hard return. It also stores all of the formatting in effect for the paragraph. Hence in order to preserve the formatting when you move or copy a paragraph, you must include the paragraph mark in the selected text. Click the Show/Hide ¶ button on the toolbar to display the paragraph mark and make sure it has been selected.

Columns add interest to a document and are implemented through the **Columns command** in the Format menu as shown in Figure 2.15. You specify the number of columns and, optionally, the space between columns. Microsoft Word does the rest, calculating the width of each column according to the left and right margins on the page and the specified (default) space between columns.

The dialog box in Figure 2.15 implements a design of three equal columns. The 2-inch width of each column is computed automatically based on left and right page margins of 1 inch each and the ¼-inch spacing between columns. The width of each column is determined by subtracting the sum of the margins and the space between the columns (a total of 2½ inches in this example) from the page width of 8½ inches. The result of the subtraction is 6 inches, which is divided by 3, resulting in a column width of 2 inches.

There is, however, one subtlety associated with column formatting, and that is the introduction of the **section**, which controls elements such as the orientation of a page (landscape or portrait), margins, page numbers, and/or the number of columns. All of the documents in the text thus far have consisted of a single section, and therefore section formatting was not an issue. It becomes important only when you want to vary an element that is formatted at the section level. You could, for example, use section formatting to create a document that has one column on its title page and two columns on the remaining pages. This requires you to divide the document into two sections through insertion of a **section break**. You then format each section independently and specify the number of columns in each section.

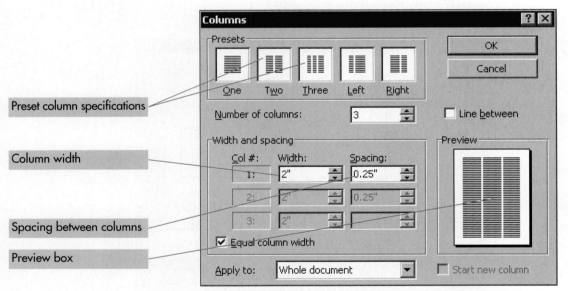

Preset column specifications

Column width

Spacing between columns

Preview box

FIGURE 2.15   *The Format Columns Command*

THE SECTION VERSUS THE PARAGRAPH

Line spacing, alignment, tabs, and indents are implemented at the paragraph level. Change any of these parameters anywhere within the current (or selected) paragraph(s) and you change *only* those paragraph(s). Margins, page numbering, orientation, and columns are implemented at the section level. Change these parameters anywhere within a section and you change the characteristics of every page within that section.

PARAGRAPH FORMATTING

Objective To implement line spacing, alignment, and indents; to implement widow and orphan protection; to box and shade a selected paragraph. Use Figure 2.16 as a guide in the exercise.

Step 1: **Select-Then-Do**

➤ Open the **Modified Tips** document from the previous exercise. If necessary, change to the Print Layout view. Click the **Zoom drop-down arrow** and click **Two Pages** to match the view in Figure 2.16a.

➤ Select the entire second page as shown in the figure. Point to the selected text and click the **right mouse button** to produce the shortcut menu. Click **Paragraph**.

Click drop-down arrow to change magnification

Click and drag to select second page

Point to selected text and click right mouse button

Print Layout View button

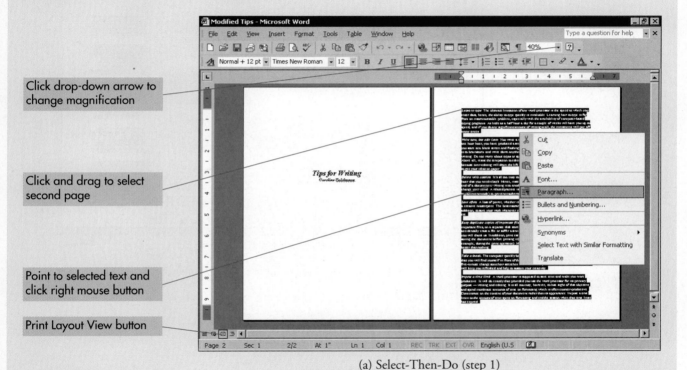

(a) Select-Then-Do (step 1)

FIGURE 2.16 *Hands-on Exercise 3*

SELECT TEXT WITH THE F8 (EXTEND) KEY

Move to the beginning of the text you want to select, then press the F8 (extend) key. The letters EXT will appear in the status bar. Use the arrow keys to extend the selection in the indicated direction; for example, press the down arrow key to select the line. You can also type any character—for example, a letter, space, or period—to extend the selection to the first occurrence of that character. Thus, typing a space or period is equivalent to selecting a word or sentence, respectively. Press Esc to cancel the selection mode.

Step 2:   **Line Spacing, Justification, and Pagination**

➤ If necessary, click the **Indents and Spacing tab** to view the options in Figure 2.16b. Click the **down arrow** on the list box for Line Spacing and select **1.5 Lines**. Click the **down arrow** on the Alignment list box and select **Justified**.

➤ Click the tab for **Line and Page Breaks**. Check the box for **Keep Lines Together**. If necessary, check the box for **Widow/Orphan Control**. Click **OK** to accept all of the settings in the dialog box.

➤ Click anywhere in the document to deselect the text and see the effects of the formatting changes.

➤ Save the document.

Click Indents and Spacing tab

Click drop-down arrow and select Justified

Click drop-down arrow and select 1.5

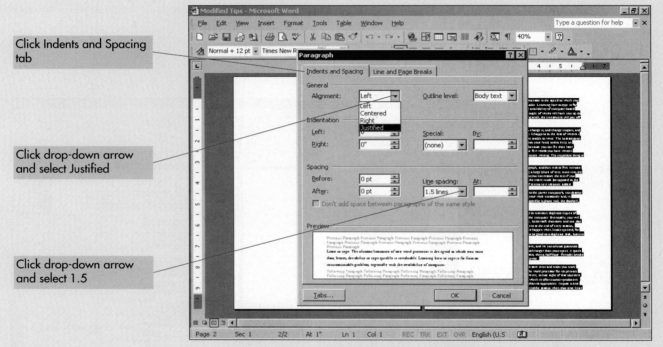

(b) Line Spacing, Justification, and Pagination (step 2)

FIGURE 2.16   *Hands-on Exercise 3 (continued)*

VIEW THE FORMATTING PROPERTIES

Open the task pane and click the down arrow in the title bar to select Formatting Properties to display complete information for the selected text in the document. The properties are displayed by Font, Paragraph, and Section, enabling you to click the plus or minus sign next to each item to view or hide the underlying details. The properties in each area are links to the associated dialog boxes. Click Alignment or Justification, for example, within the Paragraph area to open the associated dialog box, where you can change the indicated property.

Step 3: **Indents**

➤ Select the second paragraph as shown in Figure 2.16c. (The second paragraph will not yet be indented.)
➤ Pull down the **Format menu** and click **Paragraph** (or press the **right mouse button** to produce the shortcut menu and click **Paragraph**).
➤ If necessary, click the **Indents and Spacing tab** in the Paragraph dialog box. Click the **up arrow** on the Left Indentation text box to set the **Left Indent** to **.5** inch. Set the **Right indent** to **.5** inch. Click **OK**. Your document should match Figure 2.16c.
➤ Save the document.

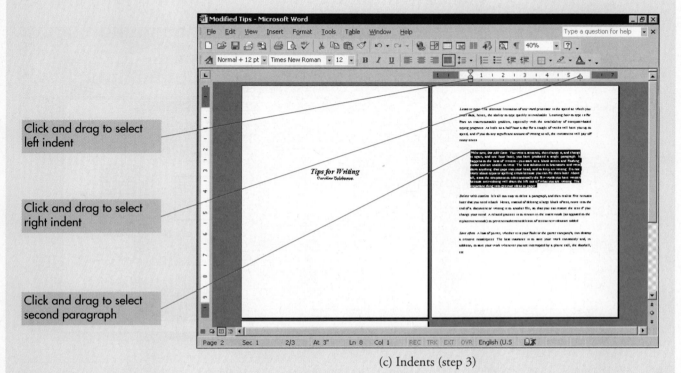

Click and drag to select left indent

Click and drag to select right indent

Click and drag to select second paragraph

(c) Indents (step 3)

FIGURE 2.16 *Hands-on Exercise 3 (continued)*

INDENTS AND THE RULER

Use the ruler to change the special, left, and/or right indents. Select the paragraph (or paragraphs) in which you want to change indents, then drag the appropriate indent markers to the new location(s). If you get a hanging indent when you wanted to change the left indent, it means you dragged the bottom triangle instead of the box. Click the Undo button and try again. (You can always use the Format Paragraph command rather than the ruler if you continue to have difficulty.)

Step 4:   **Borders and Shading**

> Pull down the **Format menu**. Click **Borders and Shading** to produce the dialog box in Figure 2.16d.
> If necessary, click the **Borders tab**. Select a style and width for the line around the box. Click the rectangle labeled **Box** under Setting. You can also experiment with a partial border by clicking in the Preview area to toggle a line on or off.
> Click the **Shading Tab**. Click the **down arrow** on the Style list box. Click **10%**.
> Click **OK** to accept the settings for both Borders and Shading. Click outside the paragraph.
> Save the document.

Click Borders tab

Click box

Selected line style

Click to see available line widths

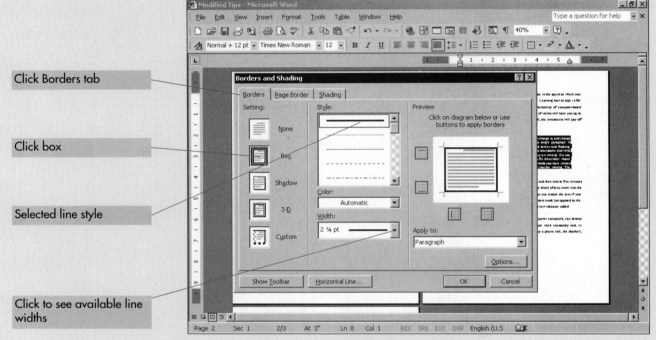

(d) Borders and Shading (step 4)

FIGURE 2.16   *Hands-on Exercise 3 (continued)*

SELECT NONCONTIGUOUS TEXT

Anyone who has used a previous version of Word will be happy to learn that you can select noncontiguous blocks of text, and then apply the same formatting to the selected text with a single command. Click and drag to select the first item, then press and hold the Ctrl key as you continue to drag the mouse over additional blocks of text. All of the selected text is highlighted within the document. Apply the desired formatting, then click anywhere in the document to deselect the text and continue working.

Step 5:   **View Many Pages**

➤ Pull down the **View menu** and click **Zoom** to display the Zoom dialog box. Click the monitor icon in the Many Pages area, then click and drag to display three pages across. Release the mouse. Click **OK**.

➤ Your screen should match the one in Figure 2.16e, which displays all three pages of the document.

➤ The Print Layout view displays both a vertical and a horizontal ruler. The boxed and indented paragraph is clearly shown in the second page.

➤ The soft page break between pages two and three occurs between tips rather than within a tip; that is, the text of each tip is kept together on the same page.

➤ Save the document a final time. Print the document at this point in the exercise and submit it to your instructor.

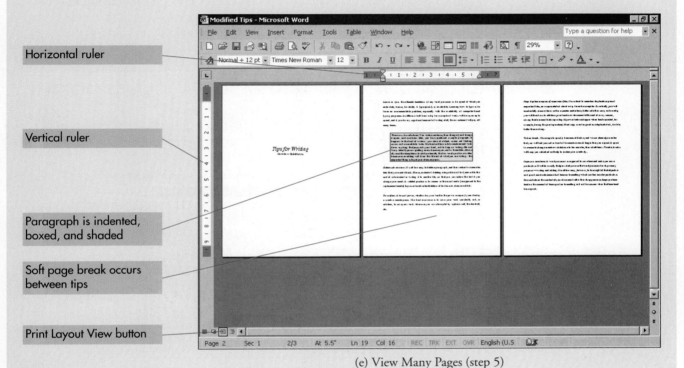

Horizontal ruler

Vertical ruler

Paragraph is indented, boxed, and shaded

Soft page break occurs between tips

Print Layout View button

(e) View Many Pages (step 5)

FIGURE 2.16   *Hands-on Exercise 3 (continued)*

THE PAGE BORDER COMMAND

You can apply a border to the title page of your document, to every page except the title page, or to every page including the title page. Click anywhere on the page, pull down the Format menu, click Borders and Shading, and click the Page Borders tab. First design the border by selecting a style, color, width, and art (if any). Then choose the page(s) to which you want to apply the border by clicking the drop-down arrow in the Apply to list box. Close the Borders and Shading dialog box.

Step 6:   **Change the Column Structure**

➤ Pull down the **File menu** and click the **Page Setup command** to display the Page Setup dialog box. Click the **Margins tab**, then change the Left and Right margins to 1″ each. Click **OK** to accept the settings and close the dialog box.

➤ Click the **down arrow** on the Zoom list box and return to **Page Width**. Press the **PgUp** or **PgDn key** to scroll until the second page comes into view.

➤ Click anywhere in the paragraph, "Write Now but Edit Later". Pull down the **Format menu**, click the **Paragraph command**, click the **Indents and Spacing tab** if necessary, then change the left and right indents to 0.

➤ All paragraphs in the document should have the same indentation as shown in Figure 2.16f. Pull down the **Format menu** and click the **Columns command** to display the Columns dialog box.

➤ Click the icon for **three columns**. The default spacing between columns is .5″, which leads to a column width of 1.83″. Click in the Spacing list box and change the spacing to **.25″**, which automatically changes the column width to 2″.

➤ Clear the box for the **Line Between** columns. Click **OK**.

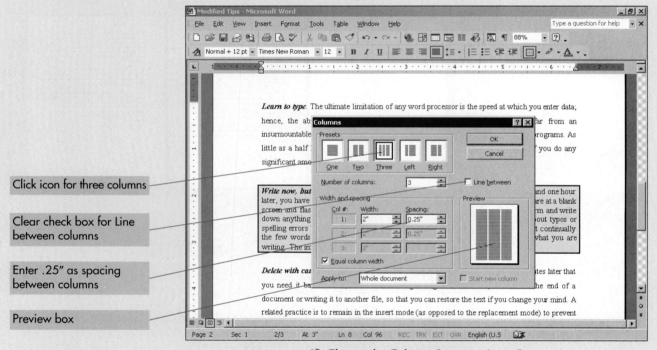

(f) Change the Column Structure (step 6)

FIGURE 2.16   *Hands-on Exercise 3 (continued)*

USE THE RULER TO CHANGE COLUMN WIDTH

Click anywhere within the column whose width you want to change, then point to the ruler and click and drag the right margin (the mouse pointer changes to a double arrow) to change the column width. Changing the width of one column in a document with equal-sized columns changes the width of all other columns so that they remain equal. Changing the width in a document with unequal columns changes only that column.

Step 7: **Insert a Section Break**

➤ Pull down the **View menu**, click the **Zoom command**, then click the **Many Pages option button**. Click and drag over 3 pages, then click **OK**. The document has switched to column formatting.

➤ Click at the beginning of the second page, immediately to the left of the first paragraph. Pull down the **Insert menu** and click **Break** to display the dialog box in Figure 2.16g.

➤ Click the **Continuous option button**, then click **OK** to accept the settings and close the dialog box.

➤ Click anywhere on the title page (before the section break you just inserted). Click the **Columns button**, then click the first column.

➤ The formatting for the first section of the document (the title page) should change to one column; the title of the document and your name are centered across the entire page.

➤ Print the document in this format for your instructor. Decide in which format you want to save the document—that is, as it exists now, or as it existed at the end of step 5. Exit Word.

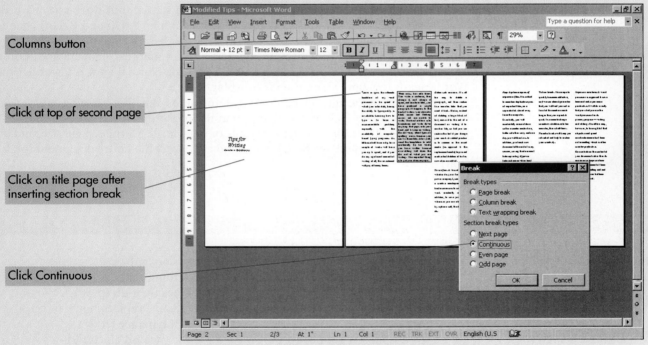

Columns button

Click at top of second page

Click on title page after inserting section break

Click Continuous

(g) Insert a Section Break (step 7)

FIGURE 2.16 *Hands-on Exercise 3 (continued)*

THE COLUMNS BUTTON

The Columns button on the Standard toolbar is the fastest way to create columns in a document. Click the button, drag the mouse to choose the number of columns, then release the mouse to create the columns. The toolbar lets you change the number of columns, but not the spacing between columns. The toolbar is also limited, in that you cannot create columns of different widths or select a line between the columns.

Many operations in Word are done within the context of select-then-do; that is, select the text, then execute the necessary command. Text may be selected by dragging the mouse, by using the selection bar to the left of the document, or by using the keyboard. Text is deselected by clicking anywhere within the document.

The Find and Replace commands locate a designated character string and optionally replace one or more occurrences of that string with a different character string. The search may be case sensitive and/or restricted to whole words. The commands may also be applied to formatting and/or special characters.

Text is moved or copied through a combination of the Cut, Copy, and Paste commands and/or the drag-and-drop facility. The contents of the Windows clipboard are modified by any subsequent Cut or Copy command, but are unaffected by the Paste command; that is, the same text can be pasted into multiple locations. The Office clipboard retains up to 24 entries that were cut or copied.

The Undo command reverses the effect of previous commands. The Undo and Redo commands work in conjunction with one another; that is, every command that is undone can be redone at a later time.

Scrolling occurs when a document is too large to be seen in its entirety. Scrolling with the mouse changes what is displayed on the screen, but does not move the insertion point. Scrolling via the keyboard (for example, PgUp and PgDn) changes what is seen on the screen as well as the location of the insertion point.

The Print Layout view displays top and bottom margins, headers and footers, and other elements not seen in the Normal view. The Normal view is faster because Word spends less time formatting the display.

The Format Paragraph command determines the line spacing, alignment, indents, and text flow, all of which are set at the paragraph level. Borders and shading are also set at the character, paragraph, or page level. Margins, page size, and orientation are set in the Page Setup command and affect the entire document (or section).

KEY TERMS

Arial (p. 64)
Automatic replacement (p. 52)
Borders and Shading command (p. 83)
Case-insensitive search (p. 52)
Case-sensitive search (p. 52)
Columns command (p. 84)
Copy command (p. 50)
Courier New (p. 64)
Cut command (p. 50)
Find command (p. 51)
First line indent (p. 77)
Font (p. 64)
Format Font command (p. 65)
Format Painter (p. 73)
Format Paragraph command (p. 81)
Go To command (p. 51)
Hanging indent (p. 77)
Hard page break (p. 69)
Highlighting (p. 73)
Hyphenation (p. 81)

Landscape orientation (p. 69)
Leader character (p. 80)
Left indent (p. 77)
Line spacing (p. 81)
Margins tab (p. 69)
Monospaced typeface (p. 65)
Nonbreaking hyphen (p. 81)
Normal view (p. 55)
Office clipboard (p. 50)
Orphan (p. 81)
Page Setup command (p. 67)
Paste command (p. 50)
Paste Special command (p. 50)
Point (p. 65)
Portrait orientation (p. 69)
Print Layout view (p. 55)
Proportional typeface (p. 65)
Replace command (p. 51)
Right indent (p. 77)
Sans serif typeface (p. 64)
Scrolling (p. 53)

Section (p. 84)
Section break (p. 84)
Select-then-do (p. 50)
Selective replacement (p. 52)
Serif typeface (p. 64)
Soft page break (p. 69)
Special indent (p. 77)
Tab stop (p. 80)
Times New Roman (p. 64)
Typeface (p. 64)
Type size (p. 65)
Type style (p. 65)
Typography (p. 64)
Underlining (p. 72)
View menu (p. 55)
Whole words only (p. 52)
Widows (p. 81)
Wild card (p. 52)
Windows clipboard (p. 50)
Zoom command (p. 55)

1. Which of the following commands does *not* place data onto the clipboard?
   (a) Cut
   (b) Copy
   (c) Paste
   (d) All of the above

2. What happens if you select a block of text, copy it, move to the beginning of the document, paste it, move to the end of the document, and paste the text again?
   (a) The selected text will appear in three places: at the original location, and at the beginning and end of the document
   (b) The selected text will appear in two places: at the beginning and end of the document
   (c) The selected text will appear in just the original location
   (d) The situation is not possible; that is, you cannot paste twice in a row without an intervening cut or copy operation

3. What happens if you select a block of text, cut it, move to the beginning of the document, paste it, move to the end of the document, and paste the text again?
   (a) The selected text will appear in three places: at the original location and at the beginning and end of the document
   (b) The selected text will appear in two places: at the beginning and end of the document
   (c) The selected text will appear in just the original location
   (d) The situation is not possible; that is, you cannot paste twice in a row without an intervening cut or copy operation

4. Which of the following are set at the paragraph level?
   (a) Alignment
   (b) Tabs and indents
   (c) Line spacing
   (d) All of the above

5. How do you change the font for *existing* text within a document?
   (a) Select the text, then choose the new font
   (b) Choose the new font, then select the text
   (c) Either (a) or (b)
   (d) Neither (a) nor (b)

6. The Page Setup command can be used to change:
   (a) The margins in a document
   (b) The orientation of a document
   (c) Both (a) and (b)
   (d) Neither (a) nor (b)

7. Which of the following is a true statement regarding indents?
   (a) Indents are measured from the edge of the page
   (b) The left, right, and first line indents must be set to the same value
   (c) The insertion point can be anywhere in the paragraph when indents are set
   (d) Indents must be set with the Format Paragraph command

8. The default tab stops are set to:
   (a) Left indents every ½ inch
   (b) Left indents every ¼ inch
   (c) Right indents every ½ inch
   (d) Right indents every ¼ inch

9. The spacing in an existing multipage document is changed from single spacing to double spacing throughout the document. What can you say about the number of hard and soft page breaks before and after the formatting change?
   (a) The number of soft page breaks is the same, but the number and/or position of the hard page breaks is different
   (b) The number of hard page breaks is the same, but the number and/or position of the soft page breaks is different
   (c) The number and position of both hard and soft page breaks is the same
   (d) The number and position of both hard and soft page breaks is different

10. Which of the following describes the Arial and Times New Roman fonts?
    (a) Arial is a sans serif font, Times New Roman is a serif font
    (b) Arial is a serif font, Times New Roman is a sans serif font
    (c) Both are serif fonts
    (d) Both are sans serif fonts

11. The find and replacement strings must be
    (a) The same length
    (b) The same case, either upper or lower
    (c) The same length and the same case
    (d) None of the above

12. You are in the middle of a multipage document. How do you scroll to the beginning of the document and simultaneously change the insertion point?
    (a) Press Ctrl+Home
    (b) Drag the scroll bar to the top of the scroll box
    (c) Both (a) and (b)
    (d) Neither (a) nor (b)

13. Which of the following substitutions can be accomplished by the Find and Replace command?
    (a) All occurrences of the words "Times New Roman" can be replaced with the word "Arial"
    (b) All text set in the Times New Roman font can be replaced by the Arial font
    (c) Both (a) and (b)
    (d) Neither (a) nor (b)

14. Which of the following deselects a selected block of text?
    (a) Clicking anywhere outside the selected text
    (b) Clicking any alignment button on the toolbar
    (c) Clicking the Bold, Italic, or Underline button
    (d) All of the above

15. Which view, and which magnification, lets you see the whole page, including top and bottom margins?
    (a) Print Layout view at 100% magnification
    (b) Print Layout view at Whole Page magnification
    (c) Normal view at 100% magnification
    (d) Normal view at Whole Page magnification

ANSWERS

1. c	**6.** c	**11.** d
2. a	**7.** c	**12.** a
3. b	**8.** a	**13.** c
4. d	**9.** b	**14.** a
5. a	**10.** a	**15.** b

1. **Formatting 101:** The document in Figure 2.17 provides practice with basic formatting. Open the partially completed document in *Chapter 2 Practice 1* and then follow the instructions within the document itself to implement the formatting. You can implement the formatting in a variety of ways—by clicking the appropriate button on the Formatting toolbar, by pulling down the Format menu and executing the indicated command, or by using a keyboard shortcut. Add your name somewhere in the document, then print the completed document for your instructor. Do not be concerned if you do not have a color printer, but indicate this to your instructor in a note at the end of the document.

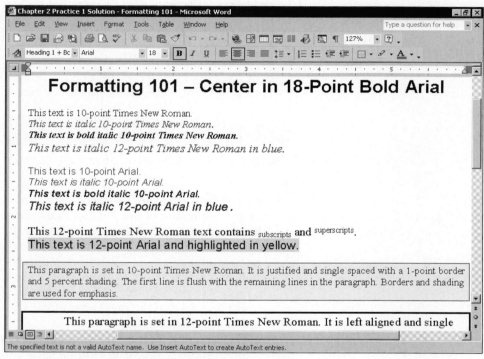

FIGURE 2.17   *Formatting 101 (Exercise 1)*

2. **Keyboard Shortcuts:** Keyboard shortcuts are especially useful if you type well because your hands can remain on the keyboard, as opposed to moving to the mouse. We never set out to memorize the shortcuts; we just learned them along the way as we continued to use Microsoft Office. It's much easier than you might think, because the same shortcuts apply to multiple applications. Ctrl+X, Ctrl+C, and Ctrl+V, for example, are the universal Windows shortcuts to cut, copy, and paste the selected text. The "X" is supposed to remind you of a pair of scissors, and the keys are located next to each other to link the commands to one another.

   Your assignment is to complete the document in *Chapter 2 Practice 2,* a portion of which can be seen in Figure 2.18. You can get the shortcut in one of two ways: by using the Help menu, or by displaying the shortcut in conjunction with the ScreenTip for the corresponding button on either the Standard or Formatting toolbar. (Pull down the Tools menu, click the Customize command to display the Customize dialog box, click the Options tab, then check the box to Show Shortcut Keys in ScreenTips.) Enter your name in the completed document, add the appropriate formatting, then submit the document to your instructor as proof you did this exercise.

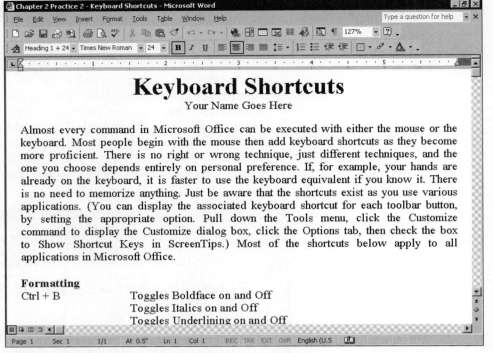

FIGURE 2.18 *Keyboard Shortcuts (Exercise 2)*

3. Moving Text: There are two basic ways to move text within a document. You can use a combination of the Cut and Paste commands, or you can simply click and drag text from one location to another. The latter technique tends to be easier if you are moving text a short distance, whereas cutting and pasting is preferable if the locations are far apart within a document. This exercise will give you a chance to practice both techniques.

   a. Open the partially completed document in *Chapter 2 Practice 3*, where you will find a list of the presidents of the United States together with the years that each man served.

   b. The list is out of order, and your assignment is to rearrange the names so that the presidents appear in chronological order. You don't have to be a historian to complete the exercise because you can use the years in office to determine the proper order.

   c. Use the Insert Hyperlink command (or click the corresponding button on the Standard toolbar) to insert a link to the White House Web site, where you can learn more about the presidents.

   d. Use the Format Columns command to display the presidents in two columns with a line down the middle as shown in Figure 2.19. You will have to implement a section break because the first two lines (the title and the hyperlink to the White House) are in one-column format, whereas the list of presidents is in two columns. You should create a second section break after the last president (George W. Bush) to balance the columns.

   e. Add your name to the completed document and submit it to your instructor as proof you completed this exercise.

   f. Start your Internet browser and connect to the White House. Select any president. Print the available biographical information for your instructor.

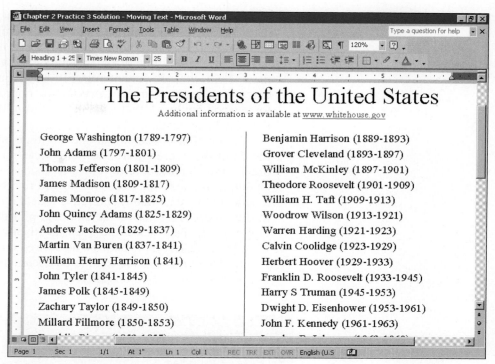

FIGURE 2.19 *Moving Text (Exercise 3)*

4. Tab Stops: Microsoft Word provides four different types of tabs that can be used to achieve a variety of formatting effects. Your assignment is to open the partially completed document in *Chapter 2 Practice 4*, then follow the instructions within the document to implement the formatting. The end result should be the document in Figure 2.20, which includes additional formatting in the opening paragraphs to boldface and italicize the key terms. Add your name somewhere in the document, then submit the completed exercise to your instructor.

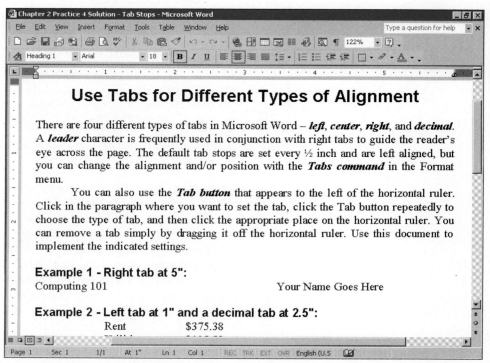

FIGURE 2.20 *Tab Stops (Exercise 4)*

5. Inserting the Date and Time: The document in Figure 2.21 describes the Insert Date and Time command and shows the various formats in which a date may appear. You need not duplicate our document exactly, but you are asked to insert the date multiple times, as both a fixed value and a field, in multiple formats. Divide your document into sections so that you can display the two sets of dates in adjacent columns. (Use the keyboard shortcut Ctrl+Shift+Enter to force a column break that will take you from the bottom of one column to the top of the next column.)

   Create your document on one day, then open it a day later to be sure that the dates that were entered as fields were updated correctly. Insert a section break after the last date to return to a single column format, then add a concluding paragraph that describes how to remove the shading from a date field. In essence any date that is entered as a field is shaded by default, as can be seen in our figure. To remove the shading, pull down the Tools menu, click the Options command, select the View tab, then click the drop-down arrow in the Field Shading list box to choose the desired option.)

   Add your name to the completed document and submit it to your instructor as proof you completed this exercise.

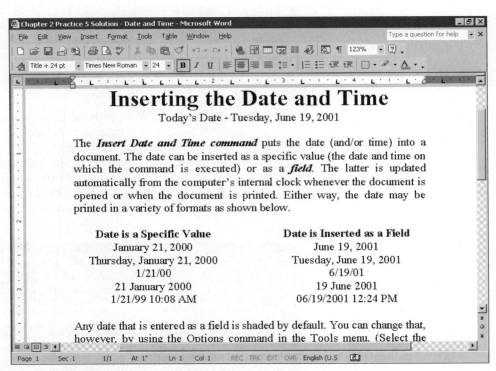

FIGURE 2.21 *Inserting the Date and Time (Exercise 5)*

6. Tips for Internet Explorer: A partially completed version of the document in Figure 2.22 can be found in the file *Chapter 2 Practice 6*. Your assignment is to open that document, then format the various tips for Internet Explorer in an attractive fashion. You need not follow our formatting exactly, but you are to apply uniform formatting throughout the document. Use one set of specifications for the heading of each tip (e.g., Arial 10-point bold) and a different format for the associated text. Use the Format Painter to copy formatting within the document. Insert a cover page that includes your name and the source of the information, then print the entire document for your instructor.

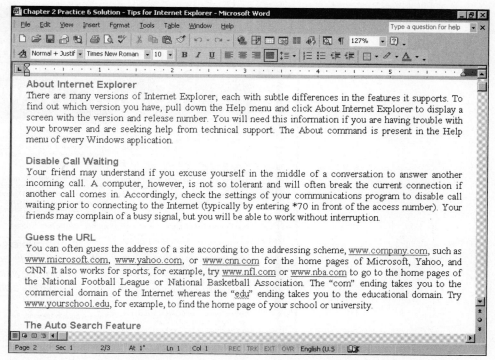

Chapter 2 Practice 6 Solution - Tips for Internet Explorer - Microsoft Word

FIGURE 2.22 *Tips for Internet Explorer (Exercise 6)*

7. **A Simple Newsletter:** Create a simple newsletter such as the one in Figure 2.23. There is no requirement to write meaningful text, but your document will be more interesting if you choose a theme and follow it throughout. (The text of our document contains suggestions for creating the document.) The newsletter should have a meaningful name (e.g., "A Simple Newsletter"), and supporting headings for the various paragraphs ("Choose a Theme", "Create the Masthead", and so on.) The text within each paragraph can consist of the same sentences that are copied throughout the document. The design of the newsletter is up to you. The document in Figure 2.23 has a formal appearance, but you can modify that design in any way you like. Some suggestions:

   a. Change the default margins of your document before you begin. You are using columns, and left and right margins of a half or three-quarters of an inch are more appropriate than the default values of 1.25 inches. Reduce the top margins as well.

   b. Create a sample heading and associated text, and format both to be sure that you have all of the necessary specifications. You can use the Line and Page Breaks tab within the Format Paragraph command to force the heading to appear with the text, and further to force the text to appear together in one paragraph. That way you can avoid awkward column breaks.

   c. Use the Columns command to fine-tune the dimensions of the columns and/or to add a line between the columns. You can use columns of varying width to add interest to the document.

   d. Choose one or two important sentences and create a pull-quote within the newsletter. Not only does this break up the text, but it calls attention to an important point.

   e. You can create a reverse, light text on a dark background, as in the masthead of our newsletter, by specifying 100% shading within the Borders and Shading command. You can also use a right tab to force an entry (your name) to align with the right margin.

   f. Try to design your newsletter with pencil and paper before you get to the computer. Print the completed newsletter for your instructor.

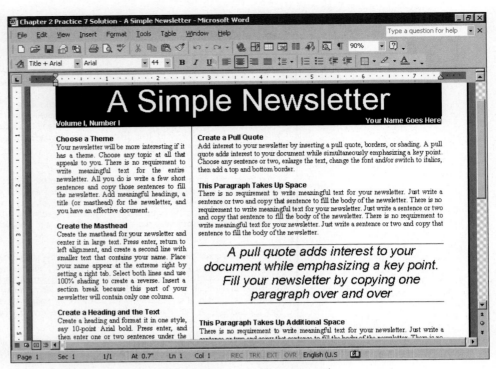

FIGURE 2.23 *A Simple Newsletter (Exercise 7)*

8. Formatting at Three Levels: You will find an unformatted version of the document in Figure 2.24 in the file *Chapter 2 Practice 8*. Open the document and match the formatting in Figure 2.24. (Use an appropriate point size for any formatting specification that is not visible within Figure 2.24.) Substitute your name as indicated, then print the completed document for your instructor.

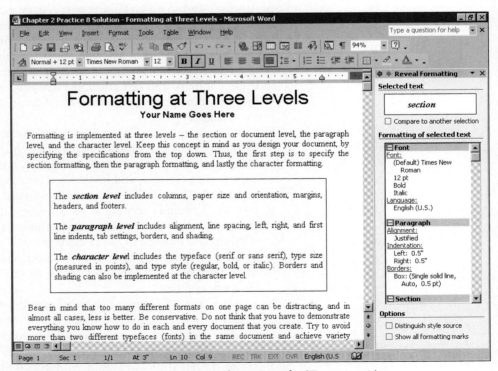

FIGURE 2.24 *Formatting at Three Levels (Exercise 8)*

9. **Viewing and Editing Comments:** The document in Figure 2.25 has been formatted for you. Look closely, however, and you will see that comments have been added to the first three tips. The comments appear in different colors to indicate that they were added by different people, in this case, Bob, Maryann, and a hypothetical student. Your assignment is to open the *Chapter 2 Practice 9* document and add additional comments of your own. Proceed as follows:

a. Read the entire document, then choose at least five tips and insert your own comment. Click where you want the comment to go, then pull down the Insert menu, click Comment, and enter the text of your comment.

b. Delete the comment that is associated with the Word Count toolbar.

c. Add a title page that contains your name and today's date.

d. Print the completed document to show the comments that you have added. Pull down the File menu, click the Print command, click the down arrow in the Print What area, and select Document Showing Markup.

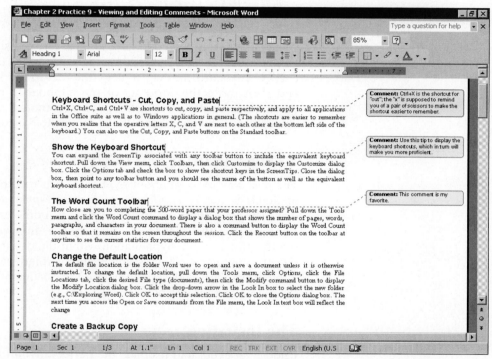

FIGURE 2.25   *Viewing and Editing Comments (Exercise 9)*

ON YOUR OWN

Your First Consultant's Job

Go to a real installation, such as a doctor's or an attorney's office, the company where you work, or the computer lab at school. Determine the backup procedures that are in effect, then write a one-page report indicating whether the policy is adequate and, if necessary, offering suggestions for improvement. Your report should be addressed to the individual in charge of the business, and it should cover all aspects of the backup strategy—that is, which files are backed up and how often, and what software is used for the backup operation. Use appropriate emphasis (for example, bold italics) to identify any potential problems. This is a professional document (it is your first consultant's job), and its appearance must be perfect in every way.

Computers Past and Present

The ENIAC was the scientific marvel of its day and the world's first operational electronic computer. It could perform 5,000 additions per second, weighed 30 tons, and took 1,500 square feet of floor space. The price was a modest $486,000 in 1946 dollars. The story of the ENIAC and other influential computers of the author's choosing is found in the file *History of Computers,* which we forgot to format, so we are asking you to do it for us.

Be sure to use appropriate emphasis for the names of the various computers. Create a title page in front of the document, then submit the completed assignment to your instructor. If you are ambitious, you can enhance this assignment by using your favorite search engine to look for computer museums on the Web. Visit one or two sites, and include this information on a separate page at the end of the document. One last task, and that is to update the description of Today's PC (the last computer in the document).

The Preamble to the Constitution

Use your favorite search engine to locate a Web site that contains the text of the United States constitution. Click and drag to select the text of the Preamble, use the Ctrl+C keyboard shortcut to copy the text to the Windows clipboard, start Word, and then paste the contents of the clipboard into the document. Format the Preamble in an attractive fashion, add a footnote that points to the Web page where you obtained the text, then add your name to the completed document.

To Hyphenate or Not to Hyphenate

The best way to learn about hyphenation is to experiment with an existing document. Open the *To Hyphenate or Not to Hyphenate* document that is on the data disk. The document is currently set in 12-point type with hyphenation in effect. Experiment with various formatting changes that will change the soft line breaks to see the effect on the hyphenation within the document. You can change the point size, the number of columns, and/or the right indent. You can also suppress hyphenation altogether, as described within the document. Summarize your findings in a short note to your instructor.

The Invitation

Choose an event and produce the perfect invitation. The possibilities are endless and limited only by your imagination. You can invite people to your wedding or to a fraternity party. Your laser printer and abundance of fancy fonts enable you to do anything a professional printer can do. Special paper will add the finishing touch. Go to it—this assignment is a lot of fun.

One Space after a Period

Touch typing classes typically teach the student to place two spaces after a period. The technique worked well in the days of the typewriter and monospaced fonts, but it creates an artificially large space when used with proportional fonts and a word processor. Select any document that is at least several paragraphs in length and print the document with the current spacing. Use the Find and Replace commands to change to the alternate spacing, then print the document a second time. Which spacing looks better to you? Submit both versions of the document to your instructor with a brief note summarizing your findings.

CHAPTER 3

Enhancing a Document: The Web and Other Resources

OBJECTIVES:

AFTER READING THIS CHAPTER YOU WILL BE ABLE TO:

1. Describe the resources in the Microsoft Media Gallery; insert clip art and/or a photograph into a document.
2. Use the Format Picture command to wrap text around a clip art image; describe various tools on the Picture toolbar.
3. Use WordArt to insert decorative text into a document; describe several tools on the WordArt toolbar.
4. Use the Drawing toolbar to create and modify lines and objects.
5. Download resources from the Internet for inclusion in a Word document; insert a footnote or endnote into a document to cite a reference.
6. Insert a hyperlink into a Word document; save a Word document as a Web page.
7. Use wizards and templates to create a document; list several wizards provided with Microsoft Word.
8. Define a mail merge; use the Mail Merge Wizard to create a set of form letters.

OVERVIEW

This chapter describes how to enhance a document using applications within Microsoft Office as well as resources from the Internet. We begin with a discussion of the Microsoft Media Gallery, a collection of clip art, sounds, photographs, and movies. We describe how Microsoft WordArt can be used to create special effects with text and how to create lines and objects through the Drawing toolbar.

These resources pale, however, in comparison to what is available via the Internet. Thus we also show you how to download a photograph from the Web and include it in an Office document. We describe how to add footnotes to give appropriate credit to your sources and how to further enhance a document through inclusion of hyperlinks. We also explain how to save a Word document as a Web page so that you can post the documents you create to a Web server or local area network. The chapter also describes some of the wizards and templates that are built into Word to help you create professionally formatted documents quickly and easily. We also introduce the concept of a mail merge.

ENHANCING A DOCUMENT

A Word document begins with text, but can be enhanced through the addition of objects. The document in Figure 3.1, for example, contains text, clip art, and WordArt (decorative text) and is the basis of a hands-on exercise that follows shortly. It also contains a scroll with additional text that was created through the Drawing toolbar, and the Windows logo that was added to the document through the Insert Symbol command. We describe each of these capabilities in the next few pages, then show you how to create the document.

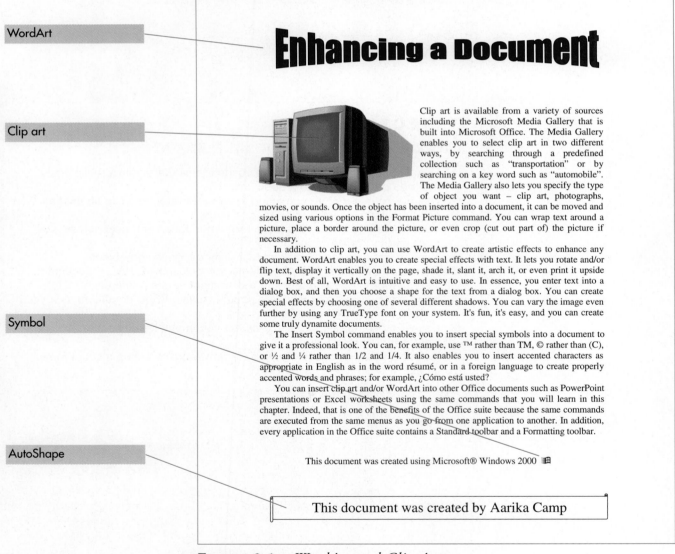

WordArt

Clip art

Symbol

AutoShape

Enhancing a Document

Clip art is available from a variety of sources including the Microsoft Media Gallery that is built into Microsoft Office. The Media Gallery enables you to select clip art in two different ways, by searching through a predefined collection such as "transportation" or by searching on a key word such as "automobile". The Media Gallery also lets you specify the type of object you want – clip art, photographs, movies, or sounds. Once the object has been inserted into a document, it can be moved and sized using various options in the Format Picture command. You can wrap text around a picture, place a border around the picture, or even crop (cut out part of) the picture if necessary.

In addition to clip art, you can use WordArt to create artistic effects to enhance any document. WordArt enables you to create special effects with text. It lets you rotate and/or flip text, display it vertically on the page, shade it, slant it, arch it, or even print it upside down. Best of all, WordArt is intuitive and easy to use. In essence, you enter text into a dialog box, and then you choose a shape for the text from a dialog box. You can create special effects by choosing one of several different shadows. You can vary the image even further by using any TrueType font on your system. It's fun, it's easy, and you can create some truly dynamite documents.

The Insert Symbol command enables you to insert special symbols into a document to give it a professional look. You can, for example, use ™ rather than TM, © rather than (C), or ½ and ¼ rather than 1/2 and 1/4. It also enables you to insert accented characters as appropriate in English as in the word résumé, or in a foreign language to create properly accented words and phrases; for example, ¿Cómo está usted?

You can insert clip art and/or WordArt into other Office documents such as PowerPoint presentations or Excel worksheets using the same commands that you will learn in this chapter. Indeed, that is one of the benefits of the Office suite because the same commands are executed from the same menus as you go from one application to another. In addition, every application in the Office suite contains a Standard toolbar and a Formatting toolbar.

This document was created using Microsoft® Windows 2000

This document was created by Aarika Camp

FIGURE 3.1   *WordArt and Clip Art*

The Media Gallery

The **Media Gallery** is accessible as a standalone application or from within multiple applications in Microsoft Office (Word, Excel, and PowerPoint, but not from Access). Either way, it is an excellent source for media objects such as clip art, sound files, photographs, and movies. There is an abundance of clip art from which to choose, so it is important to search through the available images efficiently, in order to choose the appropriate one.

The **Insert Picture command** displays a task pane in which you enter a key word (such as "basketball") that describes the picture you are looking for. The search returns a variety of potential clip art as shown in Figure 3.2a. Alternatively, you can click the down arrow in the task pane to select the Collection List as shown in Figure 3.2b. This method has you select (and then expand) various collections that may contain an appropriate image. We opened the Sports & Leisure collection where we found pictures of athletes in different sports, one of which was basketball. Look closely, and you will see that two of the pictures appear in both Figure 3.2a and 3.2b. Either way, you have ample images from which to choose.

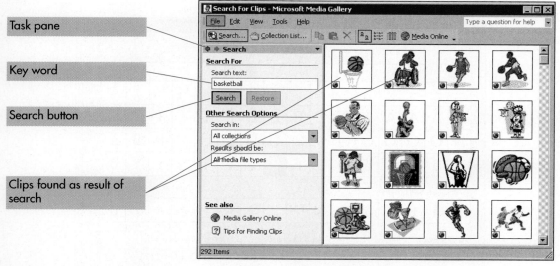

Task pane

Key word

Search button

Clips found as result of search

(a) Search by Key Word

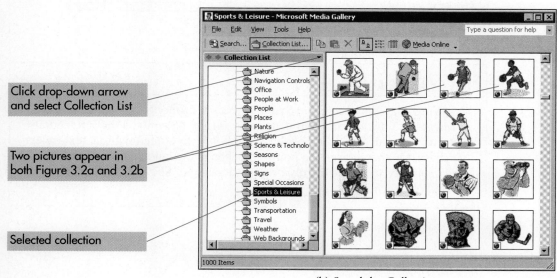

Click drop-down arrow and select Collection List

Two pictures appear in both Figure 3.2a and 3.2b

Selected collection

(b) Search by Collection

FIGURE 3.2 *The Media Gallery*

The Insert Symbol Command

The **Insert Symbol command** enables you to enter typographic symbols and/or foreign language characters into a document in place of ordinary typing—for example, ® rather than (R), © rather than (c), ½ and ¼ rather than 1/2 and 1/4, or é rather than e (as used in the word résumé). These special characters give a document a very professional look. You may have already discovered that some of this formatting can be done automatically through the **AutoCorrect** feature that is built into Word. If, for example, you type the letter "c" enclosed in parentheses, it will automatically be converted to the copyright symbol. Other symbols, such as accented letters like the é in résumé or those in a foreign language (e.g., ¿Cómo está usted?) have to be entered through the Insert Symbol command. (You could also create a macro, based on the Insert Symbol command, to simplify the process.)

Microsoft Office installs a variety of fonts onto your computer, each of which contains various symbols that can be inserted into a document. Selecting "normal text", however, as was done in Figure 3.3, provides access to the accented characters as well as other common symbols. Other fonts—especially the Wingdings, Webdings, and Symbols fonts—contain special symbols, including the Windows logo.

Click drop-down arrow to select font

Click to select symbol

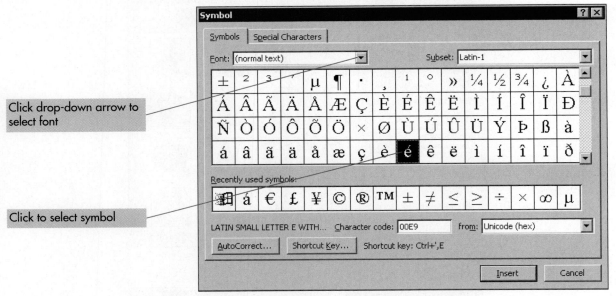

FIGURE 3.3 *Insert Symbol Command*

USE SYMBOLS AS CLIP ART

The Wingdings, Webdings, and Symbols fonts are among the best-kept secrets in Microsoft Office. Each font contains a variety of symbols that are actually pictures. You can insert any of these symbols into a document as text, select the character and enlarge the point size, change the color, then copy the modified character to create a truly original document. See practice exercise 2 at the end of the chapter.

Microsoft WordArt

Microsoft WordArt is an application within Microsoft Office that creates decorative text that can be used to add interest to a document. You can use ***WordArt*** in addition to clip art within a document, or in place of clip art if the right image is not available. You can rotate text in any direction, add three-dimensional effects, display the text vertically down the page, slant it, arch it, or even print it upside down. In short, you are limited only by your imagination.

WordArt is intuitively easy to use. In essence, you choose a style for the text from among the selections in Figure 3.4a. Then, you enter the specific text in a subsequent dialog box, after which the result is displayed as in Figure 3.4b. The finished WordArt is an object that can be moved and sized within a document, just like any other object. It's fun, it's easy, and you can create some truly unique documents.

Select a style

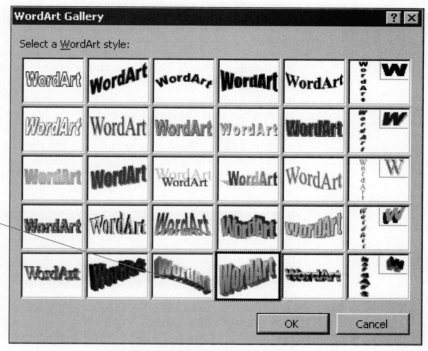

(a) Choose the Style

Enter text, which is then formatted in selected style

(b) Completed Entry

FIGURE 3.4   *Microsoft WordArt*

All clip art is created from basic shapes, such as lines, and other basic tools that are found on the *Drawing toolbar*. Select the Line tool, for example, then click and drag to create a line. Once the line has been created, you can select it and change its properties (such as thickness, style, or color) by using other tools on the Drawing toolbar. Draw a second line, or a curve, then depending on your ability, you have a piece of original clip art. You do not have to be an artist in order to use the basic tools to enhance any document.

The *drawing canvas* appears automatically whenever you select a tool from the Drawing toolbar and is indicated by a hashed line as shown in Figure 3.5. Each object within the canvas can be selected, at which point it displays its own *sizing handles*. The blue rectangle is selected in Figure 3.5. You can size an object by clicking and dragging any one of the sizing handles. We don't expect you to create clip art comparable to the images within the Media Gallery, but you can use the tools on the Drawing toolbar to modify an existing image and/or create simple shapes of your own.

The Shift key has special significance when used in conjunction with the Line, Rectangle, and Oval tools. Press and hold the Shift key as you drag the line tool horizontally or vertically to create a perfectly straight line in either direction. Press and hold the Shift key as you drag the Rectangle and Oval tool to create a square or circle, respectively. The AutoShapes button contains a series of selected shapes, such as a callout or banner, and is very useful to create simple drawings. And, as with any other drawing object, you can change the thickness, color, or fill by selecting the object and choosing the appropriate tool. It is fun and it is easy. Just be flexible and willing to experiment. We think you will be pleased at what you will be able to do.

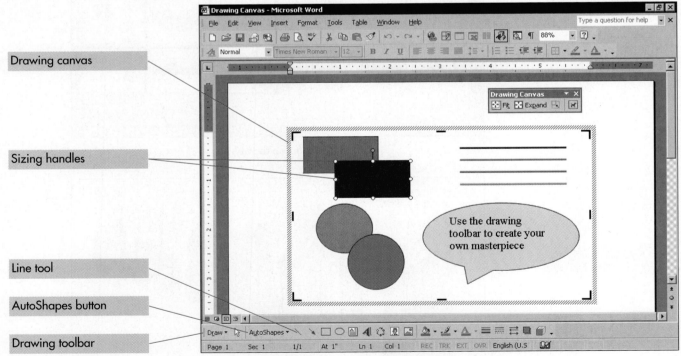

Drawing canvas

Sizing handles

Line tool

AutoShapes button

Drawing toolbar

FIGURE 3.5 *Drawing Canvas*

CHAPTER 3: ENHANCING A DOCUMENT

CLIP ART AND WORDART

Objective To insert clip art and WordArt into a document; to use the Insert Symbol command to add typographical symbols. Use Figure 3.6 as a guide in completing the exercise.

Step 1: **Insert the Clip Art**

➤ Start Word. Open the **Clip Art** and **WordArt** document in the Exploring Word folder. Save the document as **Modified Clip Art and WordArt**.

➤ Check that the insertion point is at the beginning of the document. Pull down the **Insert menu**, click (or point to) **Picture**, then click **Clip Art**. The task pane opens (if it is not already open) and displays the Media Gallery Search pane as shown in Figure 3.6a.

➤ Click in the **Search text box**. Type **computer** to search for any clip art image that is indexed with this key word, then click the **Search button** or press **enter**.

➤ The images are displayed in the Results box. Point to an image to display a drop-down arrow to its right. Click the arrow to display a context menu.

➤ Click **Insert** to insert the image into the document. Do not be concerned about its size or position at this time. Close the task pane.

➤ Save the document.

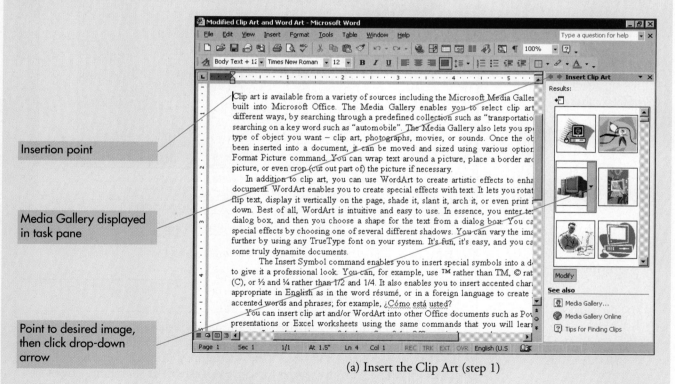

Insertion point

Media Gallery displayed in task pane

Point to desired image, then click drop-down arrow

(a) Insert the Clip Art (step 1)

FIGURE 3.6 *Hands-on Exercise 1*

Step 2: **Move and Size the Picture**

➤ Point to the picture, click the **right mouse button** to display the context-sensitive menu, then click the **Format Picture command** to display the Format Picture dialog box in Figure 3.6b.

➤ You must change the layout in order to move and size the object. Click the **Layout tab**, choose the **Square layout**, then click the option button for **Left alignment**. Click **OK** to close the dialog box.

➤ To size the picture, click and drag a corner handle (the mouse pointer changes to a double arrow) to change the length and width simultaneously. This keeps the picture in proportion.

➤ To move the picture, point to any part of the image except a sizing handle (the mouse pointer changes to a four-sided arrow), then click and drag to move the image elsewhere in the document.

➤ Save the document.

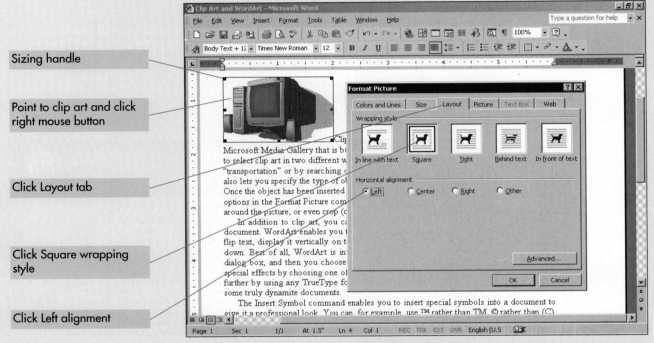

(b) Move and Size the Picture (step 2)

FIGURE 3.6 *Hands-on Exercise 1 (continued)*

SEARCH BY COLLECTION

The Media Gallery organizes its contents by collections and provides another way to select clip art. Pull down the Insert menu, click (or point to) the Picture command, then click Clip Art to open the task pane, where you can enter a key word to search for clip art. Instead of searching, however, click the link to Media Gallery at the bottom of the task pane to display the Media Gallery dialog box. Close the My Collections folder if it is open, then open the Office Collections folder, where you can explore the available images by collection.

Step 3: **WordArt**

➤ Press **Ctrl+End** to move to the end of the document. Pull down the **Insert menu**, click **Picture**, then click **WordArt** to display the WordArt Gallery dialog box in Figure 3.6c.

➤ Select the WordArt style you like (you can change it later). Click **OK**. You will see a second dialog box in which you enter the text. Enter **Enhancing a Document**. Click **OK**.

➤ The WordArt object appears in your document in the style you selected. Point to the WordArt object and click the **right mouse button** to display a shortcut menu. Click **Format WordArt** to display the Format WordArt dialog box.

➤ Click the **Layout tab**, then select **Square** as the Wrapping style. Click **OK**. It is important to select this wrapping option to facilitate placing the WordArt at the top of the document.

➤ Save the document.

Click to select desired style

Click OK

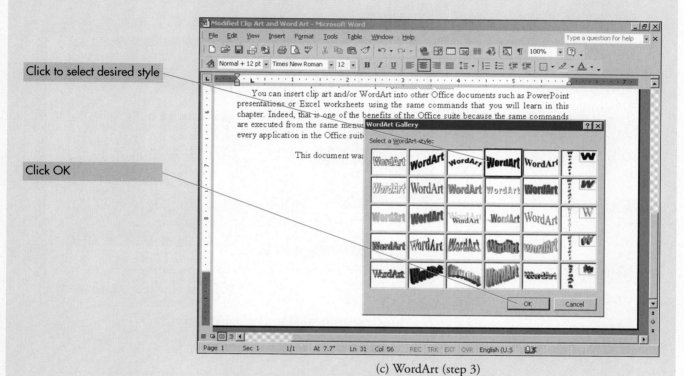

(c) WordArt (step 3)

FIGURE 3.6 *Hands-on Exercise 1 (continued)*

FORMATTING WORDART

The WordArt toolbar offers the easiest way to execute various commands associated with a WordArt object. It is displayed automatically when a WordArt object is selected and is suppressed otherwise. As with any other toolbar, you can point to a button to display a ScreenTip containing the name of the button, which is indicative of its function. The WordArt toolbar contains buttons to display the text vertically, change the style or shape, and/or edit the text.

Step 4:   **WordArt Continued**

➤ Click and drag the WordArt object to move it the top of the document. (The Format WordArt dialog box is not yet visible.)
➤ Point to the WordArt object, click the **right mouse button** to display a shortcut menu, then click **Format WordArt** to display the Format WordArt dialog box as shown in Figure 3.6d.
➤ Click the **Colors and Lines tab**, then click the **Fill Color drop-down arrow** to display the available colors. Select a different color (e.g., blue).
➤ Move and/or size the WordArt as necessary. Click the **Undo button** if necessary to cancel the action and start again.
➤ Save the document.

Click and drag WordArt object to top of file

Point to WordArt object and click right mouse button

Click Colors and Lines tab

Click to display color palette

Click desired color

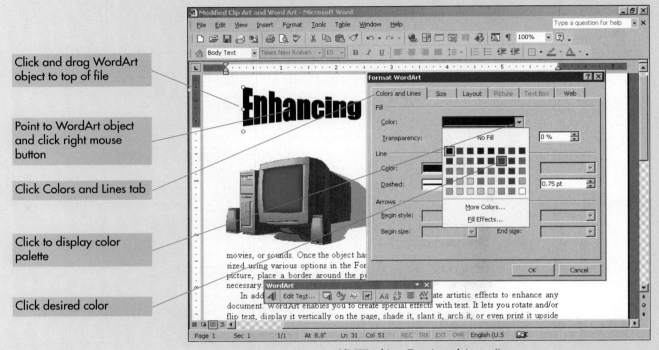

(d) WordArt Continued (step 4)

FIGURE 3.6   *Hands-on Exercise 1 (continued)*

THE THIRD DIMENSION

You can make your WordArt images even more dramatic by adding 3-D effects. You can tilt the text up or down, right or left, increase or decrease the depth, and change the shading. Pull down the View menu, click Toolbars, click Customize to display the complete list of available toolbars, then check the box to display the 3-D Settings toolbar. Select the WordArt object, then experiment with various tools and special effects. The results are even better if you have a color printer.

Step 5: **The Insert Symbol Command**

➤ Press **Ctrl+End** to move to the end of the document as shown in Figure 3.6e. If necessary, change the sentence to reflect the version of Windows that you are using, for example Windows 98, rather than Windows 2000.

➤ Click at the end of the sentence, pull down the **Insert menu**, click **Symbol**, then choose **Wingdings** from the font list box. Click the **Windows logo** (the last character in the last line), click **Insert**, then close the dialog box.

➤ Click and drag to select the newly inserted symbol. Change the font size to **24**. (One of our favorite shortcuts is to press and hold the Ctrl key as you press the square bracket to increase the font size; that is, Ctrl+] increases the font size, whereas Ctrl+[decreases the font size.)

➤ Click after the word Microsoft in the same sentence, type **(r)**, and try to watch the screen as you enter the text. The (r) will be converted to the ® registered trademark symbol by the AutoCorrect feature.

➤ Save the document.

Click drop-down arrow and select Wingdings

Click Wingdings logo

Click at end of sentence

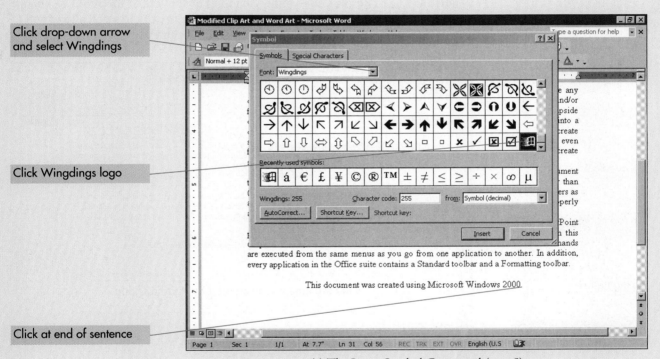

(e) The Insert Symbol Command (step 5)

FIGURE 3.6 *Hands-on Exercise 1 (continued)*

AUTOCORRECT AND AUTOFORMAT

The AutoCorrect feature not only corrects mistakes as you type by substituting one character string for another (e.g., "the" for "teh"), but it will also substitute symbols for typewritten equivalents such as © for (c), provided the entries are included in the table of substitutions. The AutoFormat feature is similar in concept and replaces common fractions such as 1/2 or 1/4 with ½ or ¼. It also converts ordinal numbers such as 1st or 2nd to 1st or 2nd.

Step 6: **Create the AutoShape**

➤ Pull down the **View menu**, click the **Toolbars command** to display the list of available toolbars, then click **Drawing toolbar**.

➤ Press the **End key** to move to the end of the line, then press the **enter key** once or twice to move below the last sentence in the document.

➤ Click the **down arrow** on the AutoShapes tool to display the menu. Click the **Stars and Banners submenu** and select the **Horizontal Scroll**.

➤ The mouse pointer changes to a tiny crosshair, and you will see a drawing canvas with an indication to create your drawing here. Press **Esc** to remove the drawing canvas (we find it easier to work without it), which in turn moves you to the bottom of the page.

➤ Click and drag to create a scroll, as shown in Figure 3.6f. Release the mouse. Right click in the scroll, click **Add Text**, change the font size to 18 point, then enter the text **This document was created by** (your name). Center the text.

➤ Click and drag the sizing handle (a circle) at the bottom of the scroll to make it narrow. Click and drag the yellow diamond at the left of the scroll to change the appearance of the scroll. The green dot at the top of the scroll allows you to rotate the scroll. Click off the scroll. Save the document.

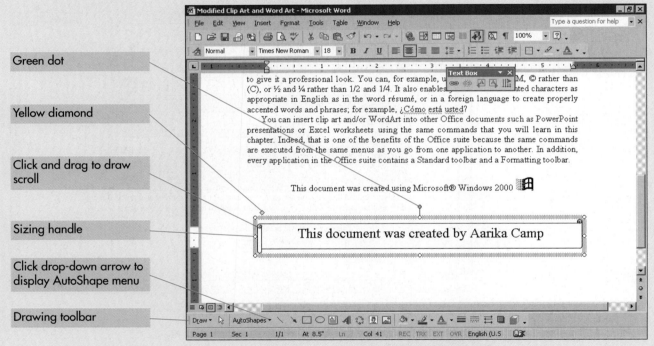

(f) Create the AutoShape (step 6)

FIGURE 3.6 *Hands-on Exercise 1 (continued)*

ORGANIZATION CHARTS AND OTHER DIAGRAMS

Microsoft Office includes a tool to create organization charts and other types of diagrams. Pull down the Insert menu and click the Diagram command to display the Diagram Gallery dialog box, where you choose the type of diagram. Click the Organization Chart, for example, and you are presented with a default chart that is the basis of a typical corporate organization chart. See practice exercise 11 at the end of the chapter.

Step 7:   **The Completed Document**

➤ Pull down the **File menu** and click the **Page Setup command** to display the Page Setup dialog box. (You can also double click the ruler below the Formatting toolbar to display the dialog box.)

➤ Click the **Margins tab** and change the top margin to **1.5 inches** (to accommodate the WordArt at the top of the document). Click **OK**.

➤ Click the **drop-down arrow** on the Zoom box and select **Whole Page** to preview the completed document as shown in Figure 3.6g. You can change the size and position of the objects from within this view. For example:
   • Select (click) the clip art to select this object and display its sizing handles.
   • Select (click) the banner to select it (and deselect the previous selection).
   • Move and size either object as necessary.

➤ Print the document and submit it to your instructor as proof that you did the exercise. Save the document. Close the document.

➤ Exit Word if you do not want to continue with the next exercise at this time.

Click drop-down arrow and select Whole Page

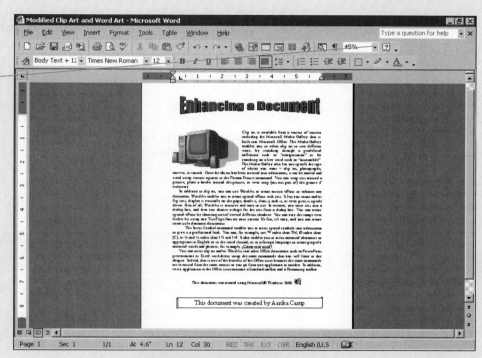

(g) The Completed Document (step 7)

FIGURE 3.6   *Hands-on Exercise 1 (continued)*

ANIMATE TEXT ON SCREEN

Select the desired text, pull down the Format menu, click the Font command to display the Font dialog box, then click the Text Effects tab. Select the desired effect such as "Blinking Background" or "Las Vegas Lights", then click OK to accept the settings and close the dialog box. The selected text should be displayed with the specified effect, which appears on the screen, but not when the document is printed. To cancel the effect, select the text, display the Font dialog box, click the Text Effects tab, select "None" as the effect then click OK.

The Internet and World Wide Web have totally changed society. Perhaps you are already familiar with the basic concepts that underlie the Internet but, if not, a brief review is in order. The *Internet* is a network of networks that connects computers anywhere in the world. The *World Wide Web* (WWW or simply, the Web) is a very large subset of the Internet, consisting of those computers that store a special type of document known as a *Web page* or *HTML document*.

The interesting thing about a Web page is that it contains references called *hyperlinks* to other Web pages, which may in turn be stored on a different computer that is located anywhere in the world. And therein lies the fascination of the Web, in that you simply click on link after link to go effortlessly from one document to the next. You can start your journey on your professor's home page, then browse through any set of links you wish to follow.

Web pages are developed in a special language called *HTML (HyperText Markup Language)*. Initially, the only way to create a Web page was to learn HTML. Microsoft Office simplifies the process because you can create the document in Word, then simply save it as a Web page. In other words, you start Word in the usual fashion, enter the text of the document with basic formatting, then use the *Save As Web Page command* to convert the document to HTML. Microsoft Word does the rest and generates the HTML statements for you. You can continue to enter text and/or change the formatting for existing text just as you can with an ordinary document.

Figure 3.7 contains the Web page you will create in the next hands-on exercise. The exercise begins by having you search the Web to locate a suitable photograph for inclusion into the document. You then download the picture to your PC and use the Insert Picture command to insert the photograph into your document. You add formatting, hyperlinks, and footnotes as appropriate, then you save the document as a Web page. The exercise is easy to do, and it will give you an appreciation for the various Web capabilities that are built into Office XP.

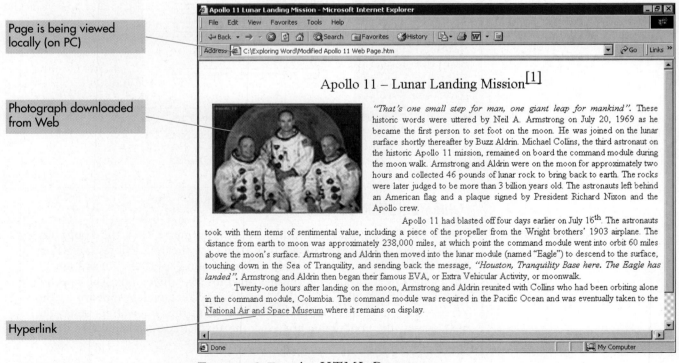

Page is being viewed locally (on PC)

Photograph downloaded from Web

Hyperlink

FIGURE 3.7 *An HTML Document*

Even if you do not place your page on the Web, you can still view it locally on your PC. This is the approach we follow in the next hands-on exercise, which shows you how to save a Word document as a Web page, then see the results of your effort in a Web browser. The Web page is stored on a local drive (e.g., on drive A or drive C) rather than on an Internet server, but it can still be viewed through Internet Explorer (or any other browser).

The ability to create links to local documents and to view those pages through a Web browser has created an entirely new way to disseminate information. Organizations of every size are taking advantage of this capability to develop an *intranet* in which Web pages are placed on a local area network for use within the organizations. The documents on an intranet are available only to individuals with access to the local area network on which the documents are stored.

THE WEB PAGE WIZARD

The Save As Web Page command converts a Word document to the equivalent HTML document for posting on a Web server. The Web Page Wizard extends the process to create a multipage Web site, complete with navigation and a professionally designed theme. The navigation options let you choose between horizontal and vertical frames so that the user can see the links and content at the same time. The design themes are quite varied and include every element on a Web page.

Copyright Protection

A *copyright* provides legal protection to a written or artistic work, giving the author exclusive rights to its use and reproduction, except as governed under the fair use exclusion as explained below. Anything on the Internet should be considered copyrighted unless the document specifically says it is in the *public domain*, in which case the author is giving everyone the right to freely reproduce and distribute the material.

Does this mean you cannot quote in your term papers statistics and other facts you find while browsing the Web? Does it mean you cannot download an image to include in your report? The answer to both questions depends on the amount of the material and on your intended use of the information. It is considered *fair use*, and thus not an infringement of copyright, to use a portion of the work for educational, nonprofit purposes, or for the purpose of critical review or commentary. In other words, you can use a quote, downloaded image, or other information from the Web, provided you cite the original work in your footnotes and/or bibliography. Facts themselves are not covered by copyright, so you can use statistical and other data without fear of infringement. You should, however, cite the original source in your document through appropriate footnotes or endnotes.

A *footnote* provides additional information about an item, such as its source, and appears at the bottom of the page where the reference occurs. An *endnote* is similar in concept but appears at the end of a document. A horizontal line separates the notes from the rest of the document. You can also convert footnotes to endnotes or vice versa.

The *Insert Reference command* inserts either a footnote or an endnote into a document, and automatically assigns the next sequential number to that note. The command adjusts for last-minute changes, either in your writing or in your professor's requirements. It will, for example, renumber all existing notes to accommodate the addition or deletion of a footnote or endnote. Existing notes are moved (or deleted) within a document by moving (deleting) the reference mark rather than the text of the footnote.

MICROSOFT WORD AND THE WEB

Objective   To download a picture from the Internet for use in a Word document; to insert a hyperlink into a Word document; to save a Word document as a Web page. Use Figure 3.8 as a reference. The exercise requires an Internet connection.

Step 1:   **Search the Web**

> ➤ Start Internet Explorer. It does not matter which page you see initially, as long as you are able to connect to the Internet and start Internet Explorer. Click the **Maximize button** so that Internet Explorer takes the entire screen.
> ➤ Click the **Search button** on the Standard Buttons toolbar to display the Search pane in the Explorer bar at the left of the Internet Explorer window. The option button to find a Web page is selected by default.
> ➤ Enter **Apollo 11** in the Find a Web page text box, then click the **Search button**. The results of the search are displayed in the left pane as shown in Figure 3.8a. The results you obtain will be different from ours.
> ➤ Check to see which search engine you used, and if necessary click the **down arrow** to the right of the Next button to select **Lycos** (the engine we used). The search will be repeated with this engine. Your results can still be different from ours, because new pages are continually added to the Web.
> ➤ Select (click) the link to Apollo 11 Home. (Enter the URL www.nasm.edu/apollo/AS11 manually if your search engine does not display this link.)
> ➤ Click the **Close button** to close the Search pane, so that your selected document takes the entire screen.

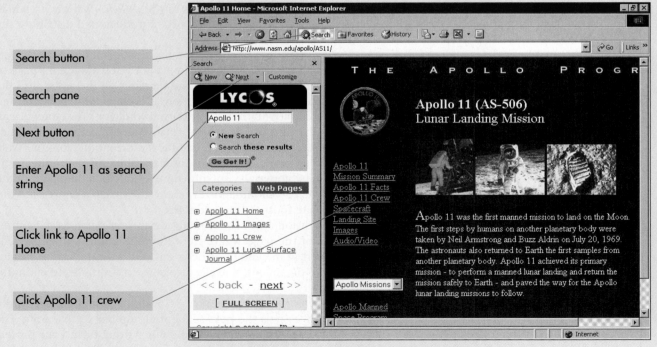

(a) Search the Web (step 1)

FIGURE 3.8   *Hands-on Exercise 2*

Step 2: **Save the Picture**

➤ Click the link to **Apollo 11 Crew** from the previous page to display the page in Figure 3.8b. Point to the picture of the astronauts, click the **right mouse button** to display a shortcut menu, then click the **Save Picture As command** to display the Save As dialog box.

- Click the **drop-down arrow** in the Save in list box to specify the drive and folder in which you want to save the graphic (e.g., in the **Exploring Word folder**).
- Internet Explorer supplies the file name and file type for you. You may change the name, but you cannot change the file type.
- Click the **Save button** to download the image. Remember the file name and location, as you will need to access the file in the next step.

➤ The Save As dialog box will close automatically after the picture has been downloaded. Click the **Minimize button** in the Internet Explorer window, since you are temporarily finished using the browser.

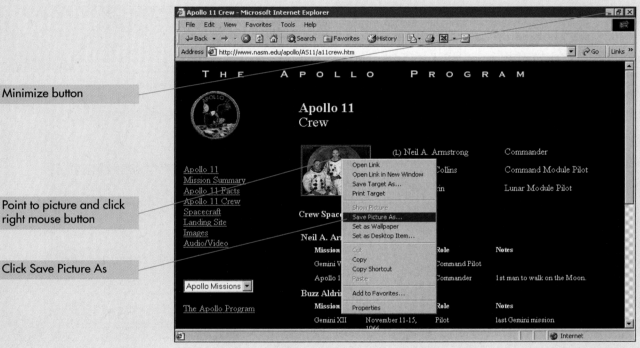

Minimize button

Point to picture and click right mouse button

Click Save Picture As

(b) Save the Picture (step 2)

FIGURE 3.8 *Hands-on Exercise 2 (continued)*

THE AUTOSEARCH FEATURE

The fastest way to initiate a search is to click in the Address box, enter the key word "go" followed by the topic you are searching for (e.g., go University of Miami), then press the enter key. Internet Explorer automatically invokes the MSN search engine and returns the relevant documents. You can also guess a Web address by typing, www.company.com, where you supply the name of the company.

Step 3: **Insert the Picture**

➤ Start Word and open the **Apollo 11 document** in the **Exploring Word folder**. Save the document as **Modified Apollo** so that you can return to the original document if necessary.

➤ Pull down the **View menu** to be sure that you are in the **Print Layout view** (or else you will not see the picture after it is inserted into the document). Pull down the **Insert menu**, point to (or click) **Picture command**, then click **From File** to display the Insert Picture dialog box shown in Figure 3.8c.

➤ Click the **down arrow** on the Look in text box to select the drive and folder where you previously saved the picture. Click the **down arrow** on the Files of type list box and specify **All files**.

➤ Select (click) **AS11_crew**, which is the file containing the picture that you downloaded earlier. Click the **drop-down arrow** on the **Views button**, then click **Preview** to display the picture prior to inserting. Click **Insert**.

➤ Save the document.

View button

Click drop-down arrow to select drive/folder

Click AS11_crew.m file

Click drop-down arrow and select All Files

Print Layout button

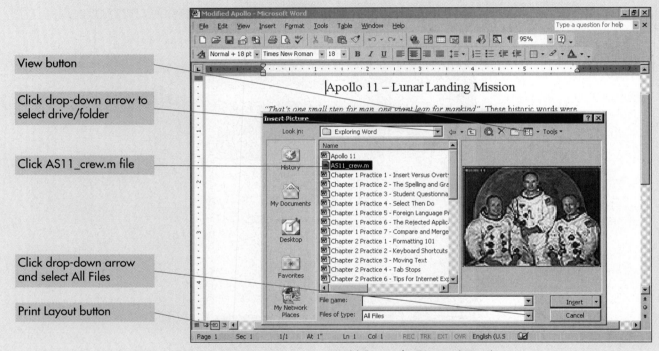

(c) Insert the Picture (step 3)

FIGURE 3.8 *Hands-on Exercise 2 (continued)*

CHANGE THE DEFAULT LOCATION

The default file location is the folder Word uses to open and save a document unless it is otherwise instructed. To change the default location, pull down the Tools menu, click Options, click the File Locations tab, click the desired File type (documents), then click the Modify command button to display the Modify Location dialog box. Click the drop-down arrow in the Look In box to select the new folder (e.g., C:\Exploring Word). Click OK to accept this selection. Click OK to close the Options dialog box. The next time you access the Open or Save commands from the File menu, the Look In text box will reflect the change.

Step 4: **Move and Size the Picture**

➤ Point to the picture after it is inserted into the document, click the **right mouse button** to display a shortcut menu, then click the **Format Picture command** to display the Format Picture dialog box.

➤ Click the **Layout tab** and choose **Square** in the Wrapping style area. Click **OK** to accept the settings and close the Format Picture dialog box.

➤ Move and/or size the picture so that it approximates the position in Figure 3.8d. Click the **Undo button** anytime that you are not satisfied with the result.

➤ Save the document.

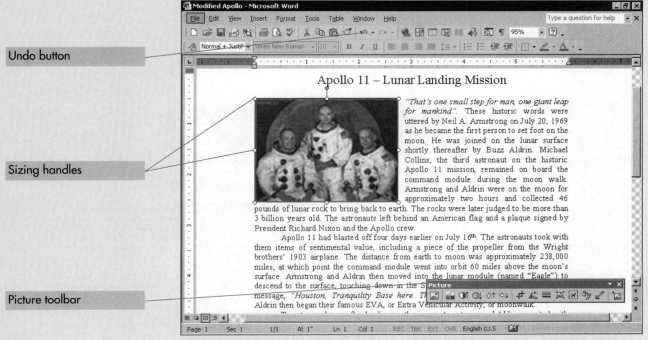

(d) Move and Size the Picture (step 4)

FIGURE 3.8 *Hands-on Exercise 2 (continued)*

CROPPING A PICTURE

The Crop tool is one of the most useful tools when dealing with a photograph as it lets you eliminate (crop) part of a picture. Select (click) the picture to display the Picture toolbar and sizing handles. (If you do not see the Picture toolbar, right click the picture to display a context-sensitive menu, then click the Show Picture Toolbar command. Click the Crop tool (the ScreenTip will display the name of the tool), then click and drag a sizing handle to crop the part of the picture you want to eliminate. Click the Crop button a second time to turn the feature off.

Step 5: **Insert a Footnote**

➤ Press **Ctrl+Home** to move to the beginning of the document, then click after Lunar Landing Mission in the title of the document. This is where you will insert the footnote.

➤ Pull down the **Insert menu**. Click **Reference**, then choose **Footnote** to display the Footnote and Endnote dialog as shown in Figure 3.8e. Check that the option buttons for **Footnotes** is selected and that the numbering starts at one. Click **Insert**.

➤ The insertion point moves to the bottom of the page, where you type the text of the footnote, which should include the Web site from where you downloaded the picture.

➤ Press **Ctrl+Home** to move to the beginning of the page, where you will see a reference for the footnote you just created. If necessary, you can move (or delete) a footnote by moving (deleting) the reference mark rather than the text of the footnote.

➤ Save the document.

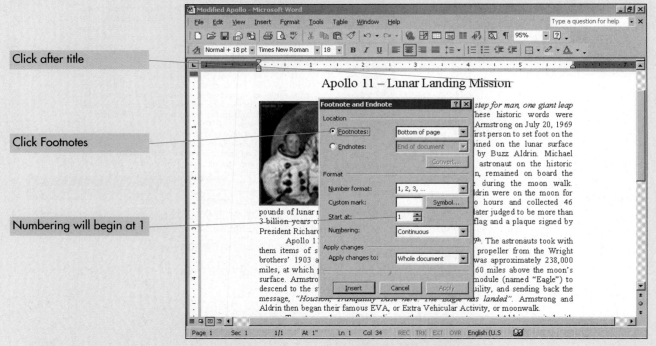

Click after title

Click Footnotes

Numbering will begin at 1

(e) Insert a Footnote (step 5)

FIGURE 3.8 *Hands-on Exercise 2 (continued)*

COPY THE WEB ADDRESS

Use the Copy command to enter a Web address from Internet Explorer into a Word document. Not only do you save time by not having to type the address yourself, but you also ensure that it is entered correctly. Click in the Address bar of Internet Explorer to select the URL, then pull down the Edit menu and click the Copy command (or use the Ctrl+C keyboard shortcut). Switch to the Word document, click at the place in the document where you want to insert the URL, pull down the Edit menu, and click the Paste command (or use the Ctrl+V keyboard shortcut).

Step 6: **Insert a Hyperlink**

➤ Scroll to the bottom of the document, then click and drag to select the text **National Air and Space Museum**.

➤ Pull down the **Insert menu** and click the **Hyperlink command** (or click the **Insert Hyperlink button** on the Standard toolbar) to display the Insert Hyperlink dialog box as shown in Figure 3.8f.

➤ National Air and Space Museum is entered automatically in the Text to display text box. Click in the Address text box to enter the address. Type **http://www.nasm.edu**.

➤ Click **OK** to accept the settings and close the dialog box. The hyperlink should appear as an underlined entry in the document.

➤ Save the document.

Insert Hyperlink button

Text is automatically entered

Click Browsed Pages

Enter address

Click and drag to select text

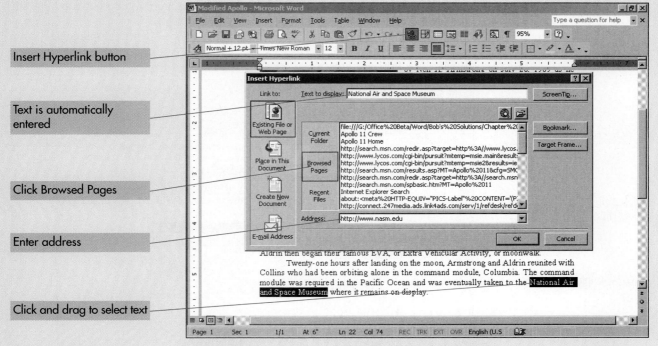

(f) Insert a hyperlink (step 6)

FIGURE 3.8   *Hands-on Exercise 2 (continued)*

CLICK TO EDIT, CTRL+CLICK TO FOLLOW

Point to a hyperlink within a Word document and you see a ToolTip that says to press and hold the Ctrl key (Ctrl+Click) to follow the link. This is different from what you usually do, because you normally just click a link to follow it. What if, however, you wanted to edit the link? Word modifies the convention so that clicking a link enables you to edit the link. Alternatively, you can right click the hyperlink to display a context-sensitive menu from where you can make the appropriate choice.

Step 7: **Create the Web Page**

➤ Pull down the **File menu** and click the **Save As Web Page command** to display the Save As dialog box as shown in Figure 3.8g. Click the **drop-down arrow** in the Save In list box to select the appropriate drive, then open the **Exploring Word folder**.

➤ Change the name of the Web page to **Modified Apollo 11 Web Page** (to differentiate it from the Word document of the same name). Click the **Change Title button** to display a dialog box in which you change the title of the Web page as it will appear in the title bar of the Web browser.

➤ Click the **Save button**. You will see a message indicating that the pictures will be left aligned. Click **Continue**.

➤ The title bar changes to reflect the name of the Web page. There are now two versions of this document in the Exploring Word folder, Modified Apollo 11, and Modified Apollo 11 Web Page. The latter has been saved as a Web page (in HTML format).

➤ Click the **Print button** on the Standard toolbar to print this page for your instructor from within Microsoft Word.

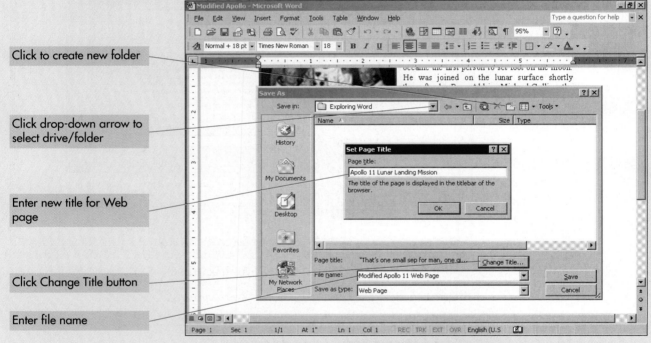

Click to create new folder

Click drop-down arrow to select drive/folder

Enter new title for Web page

Click Change Title button

Enter file name

(g) Create the Web Page (step 7)

FIGURE 3.8 *Hands-on Exercise 2 (continued)*

CREATE A NEW FOLDER

Do you work with a large number of documents? If so, it may be useful to store those documents in different folders, perhaps one folder for each course you are taking. Pull down the File menu, click the Save As command to display the Save As dialog box, then click the Create New Folder button to display the associated dialog box. Enter the name of the folder, then click OK. Once the folder has been created, use the Look In box to change to that folder the next time you open that document.

Step 8: **View the Web Page**

➤ You can view the Web page you just created even though it has not been saved on a Web server. Click the button for Internet Explorer on the Windows taskbar to return to the browser.

➤ Pull down the **File menu** and click the **Open command** to display the Open dialog box. Click the **Browse button**, then select the folder (e.g., Exploring Word) where you saved the Web page. Select (click) the **Modified Apollo 11 Web Page** document, click **Open**, then click **OK** to open the document.

➤ You should see the Web page that was created earlier as shown in Figure 3.8h, except that you are viewing the page in Internet Explorer rather than Microsoft Word. The Address bar reflects the local address (in the Exploring Word folder) of the document.

➤ Click the **Print button** on the Internet Explorer toolbar to print this page for your instructor. Does this printed document differ from the version that was printed from within Microsoft Word at the end of the previous step?

Address bar reflects local address

Print button

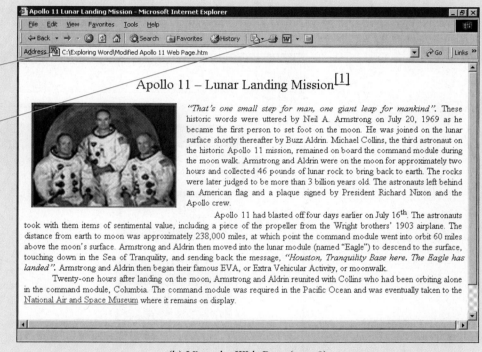

(h) View the Web Page (step 8)

FIGURE 3.8   *Hands-on Exercise 2 (continued)*

AN EXTRA FOLDER

Look carefully at the contents of the Exploring Word folder within the Open dialog box. You see the HTML document you just created, as well as a folder that was created automatically by the Save As Web Page command. The latter folder contains the objects that are referenced by the page, such as the crew's picture and a horizontal line above the footnotes. Be sure to copy the contents of this folder to the Web server in addition to your Web page if you decide to post the page.

Step 9: **Test the Web Page**

➤ This step requires an Internet connection because you will be verifying the addresses you entered earlier.

➤ Click the hyperlink to the **National Air and Space Museum** to display the Web page in Figure 3.8i. You can explore this site, or you can click the **Back button** to return to your Web page.

➤ If you are unable to connect to the Museum site, click in the Address bar and enter a different URL to see if you can connect to that site. If you connect to one site, but not the other, you should return to your original document to correct the URL.

➤ Click the **Word button** on the taskbar to return to the Web page, **right click** the hyperlink to display a context-sensitive menu, click **Edit Hyperlink**, and make the necessary correction. Save the corrected document.

➤ Click the **Browser button** on the Windows taskbar to return to the browser, click the **Refresh button** to load the corrected page, then try the hyperlink a second time.

➤ Close Internet Explorer. Exit Word if you do not want to continue with the next exercise at this time.

Back button

URL of page

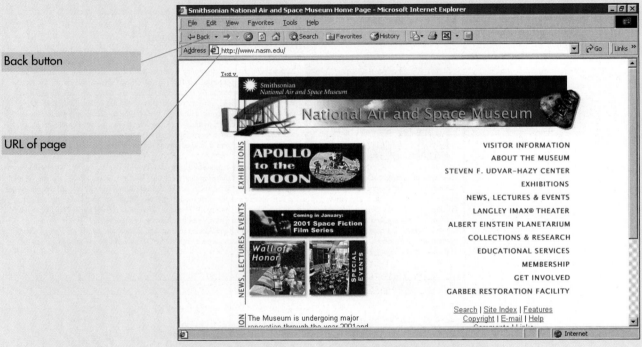

(i) Test the Web Page (step 9)

FIGURE 3.8 *Hands-on Exercise 2 (continued)*

VIEW THE HTML SOURCE CODE

Pull down the View menu in Internet Explorer and click the Source command to view the HTML statements that comprise the Web page. The statements are displayed in their own window, which is typically the Notepad accessory. Pull down the File menu in Notepad and click the Print command to print the HTML code. Do you see any relationship between the HTML statements and the Web page?

We have created some very interesting documents throughout the text, but in every instance we have formatted the document entirely on our own. It is time now to see what is available in terms of "jump starting" the process by borrowing professional designs from others. Accordingly, we discuss the wizards and templates that are built into Microsoft Word.

A *template* is a partially completed document that contains formatting, text, and/or graphics. It may be as simple as a memo or as complex as a résumé or newsletter. Microsoft Word provides a variety of templates for common documents, including a résumé, agenda, and fax cover sheet. You simply open the template, then modify the existing text as necessary, while retaining the formatting in the template. A *wizard* makes the process even easier by asking a series of questions, then creating a customized template based on your answers. A template or wizard creates the initial document for you. It's then up to you to complete the document by entering the appropriate information.

Figure 3.9 illustrates the use of wizards and templates in conjunction with a résumé. You can choose from one of three existing styles (contemporary, elegant, and professional) to which you add personal information. Alternatively, you can select the ***Résumé Wizard*** to create a customized template, as was done in Figure 3.9a.

After the Résumé Wizard is selected, it prompts you for the information it needs to create a basic résumé. You specify the style in Figure 3.9b, enter the requested information in Figure 3.9c, and choose the categories in Figure 3.9d. The wizard continues to ask additional questions (not shown in Figure 3.9), after which it displays the (partially) completed résumé based on your responses. You then complete the résumé by entering the specifics of your employment and/or additional information. As you edit the document, you can copy and paste information within the résumé, just as you would with a regular document. You can also change the formatting. It takes a little practice, but the end result is a professionally formatted résumé in a minimum of time.

Microsoft Word contains templates and wizards for a variety of other documents. (Look carefully at the tabs within the dialog box of Figure 3.9a and you can infer that Word will help you to create letters, faxes, memos, reports, legal pleadings, publications, and even Web pages. The Office Web site, www.microsoft.com/office, contains additional templates.) Consider, too, Figure 3.10, which displays four attractive documents that were created using the respective wizards. Realize, however, that while wizards and templates will help you to create professionally designed documents, they are only a beginning. *The content is still up to you.*

THIRTY SECONDS IS ALL YOU HAVE

Thirty seconds is the average amount of time a personnel manager spends skimming your résumé and deciding whether or not to call you for an interview. It doesn't matter how much training you have had or how good you are if your résumé and cover letter fail to project a professional image. Know your audience and use the vocabulary of your targeted field. Be positive and describe your experience from an accomplishment point of view. Maintain a separate list of references and have it available on request. Be sure all information is accurate. Be conscientious about the design of your résumé and proofread the final documents very carefully.

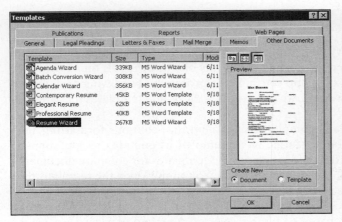

(a) Résumé Wizard

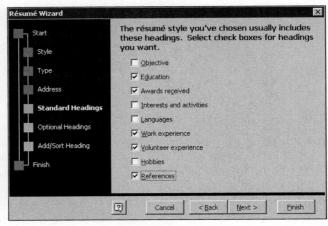

(d) Choose the Headings

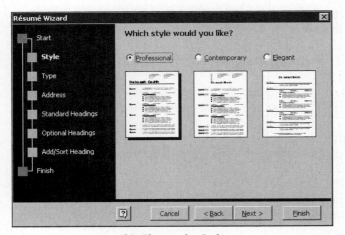

(b) Choose the Style

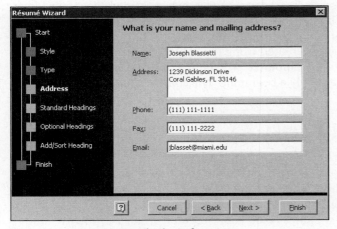

(c) Supply the Information

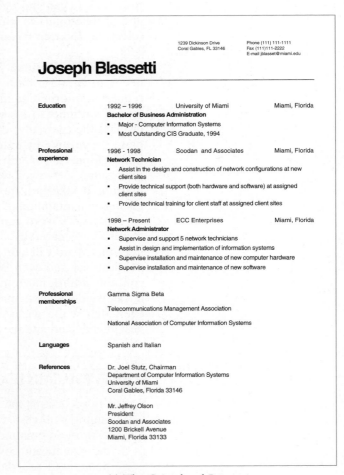

(e) The Completed Résumé

FIGURE 3.9 *Creating a Résumé*

	Sun	Mon	Tue	Wed	Thu	Fri	Sat
						1	2
June	3	4	5	6	7	8	9
	10	11	12	13	14	15	16
	17	18	19	20	21	22	23
	24	25	26	27	28	29	30
2001							

(a) Calendar

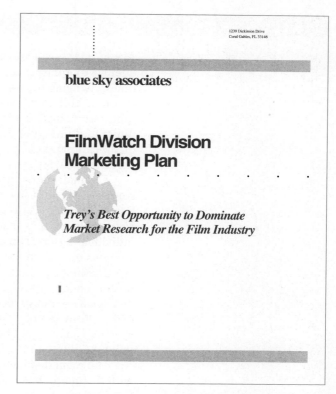

(b) Contemporary Report

INSPIRED TECHNOLOGIES
Corporate Graphics and Communications

Volume

3

Administrative
StyleSheetGuide

(c) Manual

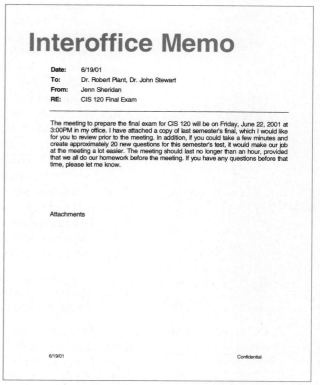

(d) Memo

FIGURE 3.10   *What You Can Do with Wizards*

A *mail merge* can create any type of standardized document, but it is used most frequently to create a set of *form letters*. In essence, it creates the same letter many times, changing the name, address, and other information as appropriate from letter to letter. You might use a mail merge to look for a job upon graduation, when you send essentially the same cover letter to many different companies. The concept is illustrated in Figure 3.11, in which John Smith has written a letter describing his qualifications, then merges that letter with a set of names and addresses, to produce the individual letters.

The mail merge process uses two files as input, a main document and a data source. A set of form letters is created as output. The *main document* (e.g., the cover letter in Figure 3.11a) contains standardized text, together with one or more *merge fields* that serve as place holders for the variable data that will be inserted in the individual letters. The data source (the set of names and addresses in Figure 3.11b) contains the information that varies from letter to letter.

The first row in the data source is called the header row and identifies the fields in the remaining rows. Each additional row contains the data to create one letter and is called a data record. Every data record contains the same fields in the same order—for example, Title, FirstName, LastName, and so on. (The fields can also be specified collectively, but for purposes of illustration, we will show the fields individually.)

The main document and the data source work in conjunction with one another, with the merge fields in the main document referencing the corresponding fields in the data source. The first line in the address of Figure 3.11a, for example, contains three entries in angle brackets, <<Title>> <<FirstName>> <<LastName>>. (These entries are not typed explicitly but are entered through special commands, as described in the hands-on exercise that follows shortly.) The merge process examines each record in the data source and substitutes the appropriate field values for the corresponding merge fields as it creates the individual form letters. For example, the first three fields in the first record will produce Mr. Eric Simon. The same fields in the second record will produce Dr. Lauren Howard, and so on.

In similar fashion, the second line in the address of the main document contains the <<Company>> field. The third line contains the <<JobTitle>> field. The fourth line references the <<Address1>> field, and the last line contains the <<City>>, <<State>, and <<PostalCode>> fields. The salutation repeats the <<Title>> and <<LastName>> fields. The first sentence in the letter uses the <<Company>> field a second time. The mail merge prepares the letters one at a time, with one letter created for every record in the data source until the file of names and addresses is exhausted. The individual form letters are shown in Figure 3.11c. Each letter begins automatically on a new page.

The implementation of a mail merge is accomplished through the *Mail Merge Wizard*, which will open in the task pane and guide you through the various steps in the mail merge process. In essence there are three things you must do:

1. Create and save the main document
2. Create and save the data source
3. Merge the main document and data source to create the individual letters

The same data source can be used to create multiple sets of form letters. You could, for example, create a marketing campaign in which you send an initial letter to the entire list, and then send follow-up letters at periodic intervals to the same mailing list. Alternatively, you could filter the original mailing list to include only a subset of names, such as the individuals who responded to the initial letter. You could also use the wizard to create a different set of documents, such as envelopes and/or e-mail messages. Note, too, that you can sort the addresses to print the documents in a specified sequence, such as zip code to take advantage of bulk mail.

John Doe Computing

1239 Dickinson Drive • **Coral Gables, FL 33146** • **(305) 666-5555**

June 22, 2001

«Title» «FirstName» «LastName»
«JobTitle»
«Company»
«Address1»
«City», «State» «PostalCode»

Dear «Title» «LastName»:

I would like to inquire about a position with «Company» as an entry-level programmer. I have graduated from the University of Miami with a Bachelor's Degree in Computer Information Systems (May 2001) and I am very interested in working for you. I am proficient in all applications in Microsoft Office and also have experience with Visual Basic, C++, and Java. I have had the opportunity to design and implement a few Web applications, both as a part of my educational program, and during my internship with Personalized Computer Designs, Inc.

I am eager to put my skills to work and would like to talk with you at your earliest convenience. I have enclosed a copy of my résumé and will be happy to furnish the names and addresses of my references. You may reach me at the above address and phone number. I look forward to hearing from you.

Sincerely,

John Doe
President

(a) The Form Letter

Title	FirstName	LastName	Company	JobTitle	Address1	City	State	PostalCode
Mr.	Eric	Simon	Arnold and Joyce Computing	President	10000 Sample Road	Coral Springs	FL	33071
Dr.	Lauren	Howard	Unique Systems	President	475 LeJeune Road	Coral Springs	FL	33071
Mr.	Peter	Gryn	Gryn Computing	Director of Human Resources	1000 Federal Highway	Miami	FL	33133
Ms.	Julie	Overby	The Overby Company	President	100 Savona Avenue	Coral Gables	FL	33146

(b) The Data Source

FIGURE 3.11   *A Mail Merge*

John Doe Computing

1239 Dickinson Drive • Coral Gables, FL 33146 • (305) 666-5555

June 22, 2001

Mr. Eric Simon
Arnold and Joyce Computing
President
10000 Sample Road
Coral Springs, FL 33071

Dear Mr. Simon:

I would like to inquire about a position with your company as an entry-level programmer. I have just graduated from the University of Miami with a Bachelor's Degree in Computer Information Systems (May 2001) and I am very interested in working for you. I am proficient in all applications in Microsoft Office and also have experience with Visual Basic, C++, and Java. I have had the opportunity to design and implement a few Web applications, both as a part of my educational program, and during my internship with Personalized Computer Designs, Inc.

I am eager to put my skills to work and would like to talk with you at your earliest convenience. I have enclosed a copy of my résumé and will be happy to furnish the names and addresses of my references. You may reach me at the above address and phone number. I look forward to hearing from you.

Sincerely,

John Doe
President

John Doe Computing

1239 Dickinson Drive • Coral Gables, FL 33146 • (305) 666-5555

June 22, 2001

Dr. Lauren Howard
Unique Systems
President
475 LeJeune Road
Coral Springs, FL 33071

Dear Dr. Howard:

I would like to inquire about a position with your company as an entry-level programmer. I have just graduated from the University of Miami with a Bachelor's Degree in Computer Information Systems (May 2001) and I am very interested in working for you. I am proficient in all applications in Microsoft Office and also have experience with Visual Basic, C++, and Java. I have had the opportunity to design and implement a few Web applications, both as a part of my educational program, and during my internship with Personalized Computer Designs, Inc.

I am eager to put my skills to work and would like to talk with you at your earliest convenience. I have enclosed a copy of my résumé and will be happy to furnish the names and addresses of my references. You may reach me at the above address and phone number. I look forward to hearing from you.

Sincerely,

John Doe
President

John Doe Computing

1239 Dickinson Drive • Coral Gables, FL 33146 • (305) 666-5555

June 22, 2001

Mr. Peter Gryn
Gryn Computing
Director of Human Resources
1000 Federal Highway
Miami, FL 33133

Dear Mr. Gryn:

I would like to inquire about a position with your company as an entry-level programmer. I have just graduated from the University of Miami with a Bachelor's Degree in Computer Information Systems (May 2001) and I am very interested in working for you. I am proficient in all applications in Microsoft Office and also have experience with Visual Basic, C++, and Java. I have had the opportunity to design and implement a few Web applications, both as a part of my educational program, and during my internship with Personalized Computer Designs, Inc.

I am eager to put my skills to work and would like to talk with you at your earliest convenience. I have enclosed a copy of my résumé and will be happy to furnish the names and addresses of my references. You may reach me at the above address and phone number. I look forward to hearing from you.

Sincerely,

John Doe
President

John Doe Computing

1239 Dickinson Drive • Coral Gables, FL 33146 • (305) 666-5555

June 22, 2001

Ms. Julie Overby
The Overby Company
President
100 Savona Avenue
Coral Gables, FL 33146

Dear Ms. Overby:

I would like to inquire about a position with your company as an entry-level programmer. I have just graduated from the University of Miami with a Bachelor's Degree in Computer Information Systems (May 2001) and I am very interested in working for you. I am proficient in all applications in Microsoft Office and also have experience with Visual Basic, C++, and Java. I have had the opportunity to design and implement a few Web applications, both as a part of my educational program, and during my internship with Personalized Computer Designs, Inc.

I am eager to put my skills to work and would like to talk with you at your earliest convenience. I have enclosed a copy of my résumé and will be happy to furnish the names and addresses of my references. You may reach me at the above address and phone number. I look forward to hearing from you.

Sincerely,

John Doe
President

(c) The Printed Letters

FIGURE 3.11   *A Mail Merge (continued)*

MAIL MERGE

Objective: To create a main document and associated data source; to implement a mail merge and produce a set of form letters. Use Figure 3.12 as a guide.

Step 1: **Open the Form Letter**

➤ Open the **Form Letter** document in the Exploring Word folder. If necessary, change to the **Print Layout view** and zoom to **Page Width** as shown in Figure 3.12a.

➤ Modify the letterhead to reflect your name and address. Select **"Your Name Goes Here"**, then type a new entry to replace the selected text. Add your address information to the second line.

➤ Click immediately to the left of the first paragraph, then press the **enter key** twice to insert two lines. Press the **up arrow** two times to return to the first line you inserted.

➤ Pull down the **Insert menu** and click the **Date and Time command** to display the dialog box in Figure 3.12a. Select (click) the date format you prefer and, if necessary, check the box to **Update automatically**. Click **OK** to close the dialog box.

➤ Save the document as **Modified Form Letter** so that you can return to the original document if necessary.

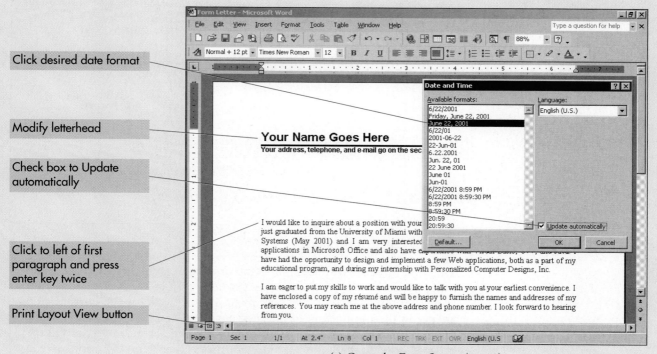

(a) Open the Form Letter (step 1)

FIGURE 3.12 *Hands-on Exercise 3*

Step 2:   **The Mail Merge Wizard**

➤ Pull down the **Tools menu**, click **Letters and Mailings**, then click **Mail Merge Wizard** to open the task pane.
➤ The option button for **Letters** is selected by default as shown in Figure 3.12b. Click **Next: Starting Document** to begin creating the document.
➤ The option button to **Use the current document** is selected. (We began the exercise by providing you with the text of the document, as opposed to having you create the entire form letter.) Click **Next: Select Recipients** to enter the list of names and addresses.
➤ Click the option button to **Type a New List**, then click the link to **Create** that appears within the task pane. This brings you to a new screen, where you enter the data for the recipients of your form letter.

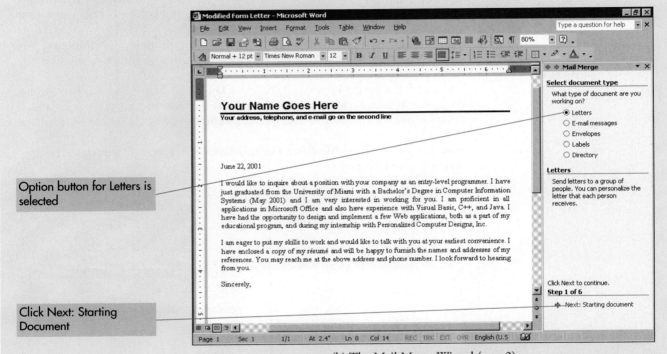

Option button for Letters is selected

Click Next: Starting Document

(b) The Mail Merge Wizard (step 2)

FIGURE 3.12   *Hands-on Exercise 3 (continued)*

THE MAIL MERGE WIZARD

The Mail Merge Wizard simplifies the process of creating form letters and other types of merge documents through step-by-step directions that appear automatically in the task pane. The options for the current step appear in the top portion of the task pane and are self-explanatory. Click the link to the next step at the bottom of the pane to move forward in the process, or click the link to the previous step to correct any mistakes you might have made.

Step 3: **Select the Recipients**

➤ Enter data for the first record, using your name and address as shown in Figure 3.12c. Type **Mr.** or **Ms.** in the Title field, then press **Tab** to move to the next (FirstName) field and enter your first name. Complete the first record.

➤ Click the **New Entry button** to enter the data for the next person. Enter your instructor's name and a hypothetical address. Enter data for one additional person, real or fictitious as you see fit. Click **Close** when you have completed the data entry.

➤ You will see the Save Address List dialog box, where you will be prompted to save the list of names and addresses. Save the file as **Names and Addresses** in the **Exploring Word folder**. The file type is specified as a Microsoft Office Address list.

➤ You will see a dialog box showing all of the records you have just entered. Click **OK** to close the dialog box. Click **Next: Write Your Letter** to continue.

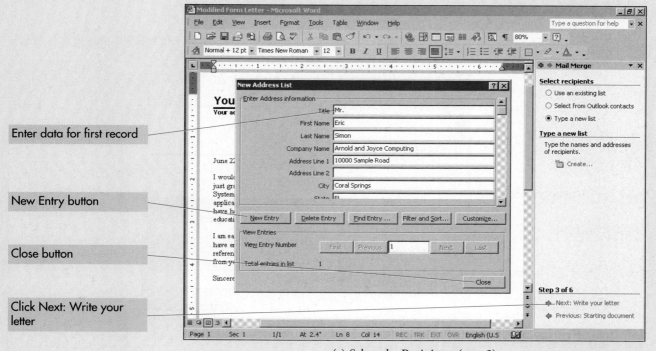

(c) Select the Recipients (step 3)

FIGURE 3.12 *Hands-on Exercise 3 (continued)*

THREE DIFFERENT FILES

A mail merge works with three different files. The main document and data source are input to the mail merge, which creates a set of merged letters as output. You can use the same data source (e.g., a set of names and addresses) with different main documents (a form letter and an envelope) and/or use the same main document with multiple data sources. You typically save, but do not print, the main document(s) and the data source(s). Conversely, you print the set of merged letters, but typically do not save them.

Step 4: **Write (Complete) the Letter**

➤ The text of the form letter is already written, but it is still necessary to insert the fields within the form letter.
➤ Click below the date and press the **enter key** once or twice. Click the link to the **Address block** to select a single entry that is composed of multiple fields (Street, City, ZipCode, and so on). Click **OK**. The AddressBlock field is inserted into the document as shown in Figure 3.12d.
➤ Press the **enter key** twice to leave a blank line after the address block. Click the link to the **Greeting line** to display the Greeting Line dialog box in Figure 3.12d.
➤ Choose the type of greeting you want. Change the comma that appears after the greeting to a colon since this is a business letter. Click **OK**. The GreetingLine field is inserted into the document and enclosed in angled brackets.
➤ Press **enter** to enter a blank line. Save the document. Click **Next: Preview Your Letters** to continue.

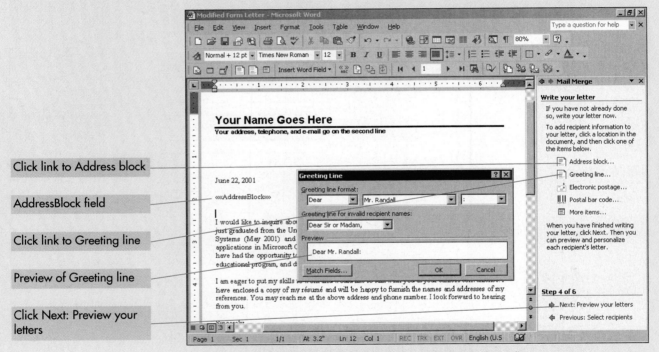

Click link to Address block

AddressBlock field

Click link to Greeting line

Preview of Greeting line

Click Next: Preview your letters

(d) Write (Complete) the Letter (step 4)

FIGURE 3.12 *Hands-on Exercise 3 (continued)*

BLOCKS VERSUS INDIVIDUAL FIELDS

The Mail Merge Wizard simplifies the process of entering field names into a form letter by supplying two predefined entries, AddressBlock and GreetingLine, which contain multiple fields that are typical of the ways in which an address and salutation appear in a conventional letter. You can still insert individual fields, by clicking in the document where you want the field to go, then clicking the Insert Merge Fields button on the Mail Merge toolbar. The blocks are easier.

Step 5: **View and Print the Letters**

➤ You should see the first form letter as shown. You can click the >> or << button in the task pane (not shown in Figure 3.12e) to move to the next or previous letter, respectively. You can also use the navigation buttons that appear on the Mail Merge toolbar.

➤ View the records individually to be sure that the form letter is correct and that the data has been entered correctly. Make corrections if necessary.

➤ Click **Next: Complete the Merge**, then click **Print** to display the dialog box in Figure 3.12e. Click **OK**, then **OK** again, to print the form letters.

➤ Click the **<<abc>>** button to display the field codes. Pull down the **File menu** and click the **Print command** to display the Print dialog box. Check the option to print the current page. Click **OK**. Submit this page to your instructor as well.

➤ Pull down the **File menu** and click the **Close command** to close the Modified Form Letter and the associated set of names and addresses. Save the documents if you are prompted to do so.

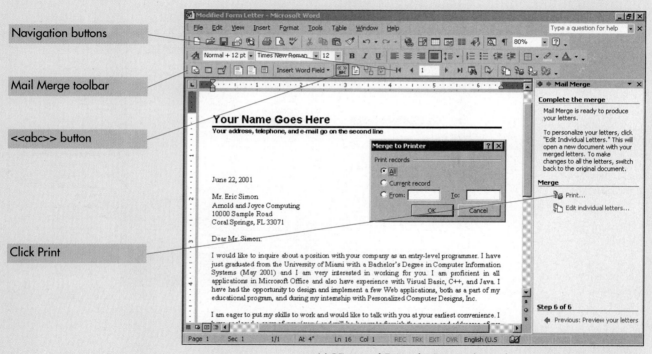

Navigation buttons

Mail Merge toolbar

<<abc>> button

Click Print

(e) View and Print the Letters (step 5)

FIGURE 3.12   *Hands-on Exercise 3 (continued)*

THE MAIL MERGE TOOLBAR

The Mail Merge toolbar appears throughout the mail merge process and contains various buttons that apply to different steps within the process. Click the <<abc>> button to display field values rather than field codes. Click the button a second time and you switch back to field codes from field values. Click the <<abc>> button to display the field values, then use the navigation buttons to view the different letters. Click the ▶ button, for example, and you move to the next letter. Click the ▶| button to display the form letter for the last record.

Step 6: **Open the Contemporary Merge Letter**

➤ Pull down the **File menu** and click the **New command** (or click the **New button** on the Standard toolbar). If necessary, pull down the **View menu** and open the **task pane**.

➤ Click the link to **General Templates** in the task pane to display the Templates dialog box, then click the **Mail Merge tab** to display the Templates dialog box in Figure 3.12f.

➤ Select (click) the **Contemporary Merge Letter**. Click the **Preview button** (if necessary) to see a thumbnail view of this document.

➤ Be sure that the **Document option button** is selected. Click **OK** to select this document and begin the merge process. You will see a form letter with the AddressBlock and GreetingLine fields already entered.

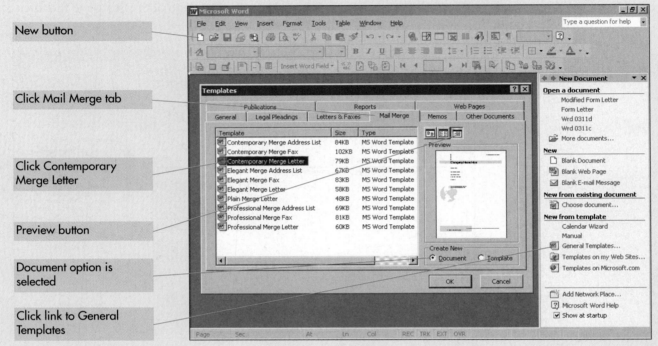

(f) Open the Contemporary Merge Letter (step 6)

FIGURE 3.12 *Hands-on Exercise 3 (continued)*

PAPER MAKES A DIFFERENCE

Most of us take paper for granted, but the right paper can make a significant difference in the effectiveness of the document, especially when you are trying to be noticed. Reports and formal correspondence are usually printed on white paper, but you would be surprised how many different shades of white there are. Other types of documents lend themselves to a specialty paper for additional impact. Consider the use of a specialty paper the next time you have an important project.

Step 7: **Select the Recipients**

➤ The option button to **Use an existing list** is selected. Click the link to **Browse** for the existing list to display the Select Data Source dialog box.
➤ We will use the same data source that you created earlier. (You could also use an Access database as the source of your data.)
➤ Click the **down arrow** on the Look in box to select the Exploring Word folder. Click the **down arrow** on the File type list box to select **Microsoft Office Address Lists**. Select the **Names and Addresses** file from step 3. Click **Open**.
➤ You should see the Mail Merge Recipients dialog box in Figure 3.12g that contains the records you entered earlier. You can use this dialog box to modify existing data, to change the order in which the form letters will appear, and/or to choose which recipients are to receive the form letter.
➤ Click **OK** to close the dialog box. Click **Next: Write Your Letter** to continue.

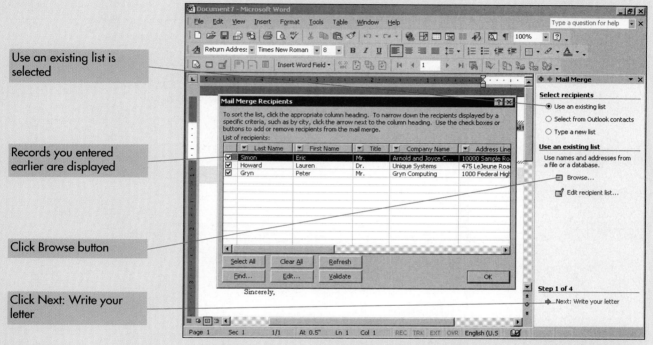

Use an existing list is selected

Records you entered earlier are displayed

Click Browse button

Click Next: Write your letter

(g) Select the Recipients (step 7)

FIGURE 3.12 *Hands-on Exercise 3 (continued)*

EDIT THE RECIPIENTS LIST

Use the Mail Merge Recipients dialog box to add, edit, or delete data for any existing recipient. Select the record you want to change, then click the Edit button to display a dialog box where you change existing information (and/or where you can delete an existing entry or add a new entry). You can display the dialog box at any time during the mail merge process by clicking the Mail Merge Recipients button on the Mail Merge toolbar.

Step 8:   **Write the Form Letter**

➤ The form letter has been created as a template as shown in Figure 3.12h. The AddressBlock and GreetingLine fields have been entered for you.

➤ Click and drag in **Type Your Letter Here** that appears in the form letter and enter two or three sentences of your own choosing. Our letter indicates that we are seeking to acquire one or more of the consulting firms on the mailing list.

➤ Continue to personalize the form letter by replacing the text in the original template. Click at the upper right of the letter and enter your return address. Use your name for the company name.

➤ Replace the signature lines with your name and title. Select the line at the bottom of the page that reads [Click here and type a slogan] and enter a slogan of your own.

➤ Save the document as **Contemporary Merge Letter** in the Exploring Word folder. Click the link to **Next: Preview your letter**.

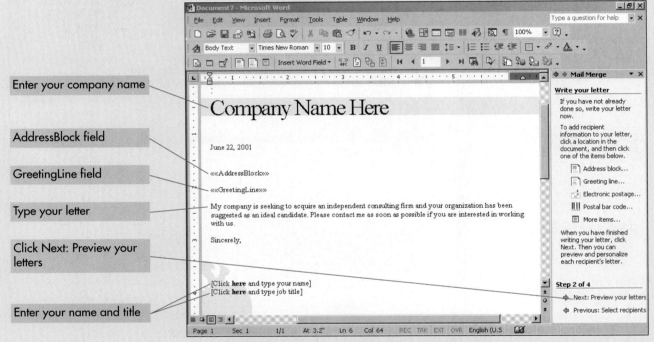

(h) Write the Form Letter (step 8)

FIGURE 3.12   *Hands-on Exercise 3 (continued)*

ENVELOPES AND MAILING LABELS

The set of form letters is only the first step in a true mail merge because you also have to create the envelopes and/or mailing labels to physically mail the letters. Start the Mail Merge wizard as you normally do, but this time specify labels (or envelopes) instead of a form letter. Follow the instructions provided by the wizard using the same data source as for the form letters. See practice exercise 8 at the end of the chapter.

Step 9: **Complete the Merge**

➤ You should see the first form letter. The name and address of this recipient are the same as in the set of form letters created earlier. Click **Next: Complete the Merge** to display the screen in Figure 3.12i.

➤ Use the navigation buttons on the Mail Merge toolbar to view the three form letters. Click the link to **Print . . .** (or click the **Merge to Printer button** on the Mail Merge toolbar).

➤ Click the option button to print all the letters, then click **OK** to display the Print dialog box. Click **OK** to print the individual form letters.

➤ Exit Word. Save the form letter and/or the names and addresses document if you are asked to do so.

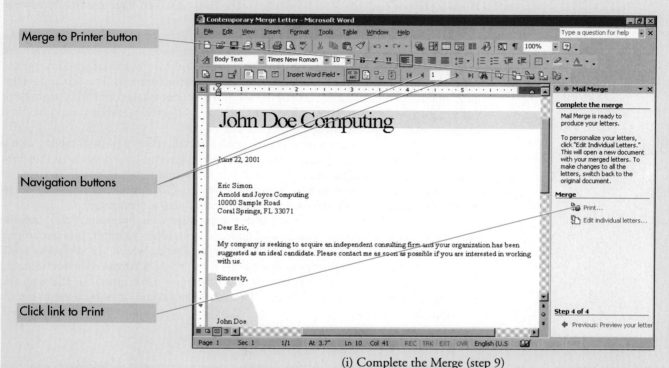

(i) Complete the Merge (step 9)

FIGURE 3.12 *Hands-on Exercise 3 (continued)*

EDIT THE INDIVIDUAL LETTERS

Click the Merge to File button (or click the link to Edit individual letters in the task pane) to create a third document (called Letters1 by default) consisting of the individual form letters. There are as many pages in this document as there are records in the address file. You can view and/or edit the individual letters from this document, then print the entire set of merged letters. You need not save this document, however, unless you actually made changes to the individual letters.

The Microsoft Media Gallery contains clip art, sound files, photographs, and movies and it is accessible from any application in Microsoft Office. The Insert Picture command is used to insert clip art into a document through the task pane. Microsoft WordArt is an application within Microsoft Office that creates decorative text, which can be used to add interest to a document.

The Insert Symbol command provides access to special characters, making it easy to place typographic characters into a document. The symbols can be taken from any font and can be displayed in any point size.

Resources (such as clip art or photographs) can be downloaded from the Web for inclusion in a Word document. Web pages are written in a language called HTML (HyperText Markup Language). The Save As Web Page command saves a Word document as a Web page.

A copyright provides legal protection to a written or artistic work, giving the author exclusive rights to its use and reproduction, except as governed under the fair use exclusion. Anything on the Internet should be considered copyrighted unless the document specifically says it is in the public domain. The fair use exclusion enables you to use a portion of the work for educational, nonprofit purposes, or for the purpose of critical review or commentary. All such material should be cited through an appropriate footnote or endnote.

Wizards and templates help create professionally designed documents with a minimum of time and effort. A template is a partially completed document that contains formatting and other information. A wizard is an interactive program that creates a customized template based on the answers you supply. The resulting documentation can be modified with respect to content and/or formatting.

A mail merge creates the same letter many times, changing only the variable data, such as the addressee's name and address, from letter to letter. It is performed in conjunction with a main document and a data source, which are stored as separate documents. The mail merge can be used to create a form letter for selected records, and/or print the form letters in a sequence different from the way the records are stored in the data source. The same data source can be used to create multiple sets of form letters.

KEY TERMS

AutoCorrect (p. 106)
AutoFormat (p. 113)
Clip art (p. 109)
Copyright (p. 117)
Drawing canvas (p. 108)
Drawing toolbar (p. 108)
Endnote (p. 117)
Fair use (p. 117)
Footnote (p. 117)
Form letter (p. 130)
HTML document (p. 116)
Hyperlink (p. 116)

HyperText Markup Language
  (HTML) (p. 116)
Insert Picture command (p. 105)
Insert Reference command (p. 117)
Insert Symbol command (p. 106)
Internet (p. 116)
Intranet (p. 117)
Mail merge (p. 130)
Mail Merge Wizard (p. 130)
Main document (p. 130)
Media Gallery (p. 105)
Merge fields (p. 130)

Microsoft WordArt (p. 107)
Public domain (p. 117)
Résumé Wizard (p. 127)
Save As Web Page command
  (p. 116)
Sizing handle (p. 108)
Template (p. 127)
Web page (p. 116)
Wizard (p. 127)
WordArt (p. 107)
World Wide Web (p. 116)

1. How do you change the size of a selected object so that the height and width change in proportion to one another?
   (a) Click and drag any of the four corner handles in the direction you want to go
   (b) Click and drag the sizing handle on the top border, then click and drag the sizing handle on the left side
   (c) Click and drag the sizing handle on the bottom border, then click and drag the sizing handle on the right side
   (d) All of the above

2. The Microsoft Media Gallery:
   (a) Is accessed through the Insert Picture command
   (b) Is available in Microsoft Word, Excel, and PowerPoint
   (c) Enables you to search for a specific piece of clip art by specifying a key word in the description of the clip art
   (d) All of the above

3. How do you search for clip art using the Microsoft Media Gallery?
   (a) By entering a key word that describes the image you want
   (b) By browsing through various collections
   (c) Both (a) and (b)
   (d) Neither (a) nor (b)

4. Which of the following objects can be inserted into a document from the Microsoft Media Gallery?
   (a) Clip art
   (b) Sound
   (c) Photographs
   (d) All of the above

5. Which of the following is true about a mail merge?
   (a) The same form letter can be used with different data sources
   (b) The same data source can be used with different form letters
   (c) Both (a) and (b)
   (d) Neither (a) nor (b)

6. Which of the following best describes the documents that are associated with a mail merge?
   (a) The main document is typically saved, but not necessarily printed
   (b) The names and addresses are typically saved, but not necessarily printed
   (c) The individual form letters are printed, but not necessarily saved
   (d) All of the above

7. Which of the following is true about footnotes or endnotes?
   (a) The addition of a footnote or endnote automatically renumbers the notes that follow
   (b) The deletion of a footnote or endnote automatically renumbers the notes that follow
   (c) Both (a) and (b)
   (d) Neither (a) nor (b)

8. Which of the following is true about the Insert Symbol command?
   (a) It can insert a symbol in different type sizes
   (b) It can access any font installed on the system
   (c) Both (a) and (b)
   (d) Neither (a) nor (b)

9. Which of the following is true regarding objects and the associated toolbars?
   (a) Clicking on a WordArt object displays the WordArt toolbar
   (b) Clicking on a Picture displays the Picture toolbar
   (c) Both (a) and (b)
   (d) Neither (a) nor (b)

10. Which of the following objects can be downloaded from the Web for inclusion in a Word document?
    (a) Clip art
    (b) Photographs
    (c) Sound and video files
    (d) All of the above

11. What is the significance of the Shift key in conjunction with various tools on the Drawing toolbar?
    (a) It will draw a circle rather than an oval using the Oval tool
    (b) It will draw a square rather than a rectangle using the Rectangle tool
    (c) It will draw a horizontal or vertical line with the Line tool
    (d) All of the above

12. What happens if you enter the text www.intel.com into a document?
    (a) The entry is converted to a hyperlink, and further, the text will be underlined and displayed in a different color
    (b) The associated page will be opened provided your computer has access to the Internet
    (c) Both (a) and (b)
    (d) Neither (a) nor (b)

13. Which of the following is a true statement about wizards?
    (a) They are accessed from the General Templates link on the task pane
    (b) They always produce a finished document with no further modification necessary
    (c) Both (a) and (b)
    (d) Neither (a) nor (b)

14. Which of the following is true about an HTML document that was created from within Microsoft Word?
    (a) It can be viewed locally
    (b) It can be viewed via the Web provided it is uploaded onto a Web server
    (c) Both (a) and (b)
    (d) Neither (a) nor (b)

15. Which of the following are created as a result of the Save As Web Page command, given that the document is called "My Home Page"?
    (a) An HTML document called "My Home Page"
    (b) A "My Home Page" folder that contains the objects that appear on the associated page
    (c) Both (a) and (b)
    (d) Neither (a) nor (b)

ANSWERS

1. a	**6.** d	**11.** d
2. d	**7.** c	**12.** a
3. c	**8.** c	**13.** a
4. d	**9.** c	**14.** c
5. c	**10.** d	**15.** c

1. Travel World: You have been hired as an intern for the Travel World agency and asked to create a flyer to distribute on campus. The only requirement is to include the travel agent's name and e-mail address. (Our information appears at the bottom of the page and is not visible in Figure 3.13.) Use any combination of clip art or photographs to make the flyer as attractive as possible. Be sure to spell check the completed flyer, then print the document for your instructor.

FIGURE 3.13 *Travel World (Exercise 1)*

2. Symbols as Clip Art: The installation of Microsoft Windows and/or Microsoft Office provides multiple fonts that are accessible from any application. Two of the fonts, Symbols and Wingdings, contain a variety of special characters that can be inserted to create some unusual documents as shown in Figure 3.14. The "art" in these documents is not clip art per se, but symbols that are added to a document through the Insert Symbol command. Use your imagination, coupled with the fact that a font is scalable to any size, to recreate the documents in Figure 3.14. Better yet, create two documents of your own design that utilize these special fonts.

3. Create a Home Page: It's easy to create a home page. Start a new document and enter its text just as you would any other document. Use any and all formatting commands to create a document similar to the one in Figure 3.15. We suggest you use clip art, as opposed to a real picture. Pull down the File menu and use the Save As Web Page command to convert the Word document to an HTML document. Complete the document as described below:
   a. Use the Insert Hyperlink command to create a list of 3 to 5 hyperlinks. Be sure to enter accurate Web addresses for each of your sites.
   b. Select all of the links after they have been entered, then click the Bullets button on the Formatting toolbar to create a bulleted list.

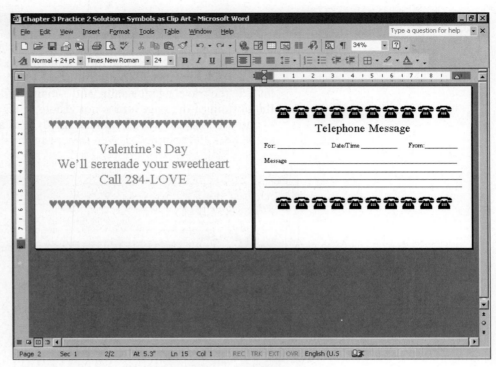

FIGURE 3.14   *Symbols as Clip Art (Exercise 2)*

FIGURE 3.15   *Create a Home Page (Exercise 3)*

c. Pull down the Format menu, click the Themes command, then select a professionally chosen design for your Web page.

d. Save the document a final time, then exit Word. Start Windows Explorer, then go to the folder containing your home page, and double click the file you just created. Internet Explorer will start automatically (because your document was saved as a Web page). You should see your document within Internet Explorer as shown in Figure 3.15. Look carefully at the Address bar and note the local address on drive C, as opposed to a Web address. Print the document for your instructor as proof you completed the assignment.

e. Creating the home page and viewing it locally is easy. Placing the page on the Web where it can be seen by anyone with an Internet connection is not as straightforward. You will need additional information from your instructor about how to obtain an account on a Web server (if that is available at your school), and further how to upload the Web page from your PC to the server.

4. A Commercial Web Page: Create a home page for a real or hypothetical business as shown in Figure 3.16, using the same general procedure as in the previous exercise. Start Word and enter the text of a new document that describes your business. Use clip art, bullets, hyperlinks, and other formatting as appropriate. Save the completed document as a Web page. Start Windows Explorer and locate the newly created document. Double click the document to open the default browser and display the page as shown in Figure 3.16, then print the page from within the browser.

There is no requirement to upload the page to the Web, but it is worth doing if you have the capability. You will need additional information from your instructor about how to obtain an account on a Web server (if that is available at your school), and further how to upload the Web page from your PC to the server.

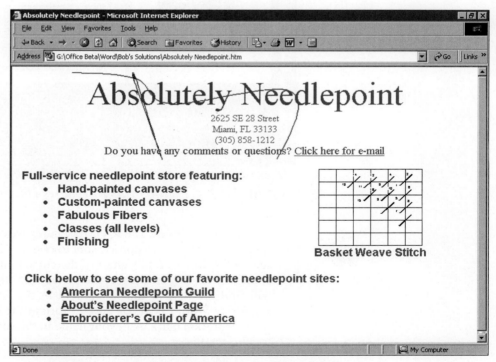

FIGURE 3.16 *Commercial Web Page (Exercise 4)*

5. Presidential Anecdotes: Figure 3.17 displays the finished version of a document containing ten presidential anecdotes. The anecdotes were taken from the book *Presidential Anecdotes,* by Paul F. Boller, Jr., published by Penguin Books (New York, 1981). Open the *Chapter 3 Practice 5* document that is found in the Exploring Word folder, then make the following changes:

   a. Add a footnote after Mr. Boller's name, which appears at the end of the second sentence, citing the information about the book. This, in turn, renumbers all existing footnotes in the document.

   b. Switch the order of the anecdotes for Lincoln and Jefferson so that the presidents appear in order. The footnotes for these references are changed automatically.

   c. Convert all of the footnotes to endnotes, as shown in the figure.

   d. Go to the White House Web site at www.whitehouse.gov and download a picture of any of the ten presidents, then incorporate that picture into a cover page. Remember to cite the reference with an appropriate footnote.

   e. Submit the completed document to your instructor.

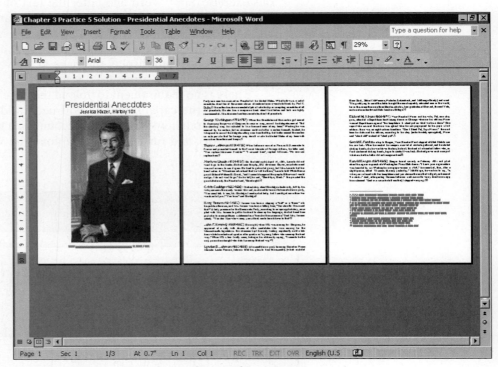

FIGURE 3.17   *Presidential Anecdotes (Exercise 5)*

6. The iCOMP® Index: The iCOMP® index was created by Intel to compare the speeds of various microprocessors to one another. This assignment asks you to search the Web to find a chart of the current index (3.0 or later), download the chart to your PC, then insert the picture into the document in Figure 3.18. You will find the text of that document in the file, *Chapter 3 Practice 6*, in the Exploring Word folder. Be sure to format the document completely, including the registration mark. Add your name to the completed document and submit it to your instructor.

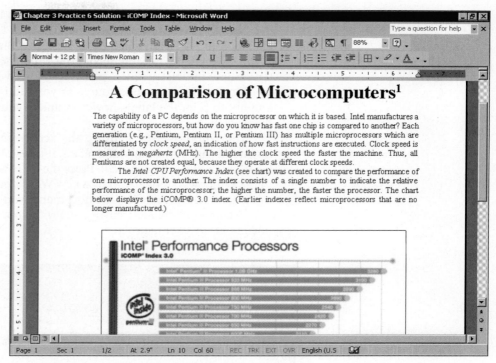

FIGURE 3.18 *The iCOMP® Index (Exercise 6)*

7. **Create an Envelope:** The Résumé Wizard will step you through the process of creating a résumé, but you need an envelope in which to mail it. Pull down the Tools menu, click Letters and Mailings, click the Envelopes and Labels command, click the Envelopes tab, then enter the indicated information. You can print the envelope and/or include it permanently in the document as shown in Figure 3.19. Do not, however, attempt to print the envelope in a computer lab at school unless envelopes are available for the printer.

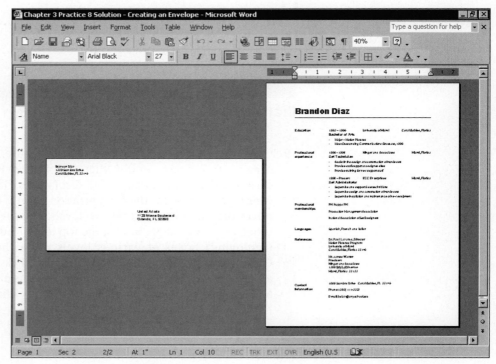

FIGURE 3.19 *Create an Envelope (Exercise 7)*

8. Mailing Labels: A mail merge creates the form letters for a mailing. That is only the first step, however, because you also have to create envelopes and/or mailing labels to physically mail the letters. Start the Mail Merge Wizard as you did in the third hands-on exercise, but this time, specify labels instead of a form letter. Follow the instructions provided by the wizard to create a set of mailing labels using the same data source as you did in the hands-on exercise. Do *not* attempt to print the labels, however, unless you actually have mailing labels for the printer.

You can, however, capture the screen in Figure 3.20 to prove to your instructor that you created the labels. It's easy. Use the mail merge to create the labels as shown in Figure 3.20. Press the Print Screen key to capture the screen to the Windows clipboard. Start a new Word document, then click the Paste button to paste the screen into the document. Add a sentence or two that describes the assignment. Include a cover page with your name, then print the completed document for your instructor.

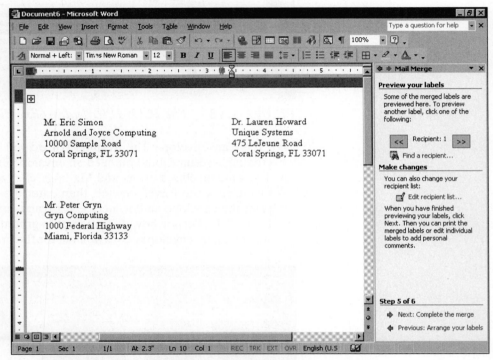

FIGURE 3.20 *Mailing Labels (exercise 8)*

9. Organization Charts: The document in Figure 3.21 shows how you can create organization charts within Microsoft Office. Pull down the Insert menu and click the Diagrams command to display the Diagram Gallery dialog box from where you can select the Organization chart. The default chart consists of four boxes that are displayed on two levels. The lower level has three subordinates reporting to the single box on the top level. You can modify the chart by adding (removing) boxes at various levels using the Insert Shape button on the Organization Chart toolbar. You can also click in any box to add the appropriate descriptive text. The organization chart is a single object that can be moved and sized within the document, just like any Windows object.

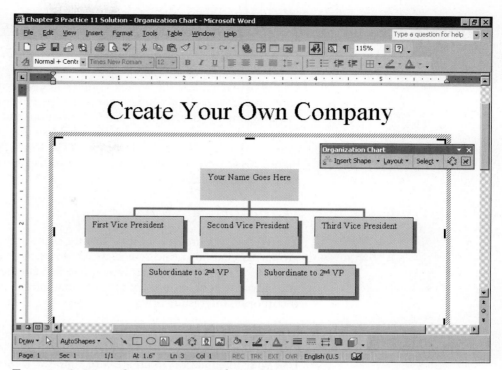

FIGURE 3.21 *Organization Chart (Exercise 9)*

10. The Calendar Wizard: The Calendar Wizard is one of several wizards that are built into Microsoft Office. Pull down the File menu, click the New command, then click General Templates in the task pane to display the associated dialog box. Click the Other documents tab to access the Calendar Wizard and create a calendar for the current month as shown in Figure 3.22.

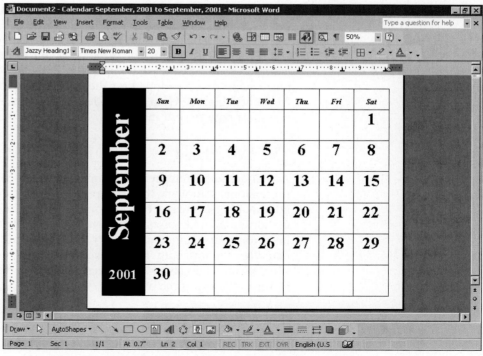

FIGURE 3.22 *The Calendar Wizard (Exercise 10)*

The Cover Page

Use WordArt and/or the Media Gallery to create a truly original cover page that you can use with all of your assignments. The cover page should include the title of the assignment, your name, course information, and date. (Use the Insert Date and Time command to insert the date as a field so that it will be updated automatically every time you retrieve the document.) The formatting is up to you. Print the completed cover page and submit it to your instructor, then use the cover page for all future assignments.

My Favorite Recording Group

The Web is a source of infinite variety, including music from your favorite rock group. You can also find music, which you can download and play, provided you have the necessary hardware. Use any search engine to find one or more sites about your favorite rock group. Try to find biographical information as well as a picture. Incorporate the results of your research into a short paper for your instructor.

The Résumé

Use your imagination to create a résumé for Benjamin Franklin or Leonardo Da Vinci, two acknowledged geniuses. The résumé is limited to one page and will be judged for content (yes, you have to do a little research on the Web) as well as appearance. You can intersperse fact and fiction as appropriate; for example, you may want to leave space for a telephone and/or a fax number, but could indicate that these devices have not yet been implemented. You can choose a format for the résumé using the Résumé Wizard, or better yet, design your own.

Macros

The Insert Symbol command can be used to insert foreign characters into a document, but this technique is too slow if you use these characters with any frequency. It is much more efficient to develop a series of macros (keyboard shortcuts) that will insert the characters for you. You could, for example, create a macro to insert an accented e, then invoke that macro through the Ctrl+e keyboard shortcut. Parallel macros could be developed for the other vowels or special characters that you use frequently. Use the Help menu to learn about macros, then summarize your findings in a short note to your instructor.

The Letterhead

A well-designed letterhead adds impact to your correspondence. Collect samples of professional stationery, then design your own letterhead, which includes your name, address, phone, and any other information you deem relevant. Include a fax number and/or e-mail address as appropriate. Use your imagination and design the letterhead for your planned career. Try different fonts and/or the Format Border command to add horizontal line(s) under the text. Consider a graphic logo, but keep it simple. You might also want to decrease the top margin so that the letterhead prints closer to the top of the page.

CHAPTER 4

Advanced Features: Outlines, Tables, Styles, and Sections

OBJECTIVES

AFTER READING THIS CHAPTER YOU WILL BE ABLE TO:

1. Create a bulleted or numbered list; create an outline using a multilevel list.
2. Describe the Outline view; explain how this view facilitates moving text within a document.
3. Describe the tables feature; create a table and insert it into a document.
4. Explain how styles automate the formatting process and provide a consistent appearance to common elements in a document.
5. Use the AutoFormat command to apply styles to an existing document; create, modify, and apply a style to selected elements of a document.
6. Define a section; explain how section formatting differs from character and paragraph formatting.
7. Create a header and/or a footer; establish different headers or footers for the first, odd, or even pages in the same document.
8. Insert page numbers into a document; use the Edit menu's Go To command to move directly to a specific page in a document.
9. Create an index and a table of contents.

OVERVIEW

This chapter presents a series of advanced features that will be especially useful the next time you have to write a term paper with specific formatting requirements. We show you how to create a bulleted or numbered list to emphasize important items within a term paper, and how to create an outline for that paper. We also introduce the tables feature, which is one of the most powerful features in Microsoft Word as it provides an easy way to arrange text, numbers, and/or graphics.

153

The second half of the chapter develops the use of styles, or sets of formatting instructions that provide a consistent appearance to similar elements in a document. We describe the AutoFormat command that assigns styles to an existing document and greatly simplifies the formatting process. We show you how to create a new style, how to modify an existing style, and how to apply those styles to text within a document. We introduce the Outline view, which is used in conjunction with styles to provide a condensed view of a document. We also discuss several items associated with longer documents, such as page numbers, headers and footers, a table of contents, and an index.

BULLETS AND LISTS

A list helps you organize information by highlighting important topics. A **bulleted list** emphasizes (and separates) the items. A **numbered list** sequences (and prioritizes) the items and is automatically updated to accommodate additions or deletions. An **outline** (or **outline numbered list**) extends a numbered list to several levels, and it too is updated automatically when topics are added or deleted. Each of these lists is created through the **Bullets and Numbering command** in the Format menu, which displays the Bullets and Numbering dialog box in Figure 4.1.

The tabs within the Bullets and Numbering dialog box are used to choose the type of list and customize its appearance. The Bulleted tab selected in Figure 4.1a enables you to specify one of several predefined symbols for the bullet. Typically, that is all you do, although you can use the Customize button to change the default spacing (of ¼ inch) of the text from the bullet and/or to choose a different symbol for the bullet.

The Numbered tab in Figure 4.1b lets you choose Arabic or Roman numerals, or upper- or lowercase letters, for a Numbered list. As with a bulleted list, the Customize button lets you change the default spacing, the numbering style, and/or the punctuation before or after the number or letter. Note, too, the option buttons to restart or continue numbering, which become important if a list appears in multiple places within a document. In other words, each occurrence of a list can start numbering anew, or it can continue from where the previous list left off.

The Outline Numbered tab in Figure 4.1c enables you to create an outline to organize your thoughts. As with the other types of lists, you can choose one of several default styles, and/or modify a style through the Customize command button. You can also specify whether each outline within a document is to restart its numbering, or whether it is to continue numbering from the previous outline.

The List Styles tab (not shown in Figure 4.1) lets you change the style (formatting specifications) associated with a list. You can change the font size, use a picture or symbol for a bullet, add color, and so on. Styles are discussed later in the chapter.

CREATING AN OUTLINE

Our next exercise explores the Bullets and Numbering command in conjunction with creating an outline for a hypothetical paper on the United States Constitution. The exercise begins by having you create a bulleted list, then asking you to convert it to a numbered list, and finally to an outline. The end result is the type of outline your professor may ask you to create prior to writing a term paper.

As you do the exercise, remember that a conventional outline is created as an outline numbered list within the Bullets and Numbering command. Text for the outline is entered in the Print Layout or Normal view, *not* the Outline view. The latter provides a completely different capability—a condensed view of a document that is used in conjunction with styles and is discussed later in the chapter. We mention this to avoid confusion should you stumble into the Outline view.

Select bullet symbol

Click to choose a different bullet symbol or change default spacing

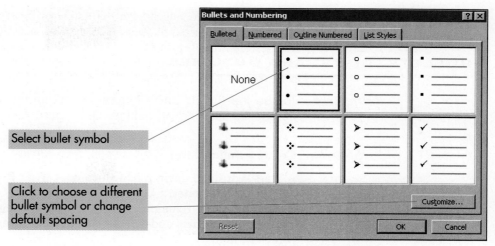

(a) Bulleted List

Select Number style

Continue numbering from previous list

Restart numbering with new list

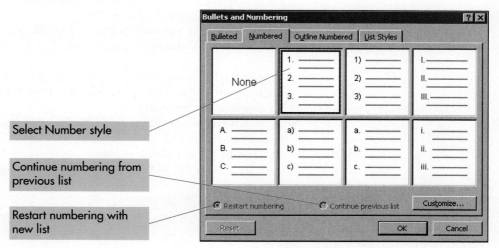

(b) Numbered List

Select Outline style

Click to modify Outline style

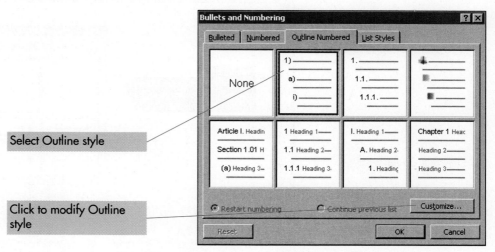

(c) Outline Numbered List

FIGURE 4.1 *Bullets and Numbering*

BULLETS, LISTS, AND OUTLINES

Objective To use the Bullets and Numbering command to create a bulleted list, a numbered list, and an outline. Use Figure 4.2 as a guide.

Step 1: **Create a Bulleted List**

> ➤ Start Word and begin a new document. Type **Preamble**, the first topic in our list, and press **enter**.
> ➤ Type the three remaining topics, **Article I—Legislative Branch**, **Article II—Executive Branch**, and **Article III—Judicial Branch**. Do not press enter after the last item.
> ➤ Click and drag to select all four topics as shown in Figure 4.2a. Pull down the **Format menu** and click the **Bullets and Numbering command** to display the Bullets and Numbering dialog box.
> ➤ If necessary, click the **Bulleted tab**, select the type of bullet you want, then click **OK** to accept this setting and close the dialog box. Bullets have been added to the list.
> ➤ Click after the words **Judicial Branch** to deselect the list and also to position the insertion point at the end of the list. Press **enter** to begin a new line. A bullet appears automatically.
> ➤ Type **Amendments**. Press **enter** to end this line and begin the next, which already has a bullet.
> ➤ Press **enter** a second time to terminate the bulleted list.
> ➤ Save the document as **US Constitution** in the **Exploring Word folder**.

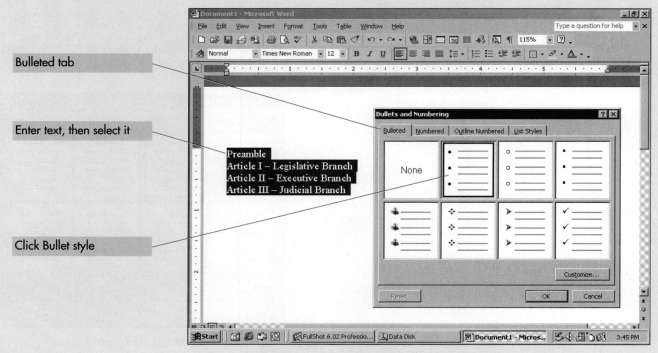

Bulleted tab

Enter text, then select it

Click Bullet style

(a) Create a Bulleted List (step 1)

FIGURE 4.2 *Hands-on Exercise 1*

Step 2: **Modify a Numbered List**

➤ Click and drag to select the five items in the bulleted list, then click the **Numbering button** on the Standard toolbar.

➤ The bulleted list has been converted to a numbered list as shown in Figure 4.2b. (The last two items have not yet been added to the list.)

➤ Click immediately after the last item in the list and press **enter** to begin a new line. Word automatically adds the next sequential number to the list.

➤ Type **History** and press **enter**. Type **The Constitution Today** as the seventh (and last) item.

➤ Click in the selection area to the left of the sixth item, **History** (only the text is selected). Now drag the selected text to the beginning of the list, in front of *Preamble*. Release the mouse.

➤ The list is automatically renumbered. *History* is now the first item, *Preamble* is the second item, and so on.

➤ Save the document.

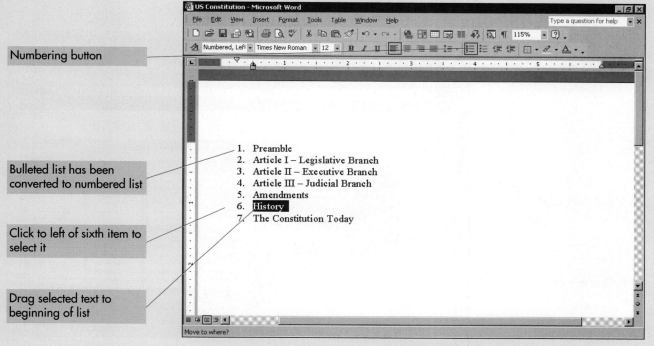

Numbering button

Bulleted list has been converted to numbered list

Click to left of sixth item to select it

Drag selected text to beginning of list

(b) Modify a Numbered List (step 2)

FIGURE 4.2   *Hands-on Exercise 1 (continued)*

THE BULLETS AND NUMBERING BUTTONS

Select the items for which you want to create a list, then click the Numbering or Bullets button on the Formatting toolbar to create a numbered or bulleted list, respectively. The buttons function as toggle switches; that is, click the button once (when the items are selected) and the list formatting is in effect. Click the button a second time and the bullets or numbers disappear. The buttons also enable you to switch from one type of list to another; that is, selecting a bulleted list and clicking the Numbering button changes the list to a numbered list, and vice versa.

Step 3: **Convert to an Outline**

➤ Click and drag to select the entire list, then click the **right mouse button** to display a context-sensitive menu.

➤ Click the **Bullets and Numbering command** to display the Bullets and Numbering dialog box in Figure 4.2c.

➤ Click the **Outline Numbered tab**, then select the type of outline you want. (Do not be concerned if the selected formatting does not display Roman numerals as we customize the outline later in the exercise.)

➤ Click **OK** to accept the formatting and close the dialog box. The numbered list has been converted to an outline, although that is difficult to see at this point.

➤ Click at the end of the third item, **Article I—Legislative Branch**. Press **enter**. The number 4 is generated automatically for the next item in the list.

➤ Press the **Tab key** to indent this item and automatically move to the next level of numbering (a lowercase *a*). Type **House of Representatives**.

➤ Press **enter**. The next sequential number (a lowercase *b*) is generated automatically. Type **Senate**.

➤ Save the document.

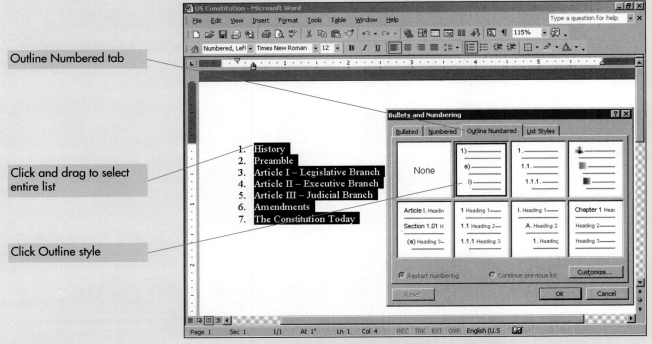

Outline Numbered tab

Click and drag to select entire list

Click Outline style

(c) Convert to an Outline (step 3)

FIGURE 4.2 *Hands-on Exercise 1 (continued)*

THE TAB AND SHIFT+TAB KEYS

The easiest way to enter text into an outline is to type continually from one line to the next, using the Tab and Shift+Tab keys as necessary. Press the enter key after completing an item to move to the next item, which is automatically created at the same level, then continue typing if the item is to remain at this level. To change the level, press the Tab key to demote the item (move it to the next lower level), or the Shift+Tab combination to promote the item (move it to the next higher level).

Step 4: **Enter Text into the Outline**

➤ Your outline should be similar in appearance to Figure 4.2d, except that you have not yet entered most of the text. Click at the end of the line containing *House of Representatives*.

➤ Press **enter** to start a new item (which begins with a lowercase *b*). Press **Tab** to indent one level, changing the letter to a lowercase *i.* Type **Length of term**. Press **enter**. Type **Requirements for office**.

➤ Click at the end of the line containing the word *Senate.* Press **enter** to start a new line (which begins with the letter *c*). Press **Tab** to indent one level, changing the letter to an *i.* Type **Length of term**, press **enter**, type **Requirements for office**, and press **enter**.

➤ Press **Shift+Tab** to move up one level. Enter the remaining text as shown in Figure 4.2.d, using the **Tab** and **Shift+Tab** keys to demote and promote the items.

➤ Save the document.

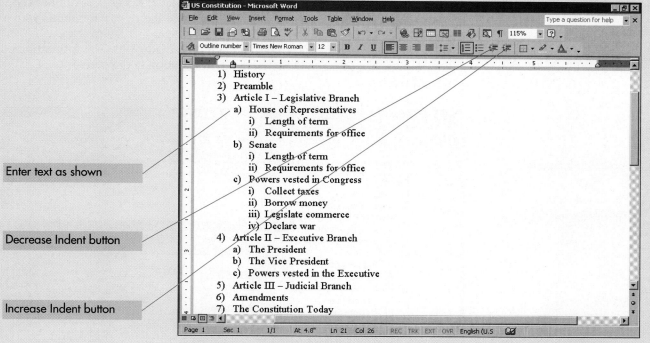

Enter text as shown

Decrease Indent button

Increase Indent button

(d) Enter Text into the Outline (step 4)

FIGURE 4.2 *Hands-on Exercise 1 (continued)*

THE INCREASE AND DECREASE INDENT BUTTONS

The Increase and Decrease Indent buttons on the Standard toolbar are another way to change the level within an outline. Click anywhere within an item, then click the appropriate button to change the level within the outline. Indentation is implemented at the paragraph level, and hence you can click the button without selecting the entire item. You can also click and drag to select multiple item(s), then click the desired button.

Step 5: **Customize the Outline**

➤ Select the entire outline, pull down the **Format menu**, then click **Bullets and Numbering** to display the Bullets and Numbering dialog box.

➤ If necessary, click the **Outline Numbered tab** and click **Customize** to display the Customize dialog box as shown in Figure 4.2e. Level **1** should be selected in the Level list box.

  • Click the **drop-down arrow** in the Number style list box and select **I, II, III** as the style.

  • Click in the Number format text box, which now contains the Roman numeral I followed by a right parenthesis. Click and drag to select the parenthesis and replace it with a period.

  • Click the **drop-down arrow** in the Number position list box. Click **right** to right-align the Roman numerals that will appear in your outline.

➤ Click the number **2** in the Level list box and select **A, B, C** as the Number style. Click in the Number format text box and replace the right parenthesis with a period.

➤ Click the number **3** in the Level list box and select **1, 2, 3** as the Number style. Click in the Number format text box and replace the right parenthesis with a period.

➤ Click **OK** to accept these settings and close the dialog box. The formatting of your outline has changed to match the customization in this step.

➤ Save the document.

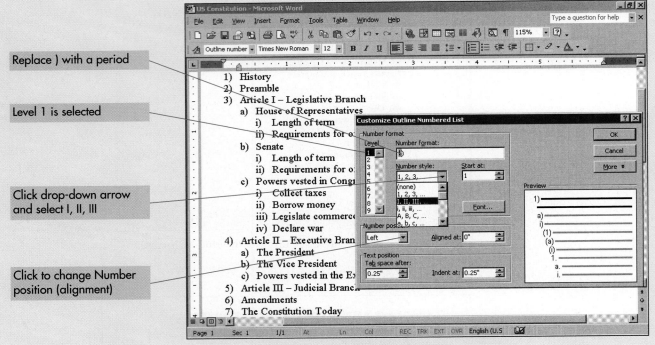

(e) Customize the Outline (step 5)

FIGURE 4.2 *Hands-on Exercise 1 (continued)*

Step 6: **The Completed Outline**

➤ Press **Ctrl+Home** to move to the beginning of the outline. The insertion point is after Roman numeral I, in front of the word *History.* Type **The United States Constitution**. Press **enter**.

➤ The new text appears as Roman numeral I and all existing entries have been renumbered appropriately. The insertion point is immediately before the word *History.* Press **enter** to create a blank line (for your name).

➤ The blank line is now Roman numeral II and *History* has been moved to Roman numeral III. Move the insertion point to the blank line.

➤ Press the **Tab key** so that the blank line (which will contain your name) is item A. This also renumbers *History* as Roman numeral II.

➤ Enter your name as shown in Figure 4.2f. Save the document, then print the outline and submit it to your instructor as proof you did this exercise.

➤ Close the document. Exit Word if you do not want to continue with the next exercise at this time.

Enter new text and your name

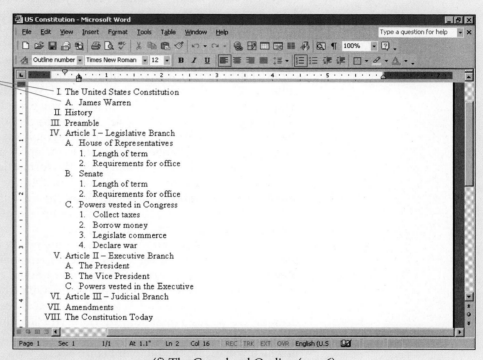

(f) The Completed Outline (step 6)

FIGURE 4.2   *Hands-on Exercise 1 (continued)*

AUTOMATIC CREATION OF A NUMBERED LIST

Word automatically creates a numbered list when you begin a paragraph with a number or letter, followed by a period, tab, or right parenthesis. Press the enter key at the end of the line and you see the next item in the sequence. To end the list, press the backspace key once, or press the enter key twice. You can also turn off the automatic numbering feature by clicking the AutoCorrect Options button that appears when you create the second item in the list and selecting Undo Automatic Numbering.

The ***tables feature*** is one of the most powerful in Word and is the basis for an almost limitless variety of documents. The study schedule in Figure 4.3a, for example, is actually a 12 × 8 (12 rows and 8 columns) table as can be seen from the underlying structure in Figure 4.3b. The completed table looks quite impressive, but it is very easy to create once you understand how a table works. You can use the tables feature to create almost any type of document. (See the practice exercises at the end of the chapter for other examples.)

The rows and columns in a table intersect to form ***cells***. Each cell is formatted independently of every other cell and may contain text, numbers and/or graphics. Commands operate on one or more cells. Individual cells can be joined together to form a larger cell as was done in the first and last rows of Figure 4.3a. Conversely, a single cell can be split into multiple cells. The rows within a table can be different heights, just as each column can be a different width. You can specify the height or width explicitly, or you can let Word determine it for you.

A cell can contain anything, even clip art as in the bottom right corner of Figure 4.3a. Just click in the cell where you want the clip art to go, then use the Insert Picture command as you have throughout the text. Use the sizing handles once the clip art has been inserted to move and/or position it within the cell.

A table is created through the ***Insert Table command*** in the ***Table menu***. The command produces a dialog box in which you enter the number of rows and columns. Once the table has been defined, you enter text in individual cells. Text wraps as it is entered within a cell, so that you can add or delete text in a cell without affecting the entries in other cells. You can format the contents of an individual cell the same way you format an ordinary paragraph; that is, you can change the font, use boldface or italics, change the alignment, or apply any other formatting command. You can select multiple cells and apply the formatting to all selected cells at once.

You can also modify the structure of a table after it has been created. The ***Insert*** and ***Delete commands*** in the Table menu enable you to add new rows or columns, or delete existing rows or columns. You can invoke other commands to shade and/or border selected cells or the entire table.

You can work with a table using commands in the Table menu, or you can use the various tools on the Tables and Borders toolbar. (Just point to a button to display a ScreenTip indicative of its function.) Some of the buttons are simply shortcuts for commands within the Table menu. Other buttons offer new and intriguing possibilities, such as the button to Change Text Direction. Note, for example, how we drew an "X" to reserve Sunday morning (for sleeping).

It's easy, and as you might have guessed, it's time for another hands-on exercise in which you create the table in Figure 4.3.

LEFT	**CENTER**	**RIGHT**

Many documents call for left, centered, and/or right aligned text on the same line, an effect that is achieved through setting tabs, or more easily through a table. To achieve the effect shown in the heading of this box, create a 1 × 3 table (one row and three columns), type the text in the three cells as needed, then use the buttons on the Formatting toolbar to left align, center, and right align the respective cells. Select the table, pull down the Format menu, click Borders and Shading, then specify None as the Border setting.

Weekly Class and Study Schedule

	Monday	Tuesday	Wednesday	Thursday	Friday	Saturday	Sunday
8:00AM							
9:00AM							
10:00AM							
11:00AM							
12:00PM							
1:00PM							
2:00PM							
3:00PM							
4:00PM							
Notes							

(a) Completed Table

(b) Underlying Structure

FIGURE 4.3 *The Tables Feature*

TABLES

Objective To create a table; to change row heights and column widths; to merge cells; to apply borders and shading to selected cells. Use Figure 4.4 as a guide for the exercise.

Step 1: **The Page Setup Command**

➤ Start Word. Click the **Tables and Borders button** on the Standard toolbar to display the Tables and Borders toolbar as shown in Figure 4.4a.

➤ The button functions as a toggle switch—click it once and the toolbar is displayed. Click the button a second time and the toolbar is suppressed. Click and drag the title bar at the left of the toolbar to anchor it under the Formatting toolbar.

➤ Pull down the **File menu** and click the **Page Setup command** to display the dialog box in Figure 4.4a.

➤ Click the **Margins tab** and click the **Landscape icon**. Change the top and bottom margins to **.75** inch.

➤ Change the left and right margins to **.5** inch each. Click **OK** to accept the settings and close the dialog box.

➤ Save the document as **My Study Schedule** in the **Exploring Word folder** that you have used throughout the text.

➤ Change to the **Print Layout view**. Zoom to **Page Width**. You are now ready to create the table.

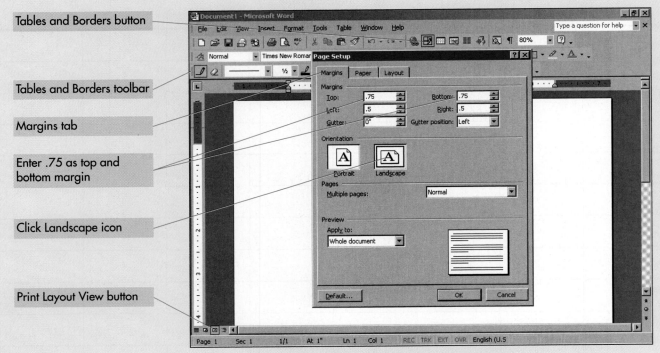

Tables and Borders button

Tables and Borders toolbar

Margins tab

Enter .75 as top and bottom margin

Click Landscape icon

Print Layout View button

(a) The Page Setup Command (step 1)

FIGURE 4.4   *Hands-on Exercise 2*

Step 2: **Create the Table**

➤ Pull down the **Table menu**, click **Insert**, and click **Table** to display the dialog box in Figure 4.4b. Enter **8** and **12** as the number of columns and rows, respectively. Click **OK** and the table will be inserted into the document.

➤ Practice selecting various elements from the table, something that you will have to do in subsequent steps:
  • To select a single cell, click inside the left grid line (the pointer changes to an arrow when you are in the proper position).
  • To select a row, click outside the table to the left of the first cell in that row.
  • To select a column, click just above the top of the column (the pointer changes to a small black arrow).
  • To select adjacent cells, drag the mouse over the cells.
  • To select the entire table, drag the mouse over the table or click the box that appears at the upper left corner of the table.

➤ Click outside the table. Save the table.

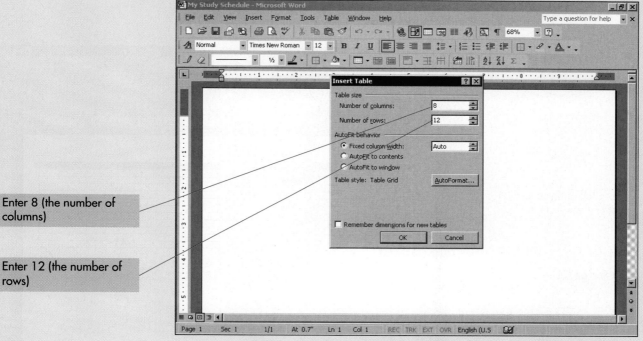

Enter 8 (the number of columns)

Enter 12 (the number of rows)

(b) Create the Table (step 2)

FIGURE 4.4 *Hands-on Exercise 2 (continued)*

TABS AND TABLES

The Tab key functions differently in a table than in a regular document. Press the Tab key to move to the next cell in the current row (or to the first cell in the next row if you are at the end of a row). Press Tab when you are in the last cell of a table to add a new blank row to the bottom of the table. Press Shift+Tab to move to the previous cell in the current row (or to the last cell in the previous row). You must press Ctrl+Tab to insert a regular tab character within a cell.

Step 3: **Merge the Cells**

➤ This step merges the cells in the first and last rows of the table. Click outside the table to the left of the first cell in the first row to select the entire first row as shown in Figure 4.4c.

➤ Pull down the **Table menu** and click **Merge Cells** (or click the **Merge Cells button** on the Tables and Borders toolbar). Click in the second row to deselect the first row, which now consists of a single cell.

➤ Click in the merged cell. Type **Weekly Class and Study Schedule** and format the text in **24 point Arial bold**. Click the **Center button** on the Formatting toolbar to center the title of the table.

➤ Click outside the table to the left of the first cell in the last row to select the entire row as shown in Figure 4.4c. Click the **Merge Cells button** on the Tables and Borders toolbar to merge these cells.

➤ Click outside the cell to deselect it, then click in the cell and type **Notes**. Press the **enter key** five times. The height of the cell increases to accommodate the blank lines. Click and drag to select the text, then format the text in **12 point Arial bold**.

➤ Save the table.

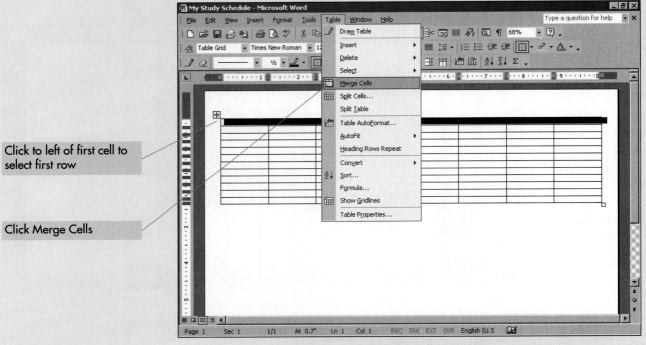

(c) Merge the Cells (step 3)

FIGURE 4.4 *Hands-on Exercise 2 (continued)*

SPLITTING A CELL

Splitting cells is the opposite of merging them. Click in any cell that you want to split, pull down the Table menu, and click the Split Cells command (or click the Split Cells button on the Tables and Borders toolbar) to display the associated dialog box. Enter the number of rows and columns that should appear after the split. Click OK to accept the settings and close the dialog box.

Step 4: **Enter the Days and Hours**

➤ Click the second cell in the second row. Type **Monday**. Press the **Tab** (or **right arrow**) **key** to move to the next cell. Type **Tuesday**. Continue until the days of the week have been entered.

➤ Select the entire row. Use the various tools on the Formatting toolbar to change the text to **10 point Arial Bold**. Click the **Center button** on the Formatting toolbar to center each day within the cell.

➤ Click the first cell in the third row. Type **8:00AM**. Press the **down arrow key** to move to the first cell in the fourth row. Type **9:00AM**. Continue in this fashion until you have entered the hourly periods up to 4:00PM. Format as appropriate. (We right aligned the time periods and changed the font to Arial bold.)

➤ Select the cells containing the hours of the day. Pull down the **Table menu**. Click **Table Properties**, then click the **Row tab** to display the Table Properties dialog box in Figure 4.4d.

➤ Click the **Specify height** check box. Click the **up arrow** until the height is **.5″**. Click the **drop-down arrow** on the Row height list box and select **Exactly**.

➤ Click the **Cell tab** in the Tables Properties dialog box, then click the **Center button**. Click **OK** to accept the settings and close the dialog box. Save the table.

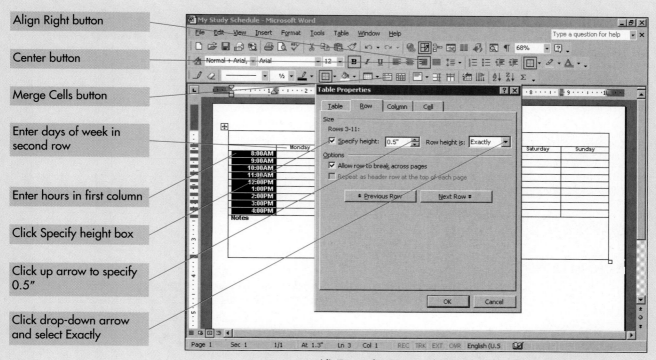

Align Right button

Center button

Merge Cells button

Enter days of week in second row

Enter hours in first column

Click Specify height box

Click up arrow to specify 0.5″

Click drop-down arrow and select Exactly

(d) Enter the Days and Hours (step 4)

FIGURE 4.4   *Hands-on Exercise 2 (continued)*

THE AUTOTEXT FEATURE

Type the first few letters of any day in the week and you will see a ScreenTip telling you to press enter to insert the completed day into your document. The days of the week are examples of AutoText (shorthand) entries that are built into Word. Pull down the Insert menu and click the AutoText command to explore the complete set of entries. You can also add your own entries to create a personal shorthand.

Step 5: **Borders and Shading**

➤ Select (click) the cell containing the title of your table. Click the **Shading Color button** on the Table and Borders toolbar to display a color palette, then choose a background color. We selected red.

➤ Click and drag to select the text within the cell. Click the **down arrow** on the **Font Color button** to display its palette, then choose **white** (that is, we want white letters on a dark background).

➤ Click and drag to select the first four cells under "Sunday", then click the **Merge Cells button** to merge these cells.

➤ Click the **down arrow** on the Line Weight tool and select **3** pt. Click the **down arrow** on the Border Color tool and select the same color you used to shade the first row.

➤ Click in the upper-left corner of the merged cell, then click and drag to draw a diagonal line as shown in Figure 4.4e. Click and drag to draw a second line to complete the cell. Save the table.

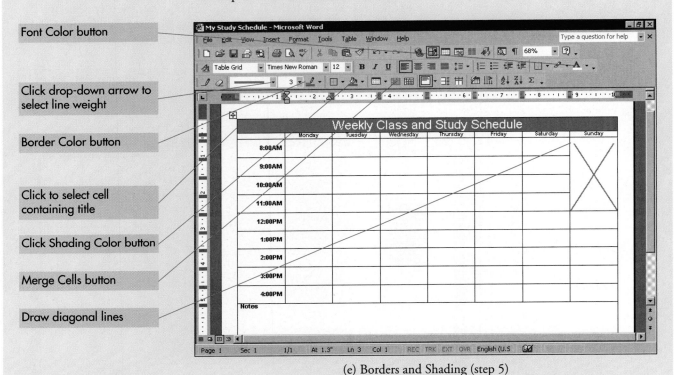

Font Color button

Click drop-down arrow to select line weight

Border Color button

Click to select cell containing title

Click Shading Color button

Merge Cells button

Draw diagonal lines

(e) Borders and Shading (step 5)

FIGURE 4.4 *Hands-on Exercise 2 (continued)*

THE AUTOFORMAT COMMAND

The AutoFormat command does not do anything that could not be done through individual formatting commands, but it does provide inspiration by suggesting attractive designs. Click anywhere in the table, pull down the Table menu, and click the Table AutoFormat command to display the associated dialog box. Choose (click) any style, click the Modify button if you want to change any aspect of the formatting, then click the Apply button to format your table in the selected style. See practice exercise 3 at the end of the chapter.

Step 6: **Insert the Clip Art**

➤ Click anywhere in the merged cell in the last row of the table. Pull down the **Insert menu**, click (or point to) **Picture**, then click **Clip Art**. The task pane opens and displays the Media Gallery Search pane as shown in Figure 4.4f.

➤ Click in the **Search** text box. Type **books** to search for any clip art image that is indexed with this key word, then click the **Search button** or press **enter**.

➤ The images are displayed in the Results box. Point to an image to display a drop-down arrow to its right. Click the arrow to display a context menu. Click **Insert** to insert the image into the document.

➤ Do not be concerned about the size or position of the image at this time.

➤ Close the task pane. Save the document.

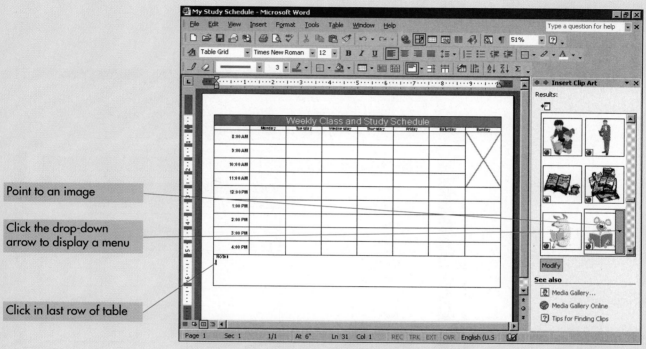

Point to an image

Click the drop-down
arrow to display a menu

Click in last row of table

(f) Insert the Clip Art (step 6)

FIGURE 4.4 *Hands-on Exercise 2 (continued)*

SEARCH BY COLLECTION

The Media Gallery organizes its contents by collections and thus provides another way to select clip art other than by a key word. Pull down the Insert menu, click (or point to) the Picture command, then click Clip Art to open the task pane, where you can enter a key word to search for clip art. Instead of searching, however, click the link to Media Gallery at the bottom of the task pane to display the Media Gallery dialog box. Collapse the My Collections folder if it is open, then expand the Office Collections folder, where you can explore the available images by collection.

Step 7: **The Finishing Touches**

➤ Select the newly inserted clip art to display the Picture toolbar, then click the **Format Picture button** to display the Format Picture dialog box. Click the **Layout tab** and choose the **Square layout**. Click **OK** to close the dialog box.

➤ Select (click) the clip art to display its sizing handles as shown in Figure 4.4g. Move and size the image as necessary within its cell.

➤ Click anywhere in the first row of the table. Pull down the **Table menu** and click the **Table Properties command** to display the associated dialog box. Change the row height to exactly **.5 inch**.

➤ Click the **down arrow** next to the **Align button** on the Tables and Borders toolbar and select **center alignment** to center the text vertically.

➤ Use the **Table Properties command** to change the row height of the second row to **.25 inch**. Center these entries vertically as well.

➤ Save the table, then print it for your instructor. Exit Word if you do not want to continue with the next exercise at this time.

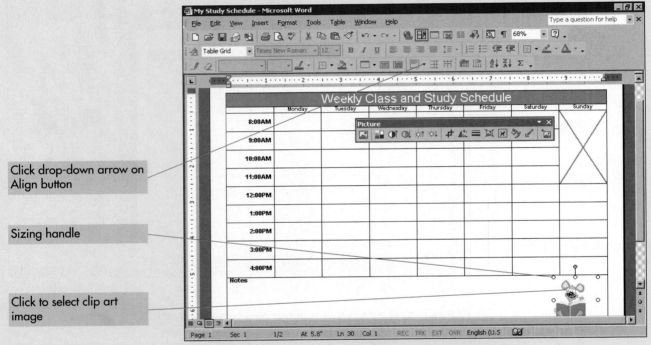

Click drop-down arrow on Align button

Sizing handle

Click to select clip art image

(g) The Finishing Touches (step 7)

FIGURE 4.4   *Hands-on Exercise 2 (continued)*

INSERTING OR DELETING ROWS AND COLUMNS

You can insert or delete rows and columns after a table has been created. To insert a row, click in any cell above or below where the new row should go, pull down the Table menu, click the Insert command, then choose rows above or below as appropriate. Follow a similar procedure to insert a column, choosing whether you want the new column to go to the left or right of the selected cell.

One characteristic of a professional document is the uniform formatting that is applied to similar elements throughout the document. Different elements have different formatting. Headings may be set in one font, color, style, and size, and the text under those headings may be set in a completely different design. The headings may be left aligned, while the text is fully justified. Lists and footnotes can be set in entirely different styles.

One way to achieve uniformity throughout the document is to use the Format Painter to copy the formatting from one occurrence of each element to the next, but this is tedious and inefficient. And if you were to change your mind after copying the formatting throughout a document, you would have to repeat the entire process all over again. A much easier way to achieve uniformity is to store the formatting information as a *style*, then apply that style to multiple occurrences of the same element within the document. Change the style and you automatically change all text defined by that style.

Styles are created on the character or paragraph level. A ***character style*** stores character formatting (font, size, and style) and affects only the selected text. A ***paragraph style*** stores paragraph formatting (such as alignment, line spacing, indents, tabs, text flow, and borders and shading, as well as the font, size, and style of the text in the paragraph). A paragraph style affects the current paragraph or multiple paragraphs if several paragraphs are selected. Styles are created and applied through the ***Styles and Formatting command*** in the Format menu as shown in Figure 4.5.

The document in Figure 4.5a consists of multiple tips for Microsoft Word. Each tip begins with a one-line heading, followed by the associated text. The task pane in the figure displays all of the styles that are in use in the document. The ***Normal style*** contains the default paragraph settings (left aligned, single spacing, and a default font) and is automatically assigned to every paragraph unless a different style is specified. The Clear Formatting style removes all formatting from selected text. It is the ***Heading 1*** and ***Body Text styles***, however, that are of interest to us, as these styles have been applied throughout the document to the associated elements. (The style assignments are done automatically through the AutoFormat command as will be explained shortly.)

The specifications for the Heading 1 and Body Text styles are shown in Figures 4.5b and 4.5c, respectively. The current settings within the Heading 1 style call for 16 point Arial bold type in blue. The text is left justified, and the heading will always appear on the same page as the next paragraph. The Body Text style is in 10 point Times New Roman and is fully justified. The preview box in both figures shows how paragraphs formatted in the style will appear. You can change the specifications of either style using any combination of buttons or associated menu commands. (Clicking the Format button in either dialog box provides access to the various commands in the Format menu.) And as indicated earlier, any changes to the style are automatically reflected in all elements that are defined by that style.

Styles automate the formatting process and provide a consistent appearance to a document. Any type of character or paragraph formatting can be stored within a style, and once a style has been defined, it can be applied to multiple occurrences of the same element within a document to produce identical formatting.

STYLES AND PARAGRAPHS

A paragraph style affects the entire paragraph; that is, you cannot apply a paragraph style to only part of a paragraph. To apply a style to an existing paragraph, place the insertion point anywhere within the paragraph, pull down the Style list box on the Formatting toolbar, then click the name of the style you want.

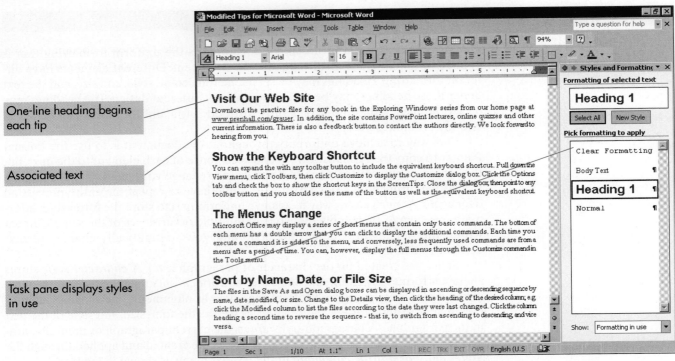

One-line heading begins
each tip

Associated text

Task pane displays styles
in use

(a) The Document

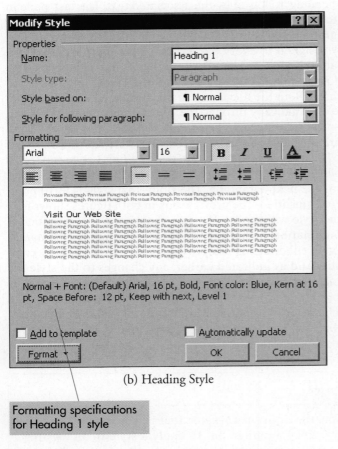

Formatting specifications
for Heading 1 style

(b) Heading Style

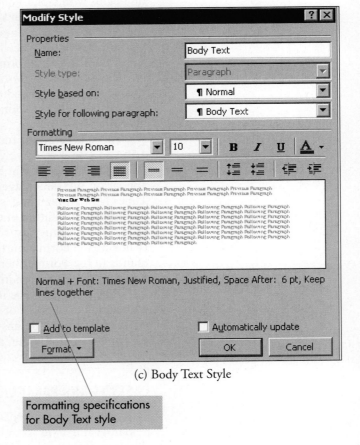

Formatting specifications
for Body Text style

(c) Body Text Style

FIGURE 4.5 *Styles*

One additional advantage of styles is that they enable you to view a document in the *Outline view*. The Outline view does not display a conventional outline (such as the multilevel list created earlier in the chapter), but rather a structural view of a document that can be collapsed or expanded as necessary. Consider, for example, Figure 4.6, which displays the Outline view of a document that will be the basis of the next hands-on exercise. The document consists of a series of tips for Microsoft Word 2002. The heading for each tip is formatted according to the Heading 1 style. The text of each tip is formatted according to the Body Text style.

The advantage of the Outline view is that you can collapse or expand portions of a document to provide varying amounts of detail. We have, for example, collapsed almost the entire document in Figure 4.6, displaying the headings while suppressing the body text. We also expanded the text for two tips (Visit Our Web Site and Moving Within a Document) for purposes of illustration.

Now assume that you want to move the latter tip from its present position to immediately below the first tip. Without the Outline view, the text would stretch over two pages, making it difficult to see the text of both tips at the same time. Using the Outline view, however, you can collapse what you don't need to see, then simply click and drag the headings to rearrange the text within the document.

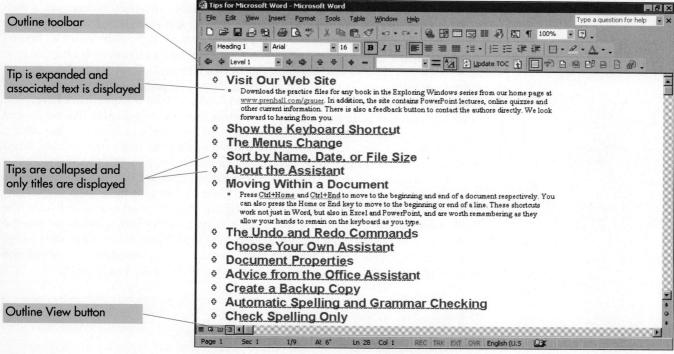

FIGURE 4.6 *The Outline View*

THE OUTLINE VERSUS THE OUTLINE VIEW

A conventional outline is created as a multilevel list within the Bullets and Numbering command. Text for the outline is entered in the Print Layout or Normal view, *not* the Outline view. The latter provides a condensed view of a document that is used in conjunction with styles.

The AutoFormat Command

Styles are extremely powerful. They enable you to impose uniform formatting within a document and they let you take advantage of the Outline view. What if, however, you have an existing and/or lengthy document that does not contain any styles (other than the default Normal style, which is applied to every paragraph)? Do you have to manually go through every paragraph in order to apply the appropriate style? The AutoFormat command provides a quick solution.

The ***AutoFormat command*** enables you to format lengthy documents quickly, easily, and in a consistent fashion. In essence, the command analyzes a document and formats it for you. Its most important capability is the application of styles to individual paragraphs; that is, the command goes through an entire document, determines how each paragraph is used, then applies an appropriate style to each paragraph. The formatting process assumes that one-line paragraphs are headings and applies the predefined Heading 1 style to those paragraphs. It applies the Body Text style to ordinary paragraphs and can also detect lists and apply a numbered or bullet style to those lists.

The AutoFormat command will also add special touches to a document if you request those options. It can replace "ordinary quotation marks" with "smart quotation marks" that curl and face each other. It will replace ordinal numbers (1st, 2nd, or 3rd) with the corresponding superscripts (1st, 2nd, or 3rd), or common fractions (1/2 or 1/4) with typographical symbols (½ or ¼).

The AutoFormat command will also replace Internet references (Web addresses and e-mail addresses) with hyperlinks. It will recognize, for example, any entry beginning with http: or www. as a hyperlink and display the entry as underlined blue text (www.microsoft.com). This is not merely a change in formatting, but an actual hyperlink to a document on the Web or corporate Intranet. It also converts entries containing an @ sign, such as rgrauer@umiami.miami.edu to a hyperlink as well. (All Word documents are Web enabled. Unlike a Web document, however, you need to press and hold the Ctrl key to follow the link and display the associated page. This is different from what you usually do, because you normally just click a link to follow it. What if, however, you wanted to edit the link? Accordingly, Word modifies the convention so that clicking a link enables you to edit the link.)

The various options for the AutoFormat command are controlled through the AutoCorrect command in the Tools menu. Once the options have been set, all formatting is done automatically by selecting the AutoFormat command from the Format menu. The changes are not final, however, as the command gives you the opportunity to review each formatting change individually, then accept the change or reject it as appropriate. (You can also format text automatically as it is entered according to the options specified under the AutoFormat As You Type tab.)

AUTOMATIC BORDERS AND LISTS

The AutoFormat As You Type option applies sophisticated formatting as text is entered. It automatically creates a numbered list any time a number is followed by a period, tab, or right parenthesis (press enter twice in a row to turn off the feature). It will also add a border to a paragraph any time you type three or more hyphens, equal signs, or underscores followed by the enter key. Pull down the Tools menu, click the AutoCorrect command, then click the AutoFormat As You Type tab and select the desired features.

STYLES

Objective To use the AutoFormat command to apply styles to an existing document; to modify existing styles; to create a new style. Use Figure 4.7 as a guide for the exercise.

Step 1: **The AutoFormat Command**

➤ Start Word. Open the document **Tips for Microsoft Word** in the **Exploring Word folder**. Save the document as **Modified Tips for Microsoft Word** so that you can return to the original if necessary.

➤ Press **Ctrl+Home** to move to the beginning of the document. Pull down the **Format menu**. Click **AutoFormat** to display the dialog box in Figure 4.7a.

➤ Click the **Options command button**. Be sure that every check box is selected to implement the maximum amount of automatic formatting. Click the **OK button** in the AutoCorrect dialog box to close the dialog box.

➤ If necessary, check the option to **AutoFormat now**, then click the **OK command button** to format the document.

➤ The status bar indicates the progress of the formatting operation, after which you will see a newly formatted document.

➤ Save the document.

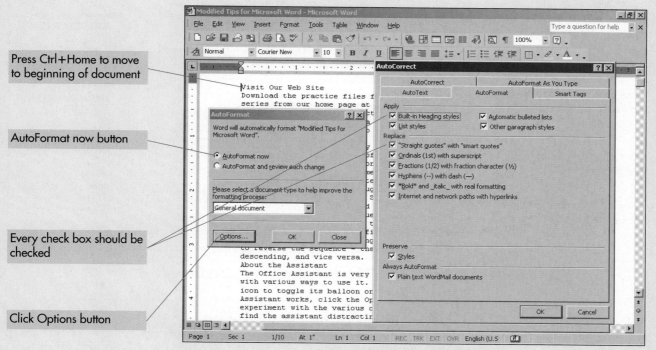

Press Ctrl+Home to move to beginning of document

AutoFormat now button

Every check box should be checked

Click Options button

(a) The AutoFormat Command (step 1)

FIGURE 4.7 *Hands-on Exercise 3*

Step 2: **Formatting Properties**

➤ Pull down the **Format menu** and click the **Reveal Formatting command** to open the task pane as shown in Figure 4.7b.

➤ Press **Ctrl+Home** to move to the beginning of the document.

➤ The task pane displays the formatting properties for the first heading in your document. Heading 1 is specified as the paragraph style within the task pane. The name of the style for the selected text (Heading 1) also appears in the Style list box at the left of the Formatting toolbar.

➤ Click in the text of the first tip to view the associated formatting properties. This time Body Text is specified as the paragraph style in the task pane. Click the title of any tip and you will see the Heading 1 style in the Style box. Click the text of any tip and you will see the Body Text style in the Style box.

➤ Click the **down arrow** to the left of the Close button in the task pane and click **Styles and Formatting** to show the styles in your document. If necessary, click the **down arrow** in the Show list box to show just the formatting in use. You will see Heading 1 and Body Text styles and an option to clear formatting.

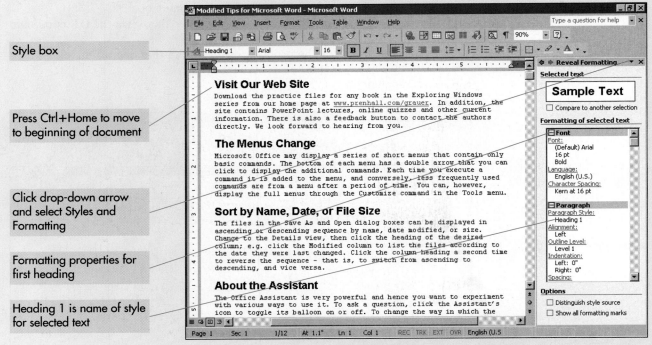

Style box

Press Ctrl+Home to move to beginning of document

Click drop-down arrow and select Styles and Formatting

Formatting properties for first heading

Heading 1 is name of style for selected text

(b) Formatting Properties (step 2)

FIGURE 4.7 *Hands-on Exercise 3 (continued)*

STYLES AND THE AUTOFORMAT COMMAND

The AutoFormat command applies the Heading 1 and Body Text styles to single- and multiple-line paragraphs, respectively. Thus, all you have to do to change the appearance of the headings or paragraphs throughout the document is change the associated style. Change the Heading 1 style, for example, and you automatically change every heading throughout the document. Change the Body Text style and you change every paragraph.

Step 3: **Modify the Body Text Style**

➤ Point to the **Body Text style** in the task pane, click the **down arrow** that appears to display a context-sensitive menu, and click **Modify** to display the Modify Style dialog box.

➤ Click the **Justify button** to change the alignment of every similar paragraph in the document. Change the font to **Times New Roman**.

➤ Click the **down arrow** next to the **Format button**, then click **Paragraph** to display the Paragraph dialog box in Figure 4.7c. If necessary, click the **Line and Page Breaks tab**.

➤ The box for Widow/Orphan control is checked by default. This ensures that any paragraph defined by the Body Text style will not be split to leave a single line at the bottom or top of a page.

➤ Check the box to **Keep Lines Together**. This is a more stringent requirement and ensures that the entire paragraph is not split. Click **OK** to close the Paragraph dialog box. Click **OK** to close the Modify Style dialog box.

➤ All of the paragraphs in the document change automatically to reflect the new definition of the Body Text style, which includes justification and ensures that the paragraph is not split across pages. Save the document.

Line and Page Breaks tab

Click drop-down arrow and select Times New Roman

Click Justify button

Check box to keep lines together

Click drop-down arrow on Format button

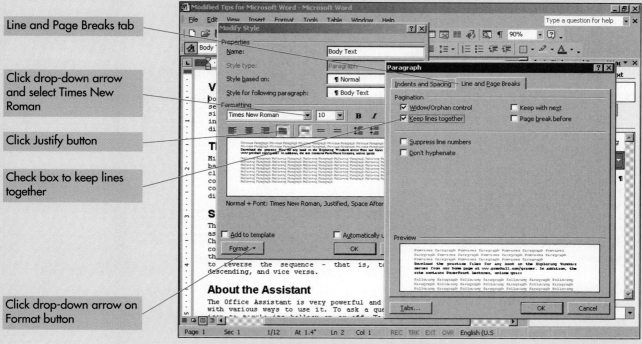

(c) Modify the Body Text Style (step 3)

FIGURE 4.7 *Hands-on Exercise 3 (continued)*

BE CAREFUL WHERE YOU CLICK

If you click the style name instead of the down arrow, you will apply the style to the selected text instead of modifying it. We know because we made this mistake. Click the Undo button to cancel the command. Click the down arrow next to the style name to display the associated menu, and click the Modify command to display the Modify Style dialog box.

➤ Point to the **Heading 1 style** in the task pane, click the **down arrow** that appears, then click **Modify** to display the Modify Style dialog box.

➤ Click the **Font Color button** to display the palette in Figure 4.7d. Click **Blue** to change the color of all of the headings in the document. The change will not take effect until you click the OK button to accept the settings and close the dialog box.

➤ Click the **Format button** toward the bottom of the dialog box, then click **Paragraph** to display the Paragraph dialog box. Click the **Indents and Spacing tab**. Change the **Spacing After** to 0. Click **OK** to accept the settings and close the Paragraph dialog box.

➤ Click **OK** to close the Modify Style dialog box. The formatting in your document has changed to reflect the changes in the Heading 1 style.

➤ Save the document.

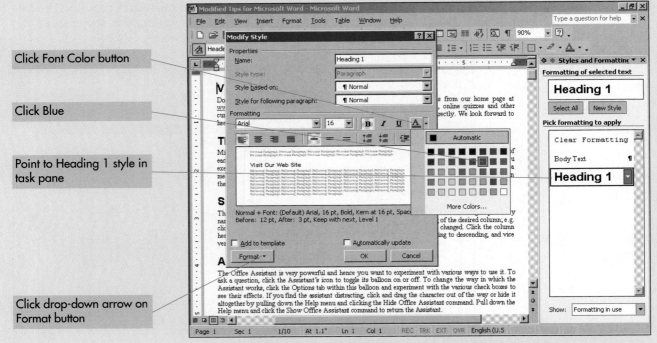

Click Font Color button

Click Blue

Point to Heading 1 style in task pane

Click drop-down arrow on Format button

(d) Modify the Heading 1 Style (step 4)

FIGURE 4.7   *Hands-on Exercise 3 (continued)*

SPACE BEFORE AND AFTER

It's common practice to press the enter key twice at the end of a paragraph (once to end the paragraph, and a second time to insert a blank line before the next paragraph). The same effect can be achieved by setting the spacing before or after the paragraph using the Spacing Before or After list boxes in the Format Paragraph command. The latter technique gives you greater flexibility in that you can specify any amount of spacing (e.g., 6 points) to leave only half a line before or after a paragraph. It also enables you to change the spacing between paragraphs more easily because the spacing information can be stored within the paragraph style.

Step 5: **The Outline View**

➤ Close the task pane. Pull down the **View menu** and click **Outline** (or click the **Outline View button** above the status bar) to display the document in Outline view.

➤ Pull down the **Edit menu** and click **Select All** (or press **Ctrl+A**) to select the entire document. Click the **Collapse button** on the Outlining toolbar to collapse the entire document so that only the headings are visible.

➤ If necessary, scroll down in the document until you can click in the heading of the tip entitled "Show the Keyboard Shortcut" as shown in Figure 4.7e. Click the **Expand button** on the Outlining toolbar to see the subordinate items under this heading.

➤ Click and drag to select the tip **Show the Keyboard Shortcut**. Point to the **plus sign** next to the selected tip (the mouse pointer changes to a double arrow), then click and drag to move the tip toward the top of the document, immediately below the first tip. Release the mouse.

➤ Save the document.

Expand button

Collapse button

Click tip heading

Outline View button

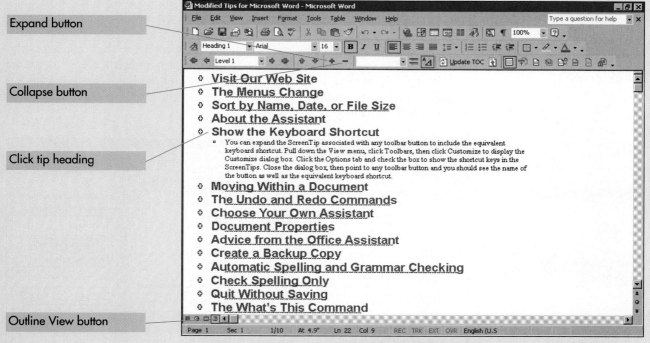

(e) The Outline View (step 5)

FIGURE 4.7   *Hands-on Exercise 3 (continued)*

THE DOCUMENT MAP

The Document Map helps you to navigate within a large document. Click the Document Map button on the Standard toolbar to divide the screen into two panes. The headings in a document are displayed in the left pane, and the text of the document is visible in the right pane. To go to a specific point in a document, click its heading in the left pane, and the insertion point is moved automatically to that point in the document, which is visible in the right pane. Click the Map button a second time to turn the feature off.

Step 6: **Create a Paragraph Style**

➤ Pull down the **View menu** and change to the **Normal view**. Pull down the **Format menu** and click **Styles and Formatting** to open the task pane as shown in Figure 4.7f.

➤ Press **Ctrl+Home** to move the insertion point to the beginning of the document, then press **Ctrl+Enter** to create a page break for a title page.

➤ Press the **up arrow** to move the insertion point to the left of the page break. Press the **enter key** twice and press the **up arrow** to move above the page break. Select the two blank lines and click **Clear Formatting** in the task pane. Press the **up arrow**.

➤ Enter the title of the document, **Tips for Microsoft Word** in **24 Points**. Change the text to **Arial Bold** in **blue**. Click the **Center button** on the Formatting toolbar. Press **enter**.

➤ The task pane displays the specifications for the text you just entered. You have created a new style, but the style is as yet unnamed. Point to the specification for the title (Arial, 24 pt, Centered) to display a down arrow, then click the arrow as shown in Figure 4.7f.

➤ Click the **Modify Style command** to display the Modify Style dialog box. Click in the **Name** text box in the Properties area and enter **Report Title** (the name of the new style). Click **OK**.

➤ Enter your name below the report title. Add a second line that references the authors of the textbook, Robert Grauer and Maryann Barber. Use a smaller point size, change the font color to blue, and center the lines. Name the associated style **Report Author**.

➤ Save the document.

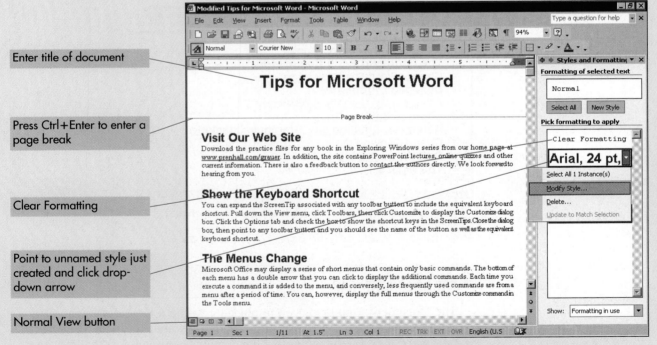

Enter title of document

Press Ctrl+Enter to enter a page break

Clear Formatting

Point to unnamed style just created and click drop-down arrow

Normal View button

(f) Create a Paragraph Style (step 6)

FIGURE 4.7 *Hands-on Exercise 3 (continued)*

Step 7: **Create a Character Style**

➤ Click and drag to select the words **Screen Tip** (that appear within the second tip). Click the **Bold** and **Italic buttons** on the Formatting toolbar so that the selected text appears in bold and italics.
➤ Once again, you have created a style as can be seen in the task pane. Point to the right of the formatting specification in the task pane, click the **down arrow**, then click the **Modify Style command** to display the Modify Style dialog box in Figure 4.7g.
➤ Click in the **Name** text box in the Properties area and enter **Emphasize** as the name of the style. Click the **down arrow** in the Style type list box and select **Character**. Click **OK**.
➤ Click and drag to select the words **practice files** that appear in the first tip, click the **down arrow** in the Style List box on the Formatting toolbar, and apply the newly created Emphasize character style to the selected text.
➤ Save the document. Close the task pane.

Enter style name

Click drop-down arrow and select Character

Click and drag to select "Screen Tip"

Point to new unnamed style and click drop-down arrow

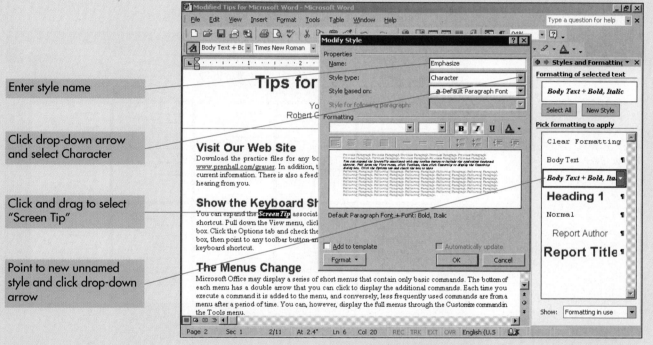

(g) Create a Character Style (step 7)

FIGURE 4.7   *Hands-on Exercise 3 (continued)*

SHOW THE KEYBOARD SHORTCUT

You can expand the ScreenTip associated with any toolbar button to include the equivalent keyboard shortcut. Pull down the View menu, click Toolbars, then click Customize to display the Customize dialog box. Click the Options tab and check the box to show the shortcut keys in the ScreenTips. Close the dialog box, then point to any toolbar button, and you should see the name of the button as well as the equivalent keyboard shortcut. There is no need to memorize the shortcuts, but they do save time.

Step 8: **The Completed Document**

➤ Change to the **Print Layout view**. Pull down the **View menu** and click the **Zoom command** to display the Zoom dialog box. Click the option button next to **Many Pages**, then click and drag the computer icon to display multiple pages. Click **OK**.

➤ You should see a multipage display similar to Figure 4.7h. The text on the individual pages is too small to read, but you can see the page breaks and overall document flow.

➤ The various tips should all be justified. Moreover each tip should fit completely on one page without spilling over to the next page according to the specifications in the Body Text style.

➤ Click above the title on the first page and press the **enter key** (if necessary) to position the title further down the page. Conversely, you could press the **Del key** to remove individual lines and move the title up the page.

➤ Save the document. Print the document only if you do not intend to do the next hands-on exercise. Exit Word if you do not want to continue with the next exercise at this time.

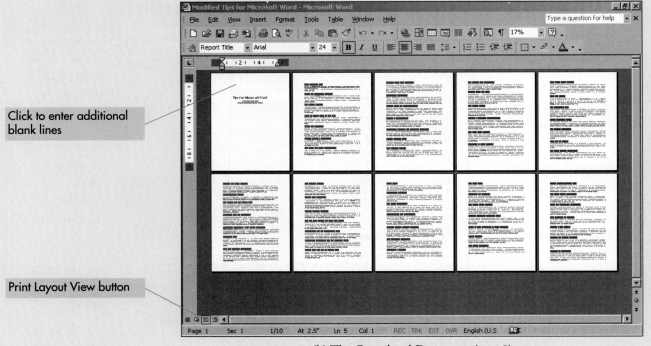

Click to enter additional blank lines

Print Layout View button

(h) The Completed Document (step 8)

FIGURE 4.7 *Hands-on Exercise 3 (continued)*

PRINT SELECTED PAGES

Why print an entire document if you want only a few pages? Pull down the File menu and click Print as you usually do, to initiate the printing process. Click the Pages option button, then enter the page numbers and/or page ranges you want; for example, 3, 6-8 will print page three and pages six through eight. You can also print multiple copies by entering the appropriate number in the Number of copies list box.

Long documents, such as term papers or reports, require additional formatting for better organization. These documents typically contain page numbers, headers and/or footers, a table of contents, and an index. Each of these elements is discussed in turn and will be illustrated in a hands-on exercise.

Page Numbers

The ***Insert Page Numbers command*** is the easiest way to place ***page numbers*** into a document and is illustrated in Figure 4.8. The page numbers can appear at the top or bottom of a page, and can be left, centered, or right aligned. Word provides additional flexibility in that you can use Roman rather than Arabic numerals, and you need not start at page number one.

The Insert Page Number command is limited, however, in that it does not provide for additional text next to the page number. You can overcome this restriction by creating a header or footer that contains the page number.

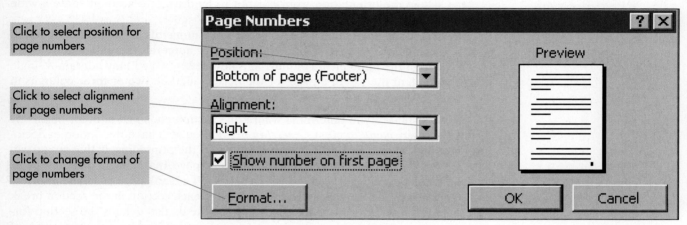

Click to select position for page numbers

Click to select alignment for page numbers

Click to change format of page numbers

FIGURE 4.8 *Page Numbers*

Headers and Footers

Headers and footers give a professional appearance to a document. A ***header*** consists of one or more lines that are printed at the top of every page. A ***footer*** is printed at the bottom of the page. A document may contain headers but not footers, footers but not headers, or both headers and footers.

Headers and footers are created from the View menu. (A simple header or footer is also created automatically by the Insert Page Number command, depending on whether the page number is at the top or bottom of a page.) Headers and footers are formatted like any other paragraph and can be centered, left or right aligned. They can be formatted in any typeface or point size and can include special codes to automatically insert the page number, date, and/or time a document is printed.

The advantage of using a header or footer (over typing the text yourself at the top or bottom of every page) is that you type the text only once, after which it appears automatically according to your specifications. In addition, the placement of the headers and footers is adjusted for changes in page breaks caused by the insertion or deletion of text in the body of the document.

Headers and footers can change continually throughout a document. The Page Setup dialog box (in the File menu) enables you to specify a different header or footer for the first page, and/or different headers and footers for the odd and even pages. If, however, you wanted to change the header (or footer) midway through a document, you would need to insert a section break at the point where the new header (or footer) is to begin.

Sections

Formatting in Word occurs on three levels. You are already familiar with formatting at the character and paragraph levels that have been used throughout the text. Formatting at the section level controls headers and footers, page numbering, page size and orientation, margins, and columns. All of the documents in the text so far have consisted of a single *section*, and thus any section formatting applied to the entire document. You can, however, divide a document into sections and format each section independently.

Formatting at the section level gives you the ability to create more sophisticated documents. You can use section formatting to:

- Change the margins within a multipage letter, where the first page (the letter-head) requires a larger top margin than the other pages in the letter.
- Change the orientation from portrait to landscape to accommodate a wide table at the end of the document.
- Change the page numbering to use Roman numerals at the beginning of the document for a table of contents and Arabic numerals thereafter.
- Change the number of columns in a newsletter, which may contain a single column at the top of a page for the masthead, then two or three columns in the body of the newsletter.

In all instances, you determine where one section ends and another begins by using the *Insert menu* to create a *section break*. You also have the option of deciding how the section break will be implemented on the printed page; that is, you can specify that the new section continue on the same page, that it begin on a new page, or that it begin on the next odd or even page even if a blank page has to be inserted.

Word stores the formatting characteristics of each section in the section break at the end of a section. Thus, deleting a section break also deletes the section formatting, causing the text above the break to assume the formatting characteristics of the next section.

Figure 4.9 displays a multipage view of a ten-page document. The document has been divided into two sections, and the insertion point is currently on the fourth page of the document (page four of ten), which is also the first page of the second section. Note the corresponding indications on the status bar and the position of the headers and footers throughout the document.

Figure 4.9 also displays the Header and Footer toolbar, which contains various icons associated with these elements. As indicated, a header or footer may contain text and/or special codes—for example, the word "page" followed by a code for the page number. The latter is inserted into the header by clicking the appropriate button on the Header and Footer toolbar. Remember, headers and footers are implemented at the section level. Thus, changing a header or footer within a document requires the insertion of a section break.

Table of Contents

A *table of contents* lists headings in the order they appear in a document and the page numbers where the entries begin. Word will create the table of contents automatically, provided you have identified each heading in the document with a built-in heading style (Heading 1 through Heading 9). Word will also update the table automatically to accommodate the addition or deletion of headings and/or changes in page numbers brought about through changes in the document.

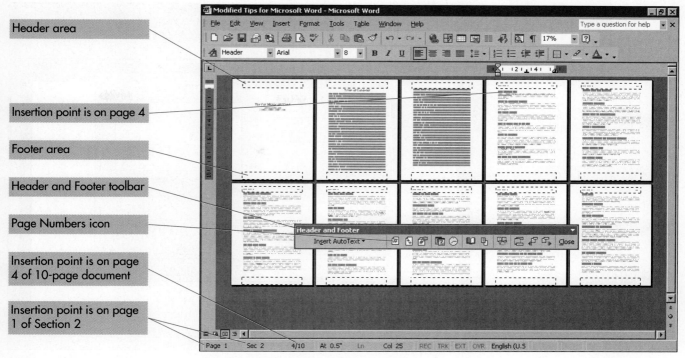

Header area

Insertion point is on page 4

Footer area

Header and Footer toolbar

Page Numbers icon

Insertion point is on page 4 of 10-page document

Insertion point is on page 1 of Section 2

FIGURE 4.9   *Headers and Footers*

The table of contents is created through the ***Index and Tables command*** from the Insert menu as shown in Figure 4.10a. You have your choice of several predefined formats and the number of levels within each format; the latter correspond to the heading styles used within the document. You can also choose the ***leader character*** and whether or not to right align the page numbers.

Creating an Index

An ***index*** is the finishing touch in a long document. Word will create an index automatically provided that the entries for the index have been previously marked. This, in turn, requires you to go through a document, and one by one, select the terms to be included in the index and mark them accordingly. It's not as tedious as it sounds. You can, for example, select a single occurrence of an entry and tell Word to mark all occurrences of that entry for the index. You can also create cross-references, such as "see also Internet."

After the entries have been specified, you create the index by choosing the appropriate settings in the Index and Tables command as shown in Figure 4.10b. You can choose a variety of styles for the index just as you can for the table of contents. Word will put the index entries in alphabetical order and will enter the appropriate page references. You can also create additional index entries and/or move text within a document, then update the index with the click of a mouse.

The Go To Command

The ***Go To command*** moves the insertion point to the top of a designated page. The command is accessed from the Edit menu by pressing the F5 function key, or by double clicking the Page number on the status bar. After the command has been executed, you are presented with a dialog box in which you enter the desired page number. You can also specify a relative page number—for example, P +2 to move forward two pages, or P −1 to move back one page.

Preview box

Page numbers

Leader character

Predefined formats

Number of levels

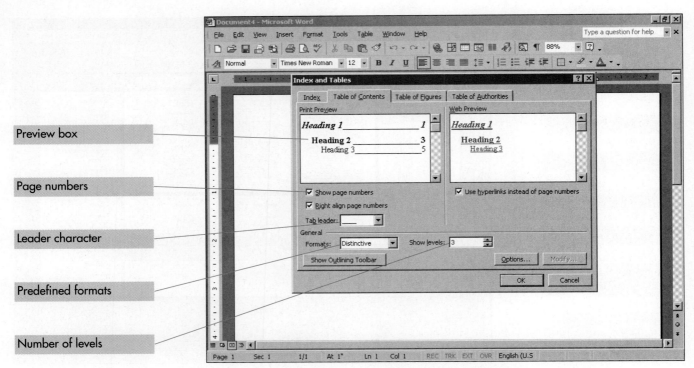

(a) Table of Contents

Preview box

Number of columns

Predefined formats

Mark Entry button

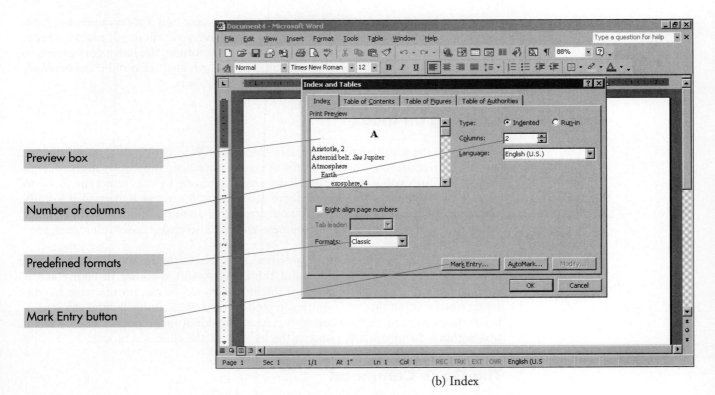

(b) Index

FIGURE 4.10 *Index and Tables Command*

WORKING IN LONG DOCUMENTS

Objective To create a header (footer) that includes page numbers; to insert and update a table of contents; to add an index entry; to insert a section break and demonstrate the Go To command; to view multiple pages of a document. Use Figure 4.11 as a guide for the exercise.

Step 1: **Applying a Style**

> ➤ Open the **Modified Tips for Word document** from the previous exercise. Zoom to **Page Width**. Scroll to the top of the second page.
> ➤ Click to the left of the first tip title. (If necessary, click the **Show/Hide ¶ button** on the Standard toolbar to hide the paragraph marks.)
> ➤ Type **Table of Contents**. Press the **enter key** two times.
> ➤ Click anywhere within the phrase "Table of Contents". Click the **down arrow** on the **Styles** list box to pull down the styles for this document as shown in Figure 4.11a.
> ➤ Click **Report Title** (the style you created at the end of the previous exercise). "Table of Contents" is centered in 24 point blue Arial bold according to the definition of Report Title.

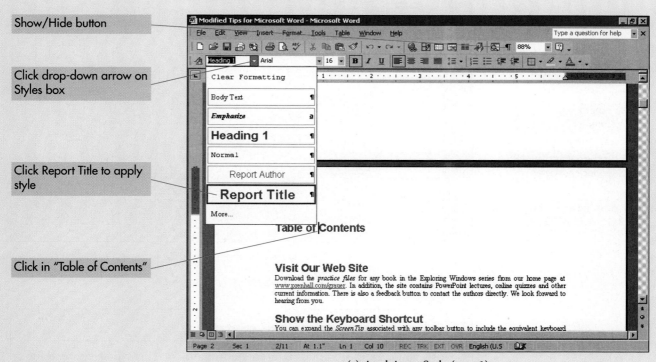

Show/Hide button

Click drop-down arrow on Styles box

Click Report Title to apply style

Click in "Table of Contents"

(a) Applying a Style (step 1)

FIGURE 4.11 *Hands-on Exercise 4*

Step 2: **Table of Contents**

➤ If necessary, change to the **Print Layout view**. Click the line immediately under the title for the table of contents. Pull down the **View menu**. Click **Zoom** to display the associated dialog box.

➤ Click the **monitor icon**. Click and drag the **page icons** to display two pages down by five pages across as shown in the figure. Release the mouse.

➤ Click **OK**. The display changes to show all eleven pages in the document.

➤ Pull down the **Insert menu**. Click **Reference**, then click **Index and Tables**. If necessary, click the **Table of Contents tab** to display the dialog box in Figure 4.11b.

➤ Check the boxes to **Show Page Numbers** and to **Right Align Page Numbers**.

➤ Click the **down arrow** on the Formats list box, then click **Distinctive**. Click the **arrow** in the **Tab Leader list box**. Choose a dot leader. Click **OK**. Word takes a moment to create the table of contents, which extends to two pages.

➤ Save the document.

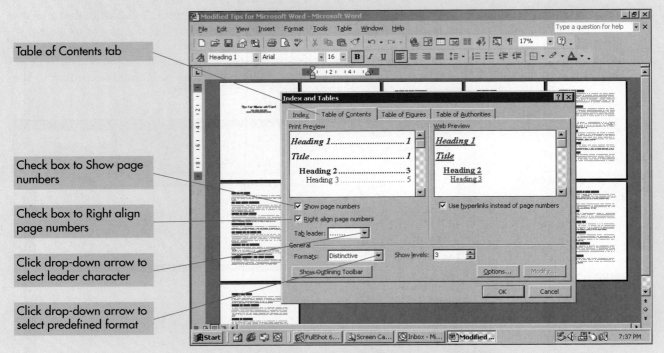

Table of Contents tab

Check box to Show page numbers

Check box to Right align page numbers

Click drop-down arrow to select leader character

Click drop-down arrow to select predefined format

(b) Table of Contents (step 2)

FIGURE 4.11 *Hands-on Exercise 4 (continued)*

AUTOFORMAT AND THE TABLE OF CONTENTS

Word will create a table of contents automatically, provided you use the built-in heading styles to define the items for inclusion. If you have not applied the styles to the document, the AutoFormat command will do it for you. Once the heading styles are in the document, pull down the Insert command, click Reference, then click Index and Tables, then click the Table of Contents command.

Step 3: **Field Codes and Field Text**

➤ Click the **arrow** on the **Zoom Control box** on the Standard toolbar. Click **Page Width** in order to read the table of contents as in Figure 4.11c.

➤ Use the **up arrow key** to scroll to the beginning of the table of contents. Press **Alt+F9**. The table of contents is replaced by an entry similar to {TOC \o "1-3"} to indicate a field code. The exact code depends on the selections you made in step 2.

➤ Press **Alt+F9** a second time. The field code for the table of contents is replaced by text.

➤ Pull down the **Edit menu**. Click **Go To** to display the dialog box in Figure 4.11c.

➤ Type **3** and press the **enter key** to go to page 3, which contains the second page of the table of contents. Click **Close**.

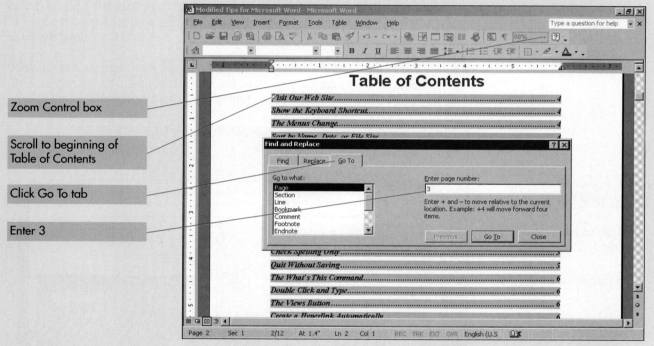

Zoom Control box

Scroll to beginning of Table of Contents

Click Go To tab

Enter 3

(c) Field Codes and Field Text (step 3)

FIGURE 4.11   *Hands-on Exercise 4 (continued)*

THE GO TO AND GO BACK COMMANDS

The F5 key is the shortcut equivalent of the Go To command and displays a dialog box to move to a specific location (a page or section) within a document. The Shift+F5 combination executes the Go Back command and returns to a previous location of the insertion point; press Shift+F5 repeatedly to cycle through the last three locations of the insertion point.

Step 4:   **Insert a Section Break**

➤ Scroll down page 3 until you are at the end of the table of contents. Click to the left of the first tip heading as shown in Figure 4.11d.

➤ Pull down the **Insert menu**. Click **Break** to display the Break dialog box. Click the **Next Page button** under Section Break types. Click **OK** to create a section break, simultaneously forcing the first tip to begin on a new page.

➤ The first tip, Visit Our Web Site, moves to the top of the next page (page 4 in the document). If the status bar already displays Page 1 Section 2, a previous user has changed the default numbering to begin each section on its own page and you can go to step 6. If not, you need to change the page numbering.

➤ Pull down the **Insert menu** and click **Page Numbers** to display the Page Numbers dialog box. Click the **drop-down arrow** in the Position list box to position the page number at the top of page (in the header).

➤ Click the **Format command button** to display the Page Number Format dialog box. Click the option button to **Start at** page 1 (i.e., you want the first page in the second section to be numbered as page 1), and click **OK** to close the Page Number Format box.

➤ Close the Page Numbers dialog box. The status bar now displays Page 1 Sec 2 to indicate that you are on page 1 in the second section. The entry 4/12 indicates that you are physically on the fourth page of a 12-page document.

Click drop-down arrow to select Top of Page

Click option button to Start at page 1

Click Format button

Click to left of first tip heading

Status bar

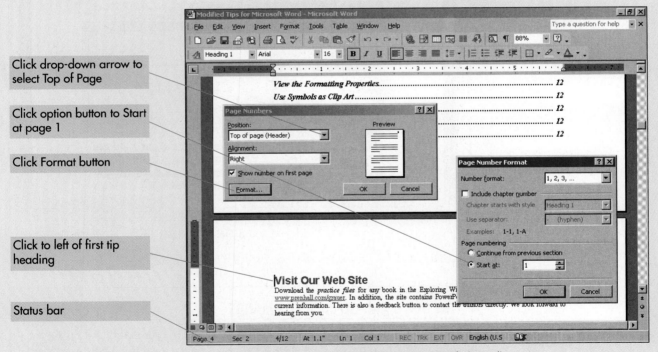

(d) Insert a Section Break (step 4)

FIGURE 4.11   *Hands-on Exercise 4 (continued)*

Step 5: **The Page Setup Command**

➤ Pull down the **File menu** and click the **Page Setup command** (or double click the **ruler**) to display the Page Setup dialog box.
➤ Click the **Layout tab** to display the dialog box in Figure 4.11e.
➤ If necessary, clear the box for Different Odd and Even Pages and for Different First Page, as all pages in this section (Section 2) are to have the same header. Click **OK**.
➤ Save the document.

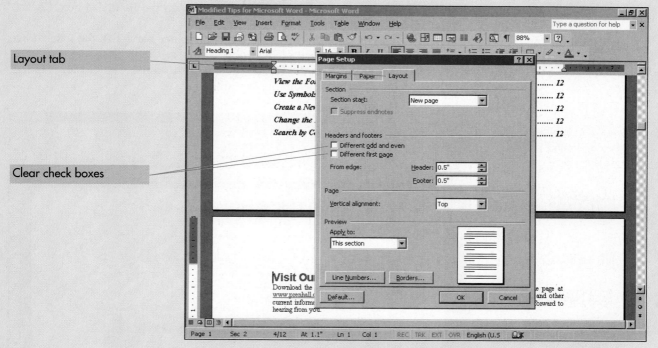

Layout tab

Clear check boxes

(e) The Page Setup Command (step 5)

FIGURE 4.11 *Hands-on Exercise 4 (continued)*

MOVING WITHIN LONG DOCUMENTS

Double click the page indicator on the status bar to display the dialog box for the Go To command from where you can go directly to any page within the document. You can also Ctrl+Click an entry in the table of contents to go directly to the text of that entry. And finally, you can use the Ctrl+Home and Ctrl+End keyboard shortcuts to move to the beginning or end of the document, respectively. The latter are universal shortcuts and apply to other Office documents as well.

Step 6: **Create the Header**

➤ Pull down the **View menu**. Click **Header and Footer** to produce the screen in Figure 4.11f. The text in the document is faded to indicate that you are editing the header, as opposed to the document.

➤ The "Same as Previous" indicator is on since Word automatically uses the header from the previous section.

➤ Click the **Same as Previous button** on the Header and Footer toolbar to toggle the indicator off and to create a different header for this section.

➤ If necessary, click in the header. Click the **arrow** on the Font list box on the Formatting toolbar. Click **Arial**. Click the **arrow** on the Font size box. Click **8**. Type **Tips for Microsoft Word**.

➤ Press the **Tab key** twice. Type **PAGE**. Press the **space bar**. Click the **Insert Page Number button** on the Header and Footer toolbar.

➤ Click the **Close button** on the Header and Footer toolbar. The header is faded, and the document text is available for editing.

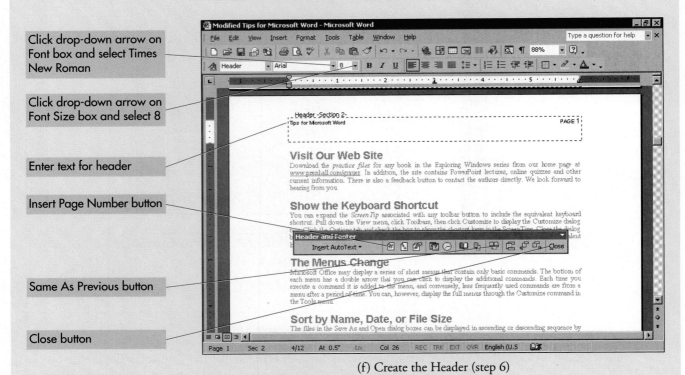

Click drop-down arrow on Font box and select Times New Roman

Click drop-down arrow on Font Size box and select 8

Enter text for header

Insert Page Number button

Same As Previous button

Close button

(f) Create the Header (step 6)

FIGURE 4.11 *Hands-on Exercise 4 (continued)*

HEADERS AND FOOTERS

If you do not see a header or footer, it is most likely because you are in the wrong view. Headers and footers are displayed in the Print Layout view but not in the Normal view. (Click the Print Layout button on the status bar to change the view.)

Step 7: **Update the Table of Contents**

➤ Press **Ctrl+Home** to move to the beginning of the document. The status bar indicates Page 1, Sec 1.
➤ Click the **Select Browse Object button** on the Vertical scroll bar, then click the **Browse by Page** icon.
➤ If necessary, click the **Next Page button** or **Previous Page button** on the vertical scroll bar (or press **Ctrl+PgDn**) to move to the page containing the table of contents.
➤ Click to the left of the first entry in the Table of Contents. Press the **F9 key** to update the table of contents. If necessary, click the **Update Entire Table button** as shown in Figure 4.11g, then click **OK**.
➤ The pages are renumbered to reflect the actual page numbers in the second section.

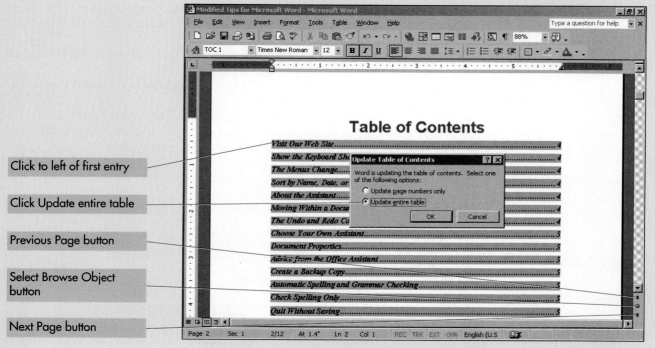

(g) Update the Table of Contents (step 7)

FIGURE 4.11   *Hands-on Exercise 4 (continued)*

SELECT BROWSE OBJECT

Click the Select Browse Object button toward the bottom of the vertical scroll bar to display a menu in which you specify how to browse through a document. Typically you browse from one page to the next, but you can browse by footnote, section, graphic, table, or any of the other objects listed. Once you select the object, click the Next or Previous buttons on the vertical scroll bar (or press Ctrl+PgDn or Ctrl+PgUp) to move to the next or previous occurrence of the selected object.

Step 8: **Create an Index Entry**

➤ Press **Ctrl+Home** to move to the beginning of the document. Pull down the **Edit menu** and click the **Find command**. Search for the first occurrence of the text "Ctrl+Home" within the document, as shown in Figure 4.11h. Close the Find and Replace dialog box.

➤ Click the **Show/Hide ¶ button** so you can see the nonprinting characters in the document, which include the index entries that have been previously created by the authors. (The index entries appear in curly brackets and begin with the letters XE.)

➤ Check that the text "Ctrl+Home" is selected within the document, then press **Alt+Shift+X** to display the Mark Index Entry dialog box. (Should you forget the shortcut, pull down the **Insert menu**, click Reference, click the **Index and Tables command**, click the **Index tab**, then click the **Mark Entry command button.**)

➤ Click the **Mark command button** to create the index entry, after which you see the field code, {XE "Ctrl+Home"}, to indicate that the index entry has been created.

➤ The Mark Index Entry dialog box stays open so that you can create additional entries by selecting additional text.

➤ Click the option button to create a **cross-reference**. Type **keyboard shortcut** in the associated text box. Click **Mark**.

➤ Click in the document, click and drag to select the text "Ctrl+End," then click in the dialog box, and the Main entry changes to Ctrl+End automatically. Click the **Mark command button** to create the index entry. Close the Mark Index Entry dialog box.

➤ Save the document.

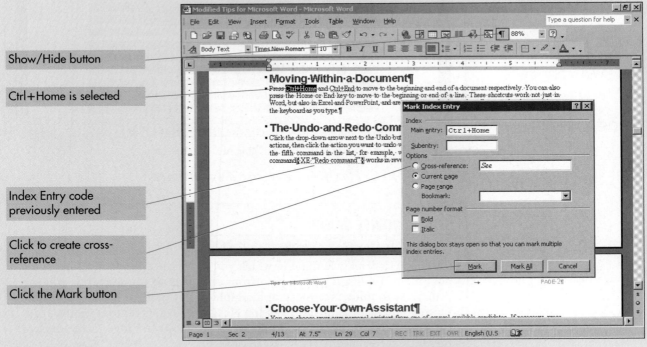

Show/Hide button

Ctrl+Home is selected

Index Entry code previously entered

Click to create cross-reference

Click the Mark button

(h) Create an Index Entry (step 8)

FIGURE 4.11   *Hands-on Exercise 4 (continued)*

Step 9: **Create the Index**

➤ Press **Ctrl+End** to move to the end of the document, where you will insert the index.

➤ Press **enter** to begin a new line.

➤ Pull down the **Insert menu**, click **Reference**, then click the **Index and Tables command** to display the Index and Tables dialog box in Figure 4.11i. Click the **Index tab** if necessary.

➤ Choose the type of index you want. We selected a **classic format** over **two columns**. Click **OK** to create the index. Click the **Undo button** if you are not satisfied with the appearance of the index, then repeat the process to create an index with a different style.

➤ Save the document.

Undo button

Preview box

Enter number of columns

Click drop-down arrow to select predefined format

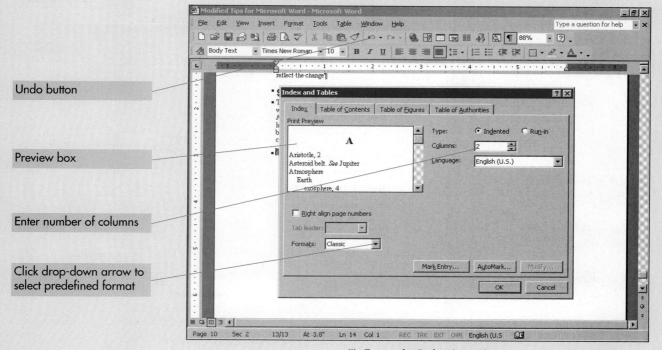

(i) Create the Index (step 9)

FIGURE 4.11   *Hands-on Exercise 4 (continued)*

AUTOMARK INDEX ENTRIES

The AutoMark command will, as the name implies, automatically mark all occurrences of all entries for inclusion in an index. To use the feature, you have to create a separate document that lists the terms you want to reference, then you execute the AutoMark command from the Index and Tables dialog box. The advantage is that it is fast. The disadvantage is that every occurrence of an entry is marked in the index so that a commonly used term may have too many page references. You can, however, delete superfluous entries by manually deleting the field codes. Click the Show/Hide button if you do not see the entries in the document.

Step 10:   **Complete the Index**

➤ Scroll to the beginning of the index and click to the left of the letter "A." Pull down the **File menu** and click the **Page Setup command** to display the Page Setup dialog box and click the **Layout tab**.

➤ Click the **down arrow** in the Section start list box and specify **New page**. Click the **down arrow** in the Apply to list box and specify **This section**. Click **OK**. The index moves to the top of a new page.

➤ Click anywhere in the index, which is contained in its own section since it is displayed over two columns. The status bar displays Page 1, Section 3, 13/13 as shown in Figure 4.11j.

➤ Save the document.

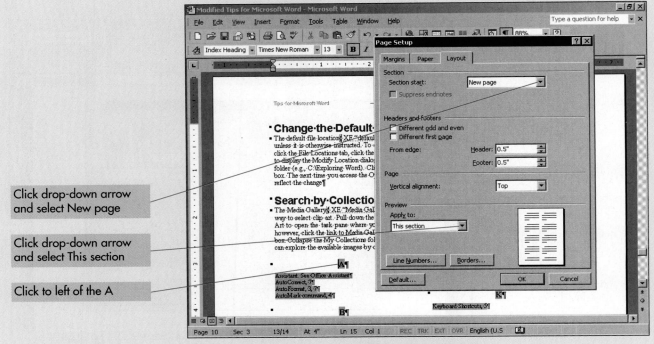

(j) Complete the Index (step 10)

FIGURE 4.11   *Hands-on Exercise 4 (continued)*

SECTION FORMATTING

Page numbering and orientation, headers, footers, and columns are implemented at the section level. Thus the index is automatically placed in its own section because it contains a different number of columns from the rest of the document. The notation on the status bar, Page 1, Section 3, 13/13 indicates that the insertion point is on the first page of section three, corresponding to the 13th page of a 13-page document.

Step 11: **The Completed Document**

➤ Pull down the **View menu**. Click **Zoom**. Click **Many Pages**. Click the **monitor icon**. Click and drag the page icon within the monitor to display two pages down by five pages. Release the mouse. Click **OK**.

➤ The completed document is shown in Figure 4.11k. The index appears by itself on the last (13th) page of the document.

➤ Save the document, then print the completed document to prove to your instructor that you have completed the exercise.

➤ Congratulations on a job well done. You have created a document with page numbers, a table of contents, and an index. Exit Word.

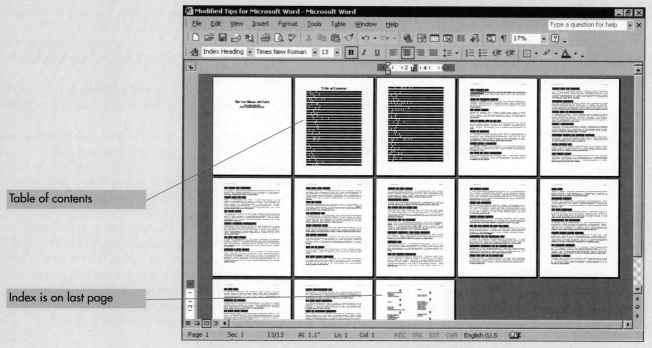

Table of contents

Index is on last page

(k) The Completed Document (step 11)

FIGURE 4.11   *Hands-on Exercise 4 (continued)*

UPDATING THE TABLE OF CONTENTS

Use a shortcut menu to update the table of contents. Point to any entry in the table of contents, then press the right mouse button to display a shortcut menu. Click Update Field, click the Update Entire Table command button, and click OK. The table of contents will be adjusted automatically to reflect page number changes as well as the addition or deletion of any items defined by any built-in heading style.

A list helps to organize information by emphasizing important topics. A bulleted or numbered list can be created by clicking the appropriate button on the Formatting toolbar or by executing the Bullets and Numbering command in the Format menu. An outline extends a numbered list to several levels.

Tables represent a very powerful capability within Word and are created through the Insert Table command in the Table menu or by using the Insert Table button on the Standard toolbar. Each cell in a table is formatted independently and may contain text, numbers, and/or graphics.

A style is a set of formatting instructions that has been saved under a distinct name. Styles are created at the character or paragraph level and provide a consistent appearance to similar elements throughout a document. Any existing styles can be modified to change the formatting of all text defined by that style.

The Outline view displays a condensed view of a document based on styles within the document. Text may be collapsed or expanded as necessary to facilitate moving text within long documents.

The AutoFormat command analyzes a document and formats it for you. The command goes through an entire document, determines how each paragraph is used, then applies an appropriate style to each paragraph.

Formatting occurs at the character, paragraph, or section level. Section formatting controls margins, columns, page orientation and size, page numbering, and headers and footers. A header consists of one or more lines that are printed at the top of every (designated) page in a document. A footer is text that is printed at the bottom of designated pages. Page numbers may be added to either a header or footer.

A table of contents lists headings in the order they appear in a document with their respective page numbers. It can be created automatically, provided the built-in heading styles were previously applied to the items for inclusion. Word will create an index automatically, provided that the entries for the index have been previously marked. This, in turn, requires you to go through a document, select the appropriate text, and mark the entries accordingly. The Edit Go To command enables you to move directly to a specific page, section, or bookmark within a document.

KEY TERMS

AutoFormat command (p. 174)
AutoMark (p. 195)
Body Text style (p. 171)
Bulleted list (p. 154)
Bullets and Numbering command (p. 154)
Cell (p. 162)
Character style (p. 171)
Delete command (p. 162)
Footer (p. 183)
Go To command (p. 185)
Header (p. 183)

Heading 1 style (p. 171)
Index (p. 185)
Index and Tables command (p. 185)
Insert menu (p. 184)
Insert Page Numbers command (p. 183)
Insert Table command (p. 162)
Leader character (p. 185)
Mark Index entry (p. 194)
Outline numbered list (p. 154)
Normal style (p. 171)
Numbered list (p. 154)

Outline (p. 154)
Outline view (p. 173)
Page numbers (p. 183)
Paragraph style (p. 171)
Section (p. 184)
Section break (p. 184)
Style (p. 171)
Styles and Formatting command (p. 171)
Table menu (p. 162)
Table of contents (p. 184)
Tables feature (p. 162)

1. Which of the following can be stored within a paragraph style?
   (a) Tabs and indents
   (b) Line spacing and alignment
   (c) Shading and borders
   (d) All of the above

2. What is the easiest way to change the alignment of five paragraphs scattered throughout a document, each of which has been formatted with the same style?
   (a) Select the paragraphs individually, then click the appropriate alignment button on the Formatting toolbar
   (b) Select the paragraphs at the same time, then click the appropriate alignment button on the Formatting toolbar
   (c) Change the format of the existing style, which changes the paragraphs
   (d) Retype the paragraphs according to the new specifications

3. The AutoFormat command will do all of the following except:
   (a) Apply styles to individual paragraphs
   (b) Apply boldface italics to terms that require additional emphasis
   (c) Replace ordinary quotes with smart quotes
   (d) Substitute typographic symbols for ordinary letters—such as © for (C)

4. Which of the following is used to create a conventional outline?
   (a) The Bullets and Numbering command
   (b) The Outline view
   (c) Both (a) and (b)
   (d) Neither (a) nor (b)

5. In which view do you see headers and/or footers?
   (a) Print Layout view
   (b) Normal view
   (c) Both (a) and (b)
   (d) Neither (a) nor (b)

6. Which of the following numbering schemes can be used with page numbers?
   (a) Roman numerals (I, II, III . . . or i, ii, iii)
   (b) Regular numbers (1, 2, 3, . . .)
   (c) Letters (A, B, C . . . or a, b, c)
   (d) All of the above

7. Which of the following is true regarding headers and footers?
   (a) Every document must have at least one header
   (b) Every document must have at least one footer
   (c) Both (a) and (b)
   (d) Neither (a) nor (b)

8. Which of the following is a *false* statement regarding lists?
   (a) A bulleted list can be changed to a numbered list and vice versa
   (b) The symbol for the bulleted list can be changed to a different character
   (c) The numbers in a numbered list can be changed to letters or roman numerals
   (d) The bullets or numbers cannot be removed

9. Page numbers can be specified in:
   (a) A header but not a footer
   (b) A footer but not a header
   (c) A header or a footer
   (d) Neither a header nor a footer

10. Which of the following is true regarding the formatting within a document?
    (a) Line spacing and alignment are implemented at the section level
    (b) Margins, headers, and footers are implemented at the paragraph level
    (c) Both (a) and (b)
    (d) Neither (a) nor (b)

11. What happens when you press the Tab key from within a table?
    (a) A Tab character is inserted just as it would be for ordinary text
    (b) The insertion point moves to the next column in the same row or the first column in the next row if you are at the end of the row
    (c) Both (a) and (b)
    (d) Neither (a) nor (b)

12. Which of the following is true, given that the status bar displays Page 1, Section 3, followed by 7/9?
    (a) The document has a maximum of three sections
    (b) The third section begins on page 7
    (c) The insertion point is on the very first page of the document
    (d) All of the above

13. The Edit Go To command enables you to move the insertion point to:
    (a) A specific page
    (b) A relative page forward or backward from the current page
    (c) A specific section
    (d) Any of the above

14. Once a table of contents has been created and inserted into a document:
    (a) Any subsequent page changes arising from the insertion or deletion of text to existing paragraphs must be entered manually
    (b) Any additions to the entries in the table arising due to the insertion of new paragraphs defined by a heading style must be entered manually
    (c) Both (a) and (b)
    (d) Neither (a) nor (b)

15. Which of the following is *false* about the Outline view?
    (a) It can be collapsed to display only headings
    (b) It can be expanded to show the entire document
    (c) It requires the application of styles
    (d) It is used to create a conventional outline

ANSWERS

1. d	**6.** d	**11.** b
2. c	**7.** d	**12.** b
3. b	**8.** d	**13.** d
4. a	**9.** c	**14.** d
5. a	**10.** d	**15.** d

1. The Résumé: Microsoft Word includes a Résumé Wizard, but you can achieve an equally good result through the tables feature. Start a new document and create a two-column table with approximately ten rows. Merge the two cells in the first row to enter your name in a distinctive font as shown in Figure 4.12. Complete the résumé by entering the various categories in the left cell of each row and the associated information in the right cell of the corresponding row. Our résumé, for example, uses right alignment for the category, but left aligns the detailed information. Select the entire table and remove the borders surrounding the individual cells. (Figure 4.12 displays gridlines, which—unlike borders—do not appear in the printed document.) Print the completed résumé for your instructor.

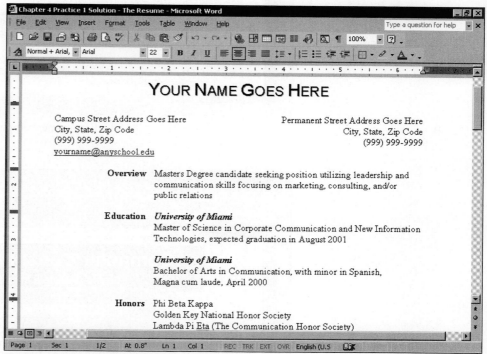

FIGURE 4.12   *The Résumé (Exercise 1)*

2. The Employment Application: A table can be the basis of almost any type of document. Use the tables feature to create a real or hypothetical employment application similar to the document in Figure 4.13a. You can follow our design or you can create your own, but try to develop an effective and attractive document. (We created the check box next to the highest degree by choosing the symbol from the Wingdings font within the Insert Symbol command.) Use appropriate spacing throughout the table, so that the completed application fills the entire page. Print the finished document for your instructor.

   Use this exercise to practice your file management skills by saving the solution in a new folder. Complete the employment application, then pull down the File menu and click the Save As command to display the Save As dialog box. Change to the Exploring Word folder, click the New folder button on the toolbar, then create a new folder as shown in Figure 4.13b. Click OK to create the folder, then click the Save button to save the document in the newly created folder. Additional folders become quite useful as you work with large numbers of documents.

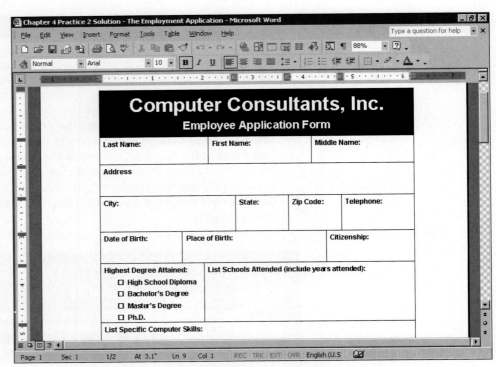

(a) The Employment Application

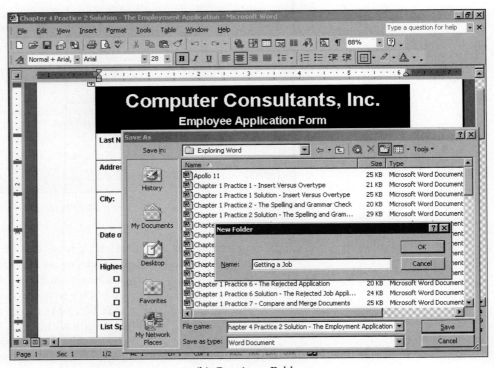

(b) Creating a Folder

FIGURE 4.13   *The Employment Application (Exercise 2)*

3. Buying a PC: The PC today is a commodity that allows the consumer to select each component. Thus, it is important to compare competing systems with respect to their features and cost. To that end, we suggest that you create a table similar to the one in Figure 4.14. You need not follow our design exactly, but you are required to leave space for at least two competing systems. Use the Table AutoFormat command to apply a format to the table. (We used the Colorful 2 design and modified the design to include a grid within the table.) You might also want to insert clip art to add interest to your table. If so, you will need to use the Format Picture command to change the layout and/or the order of the objects (the computer is to appear in front of the text.)

The table is to appear within an existing document, *Chapter 4 Practice 3*, that contains a set of tips to consider when purchasing a PC. Open the document in the Exploring Word folder and insert a page break at the beginning of the existing document. The new page is to contain the table you see in Figure 4.14. The second page will contain the tips that we provide, but it is up to you to complete the formatting. Print the document for your instructor.

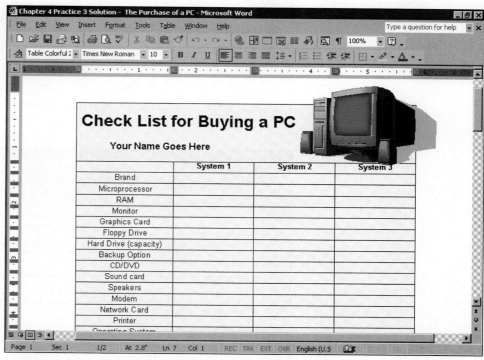

FIGURE 4.14 *Buying a PC (Exercise 3)*

BUILDS ON

HANDS-ON EXERCISE 2 PAGES 164–170

4. Section Formatting: Formatting in Microsoft Word takes place at the character, paragraph, and/or section level, with the latter controlling margins and page orientation. This assignment asks you to create the study schedule that is described in the second hands-on exercise in the chapter, after which you are to insert a title page in front of the table as shown in Figure 4.13. The title page uses portrait orientation, whereas the table uses landscape. This in turn requires you to insert a section break after the title page in order to print each section with the appropriate orientation. Print the entire document for your instructor.

5. Tips for Healthy Living: Figure 4.16 displays the first several tips in a document that contains several tips for healthier living. The unformatted version of this document can be found in the *Chapter 4 Practice 5* document in the Exploring Word folder. Open that document, then use the AutoFormat command to apply the Heading 1 and Body Text styles throughout the document. Complete the document as you see fit.

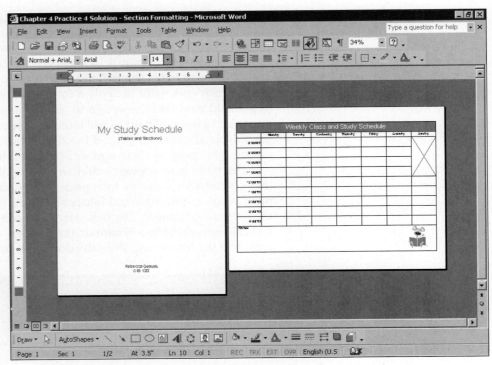

FIGURE 4.15 *Section Formatting (Exercise 4)*

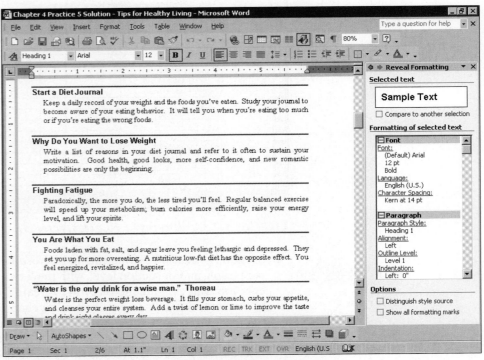

FIGURE 4.16 *Tips for Healthy Living (Exercise 5)*

6. Exporting an Outline: An outline is the basis of a PowerPoint presentation, regardless of whether it (the outline) is created in Word or PowerPoint. Open the *Chapter 4 Practice 6* document in the Exploring Word folder to display an outline for a presentation that describes e-mail. Proceed as follows:

a. Pull down the File menu, click the Send to command, then click Microsoft PowerPoint as shown in Figure 4.17. This in turn will start the PowerPoint application and create a presentation based on the Word outline.

b. Remain in PowerPoint. Pull down the Format menu and click the Slide Design command to open the task pane and view the available templates. Point to any design that is appealing to you, then click the arrow that appears after you select the design and click the Apply to All Slides command. Your presentation will be reformatted according to the selected design.

c. Select (click) the slide miniature of the first slide at the extreme left of the PowerPoint window. Pull down the Format menu and click the Slide Layout command to change the display in the task pane to the various layouts. Point to the layout at the top left of the Text Layout section (a ScreenTip will say "Title Slide"), click the arrow that appears, and click the Apply to Selected Slides command. Click in the slide where it says to "Click to add subtitle" and enter your name.

d. Pull down the File menu and click the Print command to display the Print dialog box. Click the down arrow in the Print What area and choose handouts, then specify 6 slides per page. Check the box to Frame slides, then click OK to print the handouts for your instructor.

e. Congratulations, you have just created your first PowerPoint presentation.

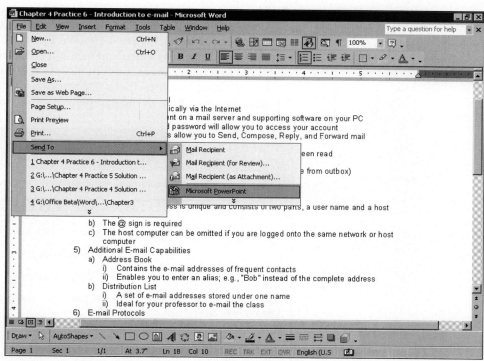

FIGURE 4.17 *Exporting an Outline (Exercise 6)*

7. Introduction to the Internet: The presentation in Figure 4.18 was created from the *Chapter 4 Practice 7* document in the Exploring Excel folder using the same instructions as in the previous exercise. This time, however, we have created a short presentation on basic Internet concepts. Add your name to the title slide and print the audience handouts for your instructor.

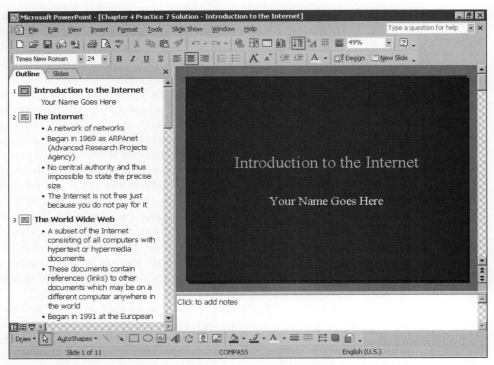

FIGURE 4.18   *Introduction to the Internet (Exercise 7)*

8. The Constitution: Use your favorite search engine to locate the text of the United States Constitution. There are many such sites on the Internet, one of which is shown in Figure 4.19. (We erased the URL, or else the assignment would be too easy.) Once you locate the document, expand the outline created in the first hands-on exercise to include information about the other provisions in the Constitution (Articles IV through VII, the Bill of Rights, and the other amendments). Submit the completed outline to your professor.

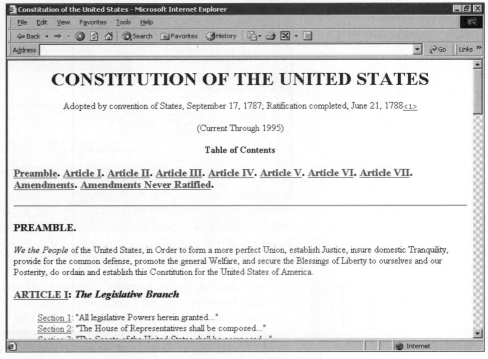

FIGURE 4.19   *The Constitution (Exercise 8)*

Tips for Windows 2000

Open the *Tips for Windows 2000* document that can be found in the Exploring Word folder. The tips are not formatted, so we would like you to use the AutoFormat command to create an attractive document. There are lots of tips, so a table of contents is also appropriate. Add a cover page with your name and date, then submit the completed document to your instructor.

Milestones in Communications

We take for granted immediate news of everything that is going on in the world, but it was not always that way. Did you know, for example, that it took five months for Queen Isabella to hear of Columbus' discovery, or that it took two weeks for Europe to learn of Lincoln's assassination? We've done some research on milestones in communications and left the file for you (*Milestones in Communications*). It runs for two, three, or four pages, depending on the formatting, which we leave to you. We would like you to include a header, and we think you should box the quotations that appear at the end of the document (it's your call as to whether to separate the quotations or group them together). Please be sure to number the completed document and don't forget a title page.

The Term Paper

Go to your most demanding professor and obtain the formatting requirements for the submission of a term paper. Be as precise as possible; for example, ask about margins, type size, and so on. What are the requirements for a title page? Is there a table of contents? Are there footnotes or endnotes, headers or footers? What is the format for the bibliography? Summarize the requirements, then indicate the precise means of implementation within Microsoft Word.

Forms, Forms, and More Forms

Every business uses a multitude of forms. Job applicants submit an employment application, sales personnel process order forms, and customers receive invoices. Even telephone messages have a form of their own. The office manager needs forms for everything, and she has come to you for help. You remember reading something about a tables feature and suggest that as a starting point. She needs more guidance, so you sit down with her and quickly design two forms that meet with her approval. Bring the two forms to class and compare your work with that of your classmates.

Writing Style

Use your favorite search engine to locate documents that describe suggested writing style for research papers. You will find different guidelines for traditional documents versus those that are published on the Web. Can you create a sample document that implements the suggested specifications? Summarize your findings in a brief note to your professor.

Essentials of
Microsoft® Windows®

OBJECTIVES

AFTER READING THIS SUPPLEMENT YOU WILL BE ABLE TO:

1. Describe the objects on the Windows desktop; use the icons on the desktop to start the associated applications.
2. Explain the significance of the common user interface; identify the elements that are present in every window.
3. Explain in general terms the similarities and differences between various versions of Windows.
4. Use the Help command to learn about Windows.
5. Format a floppy disk.
6. Differentiate between a program file and a data file; explain the significance of the icons that appear next to a file in My Computer and Windows Explorer.
7. Explain how folders are used to organize the files on a disk; use the View menu and/or the Folder Options command to change the appearance of a folder.
8. Distinguish between My Computer and Windows Explorer with respect to viewing files and folders; explain the advantages of the hierarchical view available within Windows Explorer.
9. Use Internet Explorer to download a file; describe how to view a Web page from within Windows Explorer.
10. Copy and/or move a file from one folder to another; delete a file, then recover the deleted file from the Recycle Bin.

OVERVIEW

Microsoft® Windows is a computer program (actually many programs) that controls the operation of a computer and its peripherals. The Windows environment provides a common user interface and consistent command structure for every application. You have seen the interface many times, but do you really understand it? Can

1

you move and copy files with confidence? Do you know how to back up the Excel spreadsheets, Access databases, and other Office documents that you work so hard to create? If not, now is the time to learn. This section is written for you, the computer novice, and it assumes no previous knowledge.

We begin with an introduction to the Windows desktop, the graphical user interface that enables you to work in intuitive fashion by pointing at icons and clicking the mouse. We identify the basic components of a window and describe how to execute commands and supply information through different elements in a dialog box. We introduce you to My Computer, an icon on the Windows desktop, and show you how to use My Computer to access the various components of your system. We also describe how to access the Help command.

The supplement concentrates, however, on disk and file management. We present the basic definitions of a file and a folder, then describe how to use My Computer to look for a specific file or folder. We introduce Windows Explorer, which provides a more efficient way of finding data on your system, then show you how to move or copy a file from one folder to another. We discuss other basic operations, such as renaming and deleting a file. We also describe how to recover a deleted file (if necessary) from the Recycle Bin.

There are also four hands-on exercises, which enable you to apply the conceptual discussion in the text at the computer. The exercises refer to a set of practice files (data disk) that we have created for you. You can obtain these files from our Web site (www.prenhall.com/grauer) or from a local area network if your professor has downloaded the files for you.

THE DESKTOP

Windows 95 was the first of the so-called "modern Windows" and was followed by Windows NT, Windows 98, Windows 2000, Windows Me (Millennium edition), and most recently, by Windows XP. Each of these systems is still in use. Windows 98 and its successor, Windows Me, are geared for the home user and provide extensive support for games and peripheral devices. Windows NT, and its successor Windows 2000, are aimed at the business user and provide increased security and reliability. Windows XP is the successor to all current breeds of Windows. It has a slightly different look, but maintains the conventions of its various predecessors. Hence we have called this module "Essentials of Microsoft Windows" and refer to Windows in a generic sense. (The screens were taken from Windows 2000 Professional, but could just as easily have been taken from other versions of the operating system.)

All versions of Windows create a working environment for your computer that parallels the working environment at home or in an office. You work at a desk. Windows operations take place on the *desktop* as shown in Figure 1. There are physical objects on a desk such as folders, a dictionary, a calculator, or a phone. The computer equivalents of those objects appear as icons (pictorial symbols) on the desktop. Each object on a real desk has attributes (properties) such as size, weight, and color. In similar fashion, Windows assigns properties to every object on its desktop. And just as you can move the objects on a real desk, you can rearrange the objects on the Windows desktop.

Figure 1a displays the typical desktop that appears when Windows is installed on a new computer. It has only a few objects and is similar to the desk in a new office, just after you move in. This desktop might have been taken from any of five systems—Windows 95, Windows NT, Windows 98, Windows 2000, or Windows Me—and is sometimes called "Classic Windows." The icons on this desktop are opened by double clicking. (It is possible to display an alternate desktop with underlined icons that are opened by single clicking, but that option is rarely used.) Figure 1b shows the new Windows XP desktop as it might appear on a home computer, where individual accounts are established for different users.

Double click an icon to open it

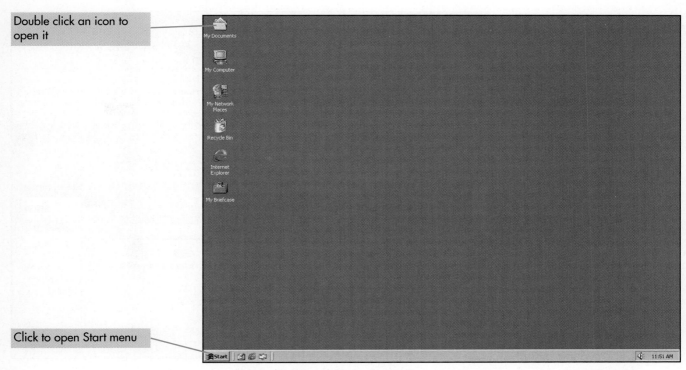

(a) Windows 95, Windows NT, Windows 98, Windows Me, and Windows 2000

Click to open Start menu

Individual desktops are established for different users

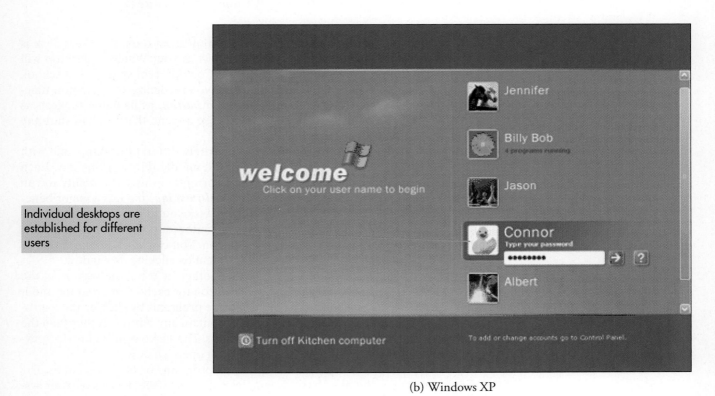

(b) Windows XP

FIGURE 1 *The Different Faces of Windows*

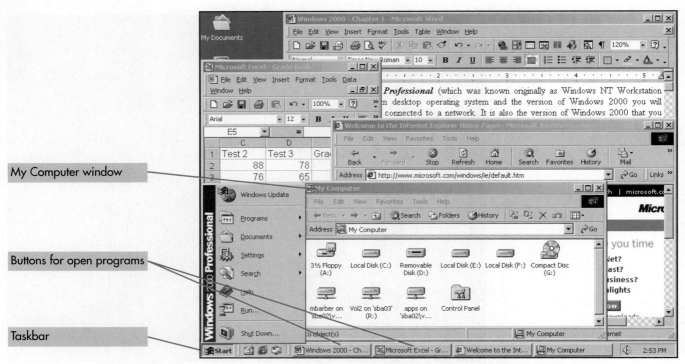

My Computer window

Buttons for open programs

Taskbar

(c) A Working Desktop (all versions of Windows)

FIGURE 1   *The Different Faces of Windows (continued)*

Do not be concerned if your desktop is different from ours. Your real desk is arranged differently from those of your friends, just as your Windows desktop will also be different. Moreover, you are likely to work on different systems—at school, at work, or at home, and thus it is important that you recognize the common functionality that is present on all desktops. The ***Start button,*** as its name suggests, is where you begin. Click the Start button and you see a menu that lets you start any program installed on your computer.

Look now at Figure 1c, which displays an entirely different desktop, one with four open windows that is similar to a desk in the middle of a working day. Each window in Figure 1c displays a program that is currently in use. The ability to run several programs at the same time is known as ***multitasking***, and it is a major benefit of the Windows environment. Multitasking enables you to run a word processor in one window, create a spreadsheet in a second window, surf the Internet in a third window, play a game in a fourth window, and so on. You can work in a program as long as you want, then change to a different program by clicking its window.

You can also change from one program to another by using the taskbar at the bottom of the desktop. The ***taskbar*** contains a button for each open program, and it enables you to switch back and forth between those programs by clicking the appropriate button. The taskbar in Figure 1a does not contain any buttons (other than the Start button) since there are no open applications. The taskbar in Figure 1c, however, contains four additional buttons, one for each open window.

The icons on the desktop are used to access programs or other functions. The ***My Computer*** icon is the most basic. It enables you to view the devices on your system, including the drives on a local area network to which you have direct access. Open My Computer in either Figure 1a or 1b, for example, and you see the objects in the My Computer window of Figure 1c. The contents of My Computer depend on the hardware of the specific computer system. Our system, for example, has one floppy drive, three local (hard or fixed) disks, a removable disk (an Iomega Zip drive), a CD-ROM, and access to various network drives. The My Computer window also contains the Control Panel folder that provides access to functions that control other elements of your computing environment. (These capabilities are not used by beginners, are generally "off limits" in a lab environment, and thus are not discussed further.)

The other icons on the desktop are also noteworthy. The **My Documents** folder is a convenient place in which to store the documents you create. **My Network Places** extends the view of your computer to include the other local area networks (if any) that your computer can access, provided you have a valid username and password. The **Recycle Bin** enables you to restore a file that was previously deleted. The Internet Explorer icon starts **Internet Explorer**, the Web browser that is built into the Windows operating system.

THE DOJ (DEPARTMENT OF JUSTICE) VERSUS MICROSOFT

A simple icon is at the heart of the multibillion dollar lawsuit brought by 19 states against Microsoft. In short, Microsoft is accused of integrating its Internet Explorer browser into the Windows operating system with the goal of dominating the market and eliminating the competition. Is Internet Explorer built into every current version of Microsoft Windows? Yes. Can Netscape Navigator run without difficulty under every current version of Microsoft Windows? The answer is also yes. As of this writing the eventual outcome of the case against Microsoft has yet to be determined.

THE COMMON USER INTERFACE

All Windows applications share a **common user interface** and possess a consistent command structure. This means that every Windows application works essentially the same way, which provides a sense of familiarity from one application to the next. In other words, once you learn the basic concepts and techniques in one application, you can apply that knowledge to every other application. Consider, for example, Figure 2, which shows open windows for My Computer and My Network Places, and labels the essential elements in each.

The contents of the two windows are different, but each window has the same essential elements. The **title bar** appears at the top of each window and displays the name of the window, My Computer and My Network Places in Figure 2a and 2b, respectively. The icon at the extreme left of the title bar identifies the window and also provides access to a control menu with operations relevant to the window such as moving it or sizing it. The **minimize button** shrinks the window to a button on the taskbar, but leaves the window in memory. The **maximize button** enlarges the window so that it takes up the entire desktop. The **restore button** (not shown in either figure) appears instead of the maximize button after a window has been maximized, and restores the window to its previous size. The **close button** closes the window and removes it from memory and the desktop.

The **menu bar** appears immediately below the title bar and provides access to **pull-down menus**. One or more **toolbars** appear below the menu bar and let you execute a command by clicking a button as opposed to pulling down a menu. The **status bar** at the bottom of the window displays information about the window as a whole or about a selected object within a window.

A vertical (or horizontal) **scroll bar** appears at the right (or bottom) border of a window when its contents are not completely visible and provides access to the unseen areas. A scroll bar does not appear in Figure 2a since all of the objects in the window are visible at the same time. A vertical scroll bar is found in Figure 2b, however, since there are other objects in the window.

Title bar

Menu bar

Toolbars

Minimize button

Maximize button

Close button

Status bar

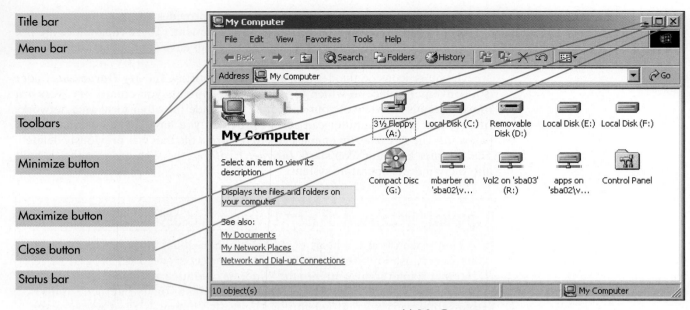

(a) My Computer

Title bar

Menu bar

Toolbars

Minimize button

Maximize button

Close button

Scroll bar

Status bar

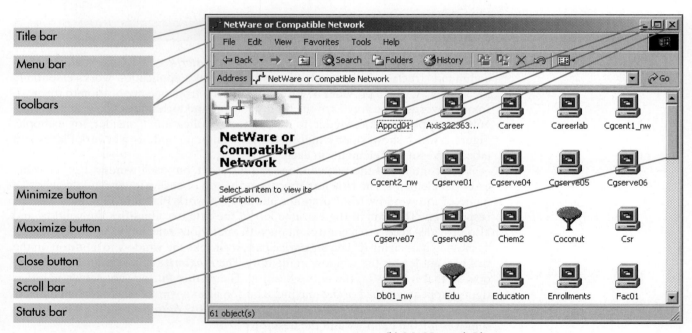

(b) My Network Places

FIGURE 2   *Anatomy of a Window*

Moving and Sizing a Window

A window can be sized or moved on the desktop through appropriate actions with the mouse. To *size a window*, point to any border (the mouse pointer changes to a double arrow), then drag the border in the direction you want to go—inward to shrink the window or outward to enlarge it. You can also drag a corner (instead of a border) to change both dimensions at the same time. To *move a window* while retaining its current size, click and drag the title bar to a new position on the desktop.

Pull-Down Menus

The menu bar provides access to *pull-down menus* that enable you to execute commands within an application (program). A pull-down menu is accessed by clicking the menu name or by pressing the Alt key plus the underlined letter in the menu name; for example, press Alt+V to pull down the View menu. (You may have to press the Alt key in order to see the underlines.) Three pull-down menus associated with My Computer are shown in Figure 3.

Commands within a menu are executed by clicking the command or by typing the underlined letter. Alternatively, you can bypass the menu entirely if you know the equivalent keystrokes shown to the right of the command in the menu (e.g., Ctrl+X, Ctrl+C, or Ctrl+V to cut, copy, or paste as shown within the Edit menu). A dimmed command (e.g., the Paste command in the Edit menu) means the command is not currently executable; some additional action has to be taken for the command to become available.

An ellipsis (. . .) following a command indicates that additional information is required to execute the command; for example, selection of the Format command in the File menu requires the user to specify additional information about the format-

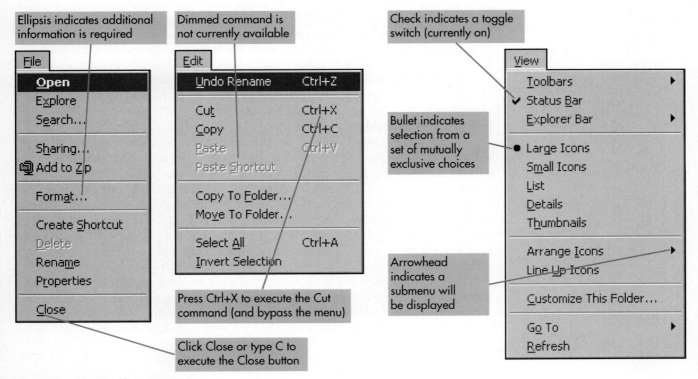

FIGURE 3 *Pull-Down Menus*

ting process. This information is entered into a dialog box (discussed in the next section), which appears immediately after the command has been selected.

A check next to a command indicates a toggle switch, whereby the command is either on or off. There is a check next to the Status Bar command in the View menu of Figure 3, which means the command is in effect (and thus the status bar will be displayed). Click the Status Bar command and the check disappears, which suppresses the display of the status bar. Click the command a second time and the check reappears, as does the status bar in the associated window.

A bullet next to an item (e.g., Large Icons in Figure 3) indicates a selection from a set of mutually exclusive choices. Click another option within the group (e.g., Small Icons) and the bullet will disappear from the previous selection (Large Icons) and appear next to the new selection (Small Icons).

An arrowhead after a command (e.g., the Arrange Icons command in the View menu) indicates that a submenu (also known as a cascaded menu) will be displayed with additional menu options.

Dialog Boxes

A *dialog box* appears when additional information is necessary to execute a command. Click the Print command in Internet Explorer, for example, and you are presented with the Print dialog box in Figure 4, requesting information about precisely what to print and how. The information is entered into the dialog box in different ways, depending on the type of information that is required. The tabs at the top of the dialog box provide access to different sets of options. The General and Paper tabs are selected in Figures 4a and 4b, respectively.

Option (Radio) buttons indicate mutually exclusive choices, one of which must be chosen, such as the page range in Figure 4a. You can print all pages, the selection (highlighted text), the current page, or a specific set of pages (such as pages 1–4), but you can choose one and only one option. Click a button to select an option, which automatically deselects the previously selected option.

A *text box* enters specific information such as the pages that will be printed in conjunction with selecting the radio button for pages. A flashing vertical bar (an I-beam) appears within the text box when the text box is active, to mark the insertion point for the text you will enter.

A *spin button* is another way to enter specific information such as the number of copies. Click the Up or Down arrow to increase or decrease the number of pages, respectively. You can also enter the information explicitly by typing it into a spin box, just as you would a text box.

Check boxes are used instead of option buttons if the choices are not mutually exclusive or if an option is not required. The Collate check box is checked in Figure 4a, whereas the Print to file box is not checked. Individual options are selected and cleared by clicking the appropriate check box, which toggles the box on and off.

A *list box* such as the Size is list box in Figure 4b displays some or all of the available choices, any one of which is selected by clicking the desired item. Just click the Down arrow on the list box to display the associated choices such as the paper source in Figure 4b. (A scroll bar appears within an open list box if all of the choices are not visible and provides access to the hidden choices.)

The *Help button* (a question mark at the right end of the title bar) provides help for any item in the dialog box. Click the button, then click the item in the dialog box for which you want additional information. The Close button (the X at the extreme right of the title bar) closes the dialog box without executing the command.

Tabs provide access to
different sets of options

Spin buttons

Check box is clear if
option is not required

Option buttons indicate
mutually exclusive choices

Text box enters
specific information

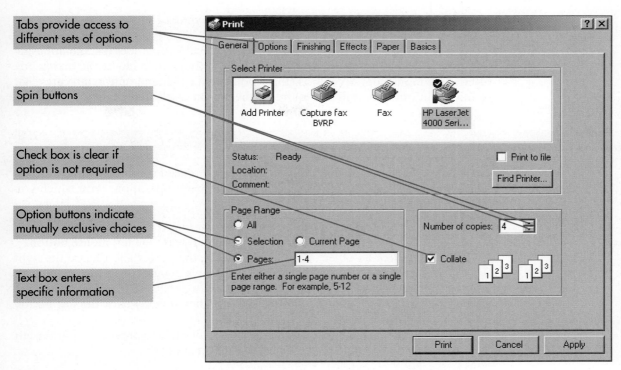

(a) General Tab

Help button

Close button

List box displays some
or all available choices

Click down arrow to
display associated choices

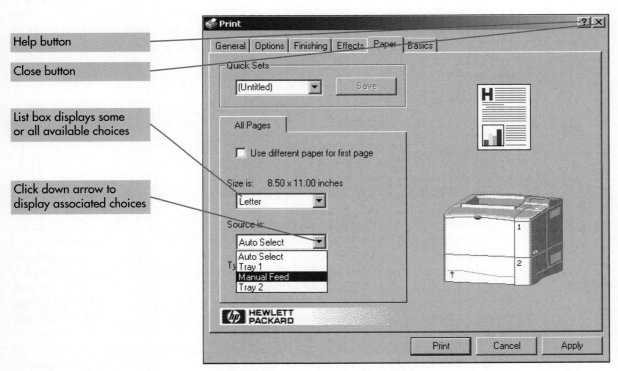

(b) Paper Tab

FIGURE 4   *Dialog Boxes*

All dialog boxes also contain one or more ***command buttons***, the function of which is generally apparent from the button's name. The Print button, in Figure 4a, for example, initiates the printing process. The Cancel button does just the opposite, and ignores (cancels) any changes made to the settings, then closes the dialog box without further action. An ellipsis (three dots) on a command button indicates that additional information will be required if the button is selected.

THE MOUSE

The mouse is indispensable to Windows and is referenced continually in the hands-on exercises throughout the text. There are five basic operations with which you must become familiar:

- To ***point*** to an object, move the mouse pointer onto the object.
- To ***click*** an object, point to it, then press and release the left mouse button.
- To ***right click*** an object, point to the object, then press and release the right mouse button. Right clicking an object displays a context-sensitive menu with commands that pertain to the object.
- To ***double click*** an object, point to it and then quickly click the left button twice in succession.
- To ***drag*** an object, move the pointer to the object, then press and hold the left button while you move the mouse to a new position.

You may also encounter a mouse with a wheel between the left and right buttons that lets you scroll through a document by rotating the wheel forward or backward. The action of the wheel, however, may change, depending on the application in use. In any event, the mouse is a pointing device—move the mouse on your desk and the mouse pointer, typically a small arrowhead, moves on the monitor. The mouse pointer assumes different shapes according to the location of the pointer or the nature of the current action. You will see a double arrow when you change the size of a window, an I-beam as you insert text, a hand to jump from one help topic to the next, or a circle with a line through it to indicate that an attempted action is invalid.

The mouse pointer will also change to an hourglass to indicate Windows is processing your command, and that no further commands may be issued until the action is completed. The more powerful your computer, the less frequently the hourglass will appear.

The Mouse versus the Keyboard

Almost every command in Windows can be executed in different ways, using either the mouse or the keyboard. Most people start with the mouse and add keyboard shortcuts as they become more proficient. There is no right or wrong technique, just different techniques, and the one you choose depends entirely on personal preference in a specific situation. If, for example, your hands are already on the keyboard, it is faster to use the keyboard equivalent. Other times, your hand will be on the mouse and that will be the fastest way. Toolbars provide still other ways to execute common commands.

In the beginning, you may wonder why there are so many different ways to do the same thing, but you will eventually recognize the many options as part of Windows' charm. It is not necessary to memorize anything, nor should you even try; just be flexible and willing to experiment. The more you practice, the faster all of this will become second nature to you.

All versions of Windows include extensive documentation with detailed information about virtually every function in Windows. It is accessed through the ***Help command*** on the Start menu, which provides different ways to search for information.

The ***Contents tab*** in Figure 5a is analogous to the table of contents in an ordinary book. The topics are listed in the left pane and the information for the selected topic is displayed in the right pane. The list of topics can be displayed in varying amounts of detail, by opening and closing the various book icons that appear. (The size of the left pane can be increased or decreased by dragging the border between the left and right pane in the appropriate direction.)

A closed book such as "Troubleshooting and Maintenance" indicates the presence of subtopics, which are displayed by opening (clicking) the book. An open book, on the other hand, such as "Internet, E-mail, and Communications," already displays its subtopics. Each subtopic is shown with one of two icons—a question mark to indicate "how to" information, or an open book to indicate conceptual information. Either way, you can click any subtopic in the left pane to view its contents in the right pane. Underlined entries in the right pane (e.g., Related Topics) indicate a hyperlink, which in turn displays additional information. Note, too, that you can print the information in the right pane by pulling down the Options menu and selecting the Print command.

The ***Index tab*** in Figure 5b is analogous to the index of an ordinary book. You enter the first several letters of the topic to look up, such as "floppy disk," choose a topic from the resulting list, and then click the Display button to view the information in the right pane. The underlined entries in the right pane represent hyperlinks, which you can click to display additional topics. And, as in the Contents window, you can print the information in the right pane by pulling down the Options menu and selecting the Print command.

The ***Search tab*** (not shown in Figure 5) displays a more extensive listing of entries than does the Index tab. It lets you enter a specific word or phrase and then it returns every topic containing that word or phrase.

The ***Favorites tab*** enables you to save the information within specified help topics as bookmarks, in order to return to those topics at a later date, as explained in the following hands-on exercise.

FORMATTING A FLOPPY DISK

You will soon begin to work on the computer, which means that you will be using various applications to create different types of documents. Each document is saved in its own file and stored on disk, either on a local disk (e.g., drive C) if you have your own computer, or on a floppy disk (drive A) if you are working in a computer lab at school.

All disks have to be formatted before they can hold data. The formatting process divides a disk into concentric circles called tracks, and then further divides each track into sectors. You don't have to worry about formatting a hard disk, as that is done at the factory prior to the machine being sold. You typically don't even have to format a floppy disk, since most floppies today are already formatted when you buy them. Nevertheless, it is very easy to format a floppy disk and it is a worthwhile exercise. Be aware, however, that formatting erases any data that was previously on a disk, so be careful not to format a disk with important data (e.g., one containing today's homework assignment). Formatting is accomplished through the ***Format command***. The process is straightforward, as you will see in the hands-on exercise that follows.

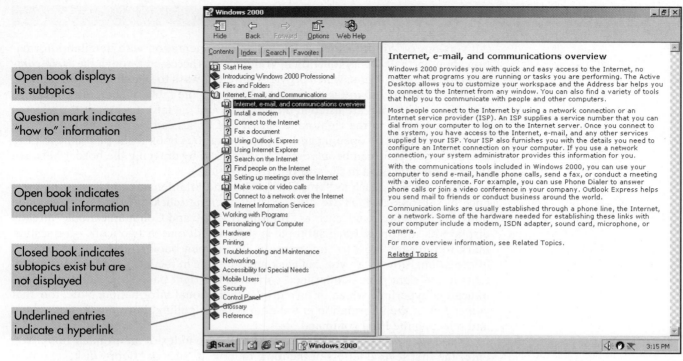

Open book displays
its subtopics

Question mark indicates
"how to" information

Open book indicates
conceptual information

Closed book indicates
subtopics exist but are
not displayed

Underlined entries
indicate a hyperlink

(a) Contents Tab

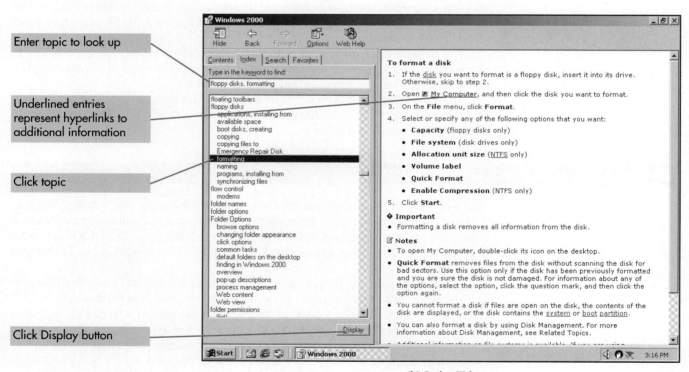

Enter topic to look up

Underlined entries
represent hyperlinks to
additional information

Click topic

Click Display button

(b) Index Tab

FIGURE 5   *The Help Command*

Welcome to Windows

Objective   To turn on the computer, start Windows, and open My Computer; to move and size a window; to format a floppy disk and use the Help command. Use Figure 6 as a guide in the exercise.

Step 1:   **Open My Computer**

➤ Start the computer by turning on the various switches appropriate to your system. Your system will take a minute or so to boot up, after which you may be asked for a **user name** and **password**.

➤ Enter this information, after which you should see the desktop in Figure 6a. It does not matter if you are using a different version of Windows.

➤ Close the Getting Started with Windows 2000 window if it appears. Do not be concerned if your desktop differs from ours.

➤ The way in which you open My Computer (single or double clicking) depends on the options in effect as described in step 2. Either way, however, you can **right click** the **My Computer icon** to display a context-sensitive menu, then click the **Open command**.

➤ The My Computer window will open on your desktop, but the contents of your window and/or its size and position will be different from ours. You are ready to go to work.

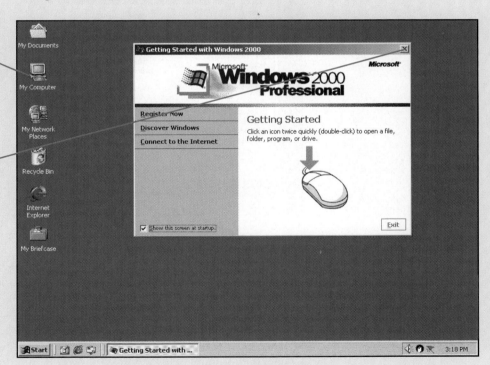

Right click My Computer and click Open from the context-sensitive menu

Click to close Getting Started with Windows 2000 window

(a) Open My Computer (step 1)

FIGURE 6   *Hands-on Exercise 1*

Step 2: **Set the Folder Options**

➤ Pull down the **Tools menu** and click the **Folder Options command** to display the Folder Options dialog box. Click the **General tab**, then set the options as shown in Figure 6b. (Your network administrator may have disabled this command, in which case you will use the default settings.)

- The Active desktop enables you to display Web content directly on the desktop. We suggest that you disable this option initially.
- Enabling Web content in folders displays the template at the left side of the window. The Windows classic option does not contain this information.
- Opening each successive folder within the same window saves space on the desktop as you browse the system. We discuss this in detail later on.
- The choice between clicking underlined items and double clicking an icon (without the underline) is personal. We prefer to double click.

➤ Click **OK** to accept the settings and close the Folder Options dialog box. The My Computer window on your desktop should be similar to ours.

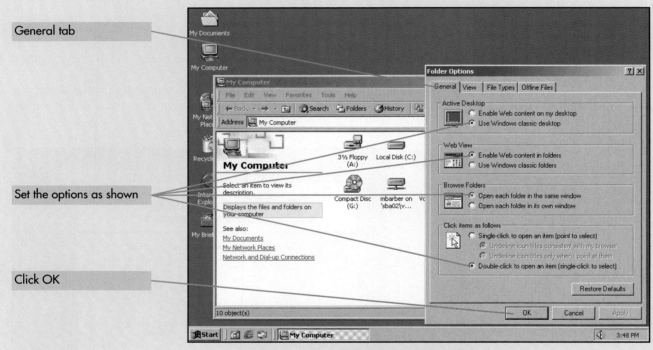

(b) Set the Folder Options (step 2)

FIGURE 6   *Hands-on Exercise 1 (continued)*

IT'S DIFFERENT IN WINDOWS 98

The Folder Options command is under the View menu in Windows 98, whereas it is found in the Tools menu in Windows 2000. Thus, to go from clicking to double clicking in Windows 98, pull down the View menu, click Folder Options, click the General tab, then choose Web style or Classic style, respectively. The procedure to display Web content in a folder is also different in Windows 98; you need to pull down the View menu and toggle the As Web Page command on.

Step 3:   **Move and Size a Window**

➤ If necessary, pull down the **View menu** and click **Large Icons** so that your My Computer window more closely resembles the window in Figure 6c.
➤ Move and size the My Computer window on your desktop to match the display in Figure 6c.
   • To change the width or height of the window, click and drag a border (the mouse pointer changes to a double arrow) in the direction you want to go.
   • To change the width and height at the same time, click and drag a corner rather than a border.
   • To change the position of the window, click and drag the title bar.
➤ Click the **minimize button** to shrink the My Computer window to a button on the taskbar. My Computer is still active in memory, however. Click the **My Computer button** on the taskbar to reopen the window.
➤ Click the **maximize button** so that the My Computer window expands to fill the entire screen. Click the **restore button** (which replaces the maximize button and is not shown in Figure 6c) to return the window to its previous size.

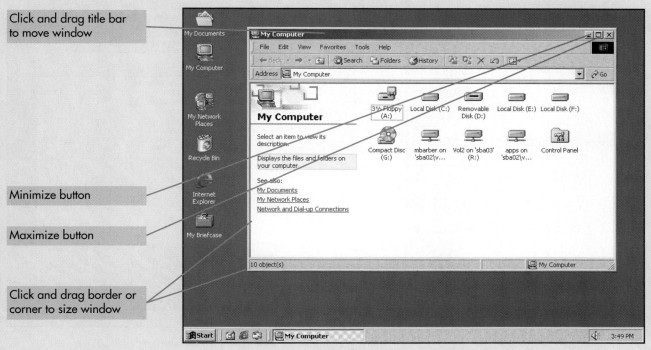

Click and drag title bar to move window

Minimize button

Maximize button

Click and drag border or corner to size window

(c) Move and Size a Window (step 3)

FIGURE 6   *Hands-on Exercise 1 (continued)*

MINIMIZING VERSUS CLOSING AN APPLICATION

Minimizing an application leaves the application open in memory and available at the click of the taskbar button. Closing it, however, removes the application from memory, which also causes it to disappear from the taskbar. The advantage of minimizing an application is that you can return to the application immediately. The disadvantage is that leaving too many applications open simultaneously may degrade performance.

Step 4: **Use the Pull-Down Menus**

➤ Pull down the **View menu**, then click the **Toolbars command** to display a cascaded menu as shown in Figure 6d. If necessary, check the commands for the **Standard Buttons** and **Address Bar**, and clear the commands for Links and Radio.

➤ Pull down the **View menu** to make or verify the following selections. (You have to pull down the View menu each time you make an additional change.)

  • The **Status Bar command** should be checked. The Status Bar command functions as a toggle switch. Click the command and the status bar is displayed; click the command a second time and the status bar disappears.)

  • Click the **Details command** to change to this view. Notice that the different views are grouped within the menu and that only one view at a time can be selected.

➤ Pull down the **View menu** once again, click (or point to) the **Explorer Bar command**, and verify that none of the options is checked.

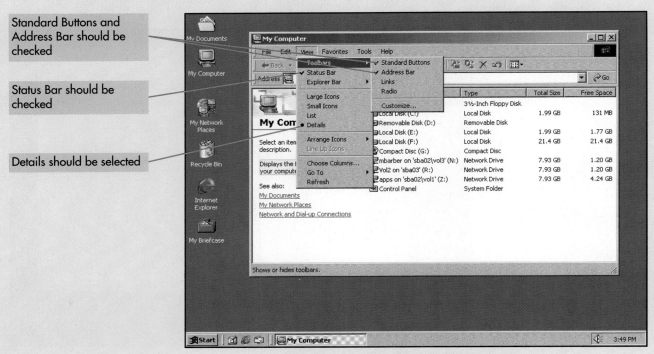

Standard Buttons and Address Bar should be checked

Status Bar should be checked

Details should be selected

(d) Use the Pull-Down Menus (step 4)

FIGURE 6 *Hands-on Exercise 1 (continued)*

DESIGNATING THE DEVICES ON A SYSTEM

The first (usually only) floppy drive is always designated as drive A. (A second floppy drive, if it were present, would be drive B.) The first hard (local) disk on a system is always drive C, whether or not there are one or two floppy drives. Additional local drives, if any, a Zip (removable storage) drive, a network drive, and/or the CD-ROM are labeled from D on.

Step 5: **Format a Floppy Disk**

➤ Place a floppy disk in drive A. Select (click) drive A, then pull down the **File menu** and click the **Format command** to display the dialog box in Figure 6e.
  • Set the **Capacity** to match the floppy disk you purchased (1.44MB for a high-density disk and 720KB for a double-density disk).
  • Click the **Volume label text box** if it's empty or click and drag over the existing label. Enter a new label (containing up to 11 characters).
  • You can check the **Quick Format box** if the disk has been previously formatted, as a convenient way to erase the contents of the disk.
➤ Click the **Start button**, then click **OK** after you have read the warning. The formatting process erases anything that is on the disk, so be sure that you do not need anything on the disk you are about to format.
➤ Click **OK** after the formatting is complete. Close the Format dialog box, then save the formatted disk for use with various exercises later in the text.
➤ Close the My Computer window.

Click to select appropriate capacity

Enter a Volume label

Quick Format box

Click OK

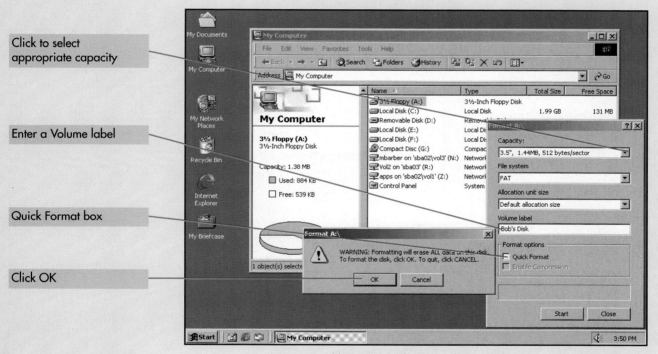

(e) Format a Floppy Disk (step 5)

FIGURE 6   *Hands-on Exercise 1 (continued)*

THE HELP BUTTON

The Help button (a question mark) appears in the title bar of almost every dialog box. Click the question mark, then click the item you want information about (which then appears in a pop-up window). To print the contents of the pop-up window, click the right mouse button inside the window, and click Print Topic. Click outside the pop-up window to close the window and continue working.

Step 6: **The Help Command**

➤ Click the **Start button** on the taskbar, then click the **Help command** to display the Help window in Figure 6f. Maximize the Help window.

➤ Click the **Contents tab**, then click a closed book such as **Hardware** to open the book and display the associated topics. Click any one of the displayed topics such as **Hardware overview** in Figure 6f.

➤ Pull down the **Options menu** and click the **Print command** to display the Print Topics dialog box. Click the option button to print the selected topic, click **OK**, then click the **Print button** in the resulting dialog box.

➤ Click the **Index tab**, type **format** (the first several letters in "Formatting disks," the topic you are searching for). Double click this topic within the list of index items. Pull down the **Options menu** and click the **Print command** to print this information as well.

➤ Submit the printed information to your instructor. Close the Help window.

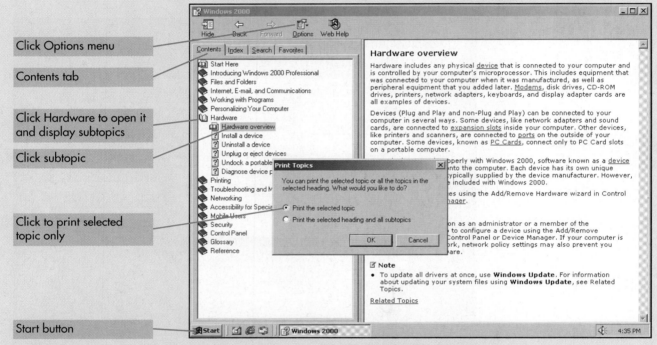

Click Options menu

Contents tab

Click Hardware to open it and display subtopics

Click subtopic

Click to print selected topic only

Start button

(f) The Help Command (step 6)

FIGURE 6 *Hands-on Exercise 1 (continued)*

THE FAVORITES TAB

Do you find yourself continually searching for the same Help topic? If so, you can make life a little easier by adding the topic to a list of favorite Help topics. Start Help, then use the Contents, Index, or Search tabs to locate the desired topic. Now click the Favorites tab in the Help window, then click the Add button to add the topic. You can return to the topic at any time by clicking the Favorites tab, then double clicking the bookmark to display the information.

Step 7:   **Shut Down the Computer**

➤ It is very important that you shut down your computer properly as opposed to just turning off the power. This enables Windows to properly close all of its system files and to save any changes that were made during the session.

➤ Click the **Start button**, click the **Shut Down command** to display the Shut Down Windows dialog box in Figure 6g. Click the **drop-down arrow** to display the desired option:

  • Logging off ends your session, but leaves the computer running at full power. This is the typical option you select in a laboratory setting.

  • Shutting down the computer ends the session and also closes Windows so that you can safely turn the power off. (Some computers will automatically turn the power off for you if this option is selected.)

  • Restarting the computer ends your sessions, then closes and restarts Windows to begin a new session.

➤ Welcome to Windows 2000!

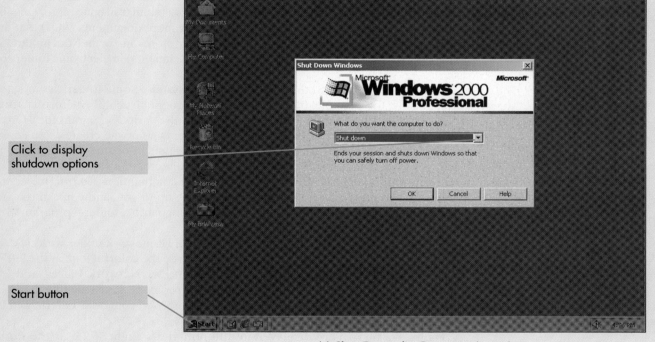

Click to display
shutdown options

Start button

(g) Shut Down the Computer (step 7)

FIGURE 6   *Hands-on Exercise 1 (continued)*

THE TASK MANAGER

The Start button is the normal way to exit Windows. Occasionally, however, an application may "hang"—in which case you want to close the problem application but leave Windows open. Press Ctrl+Alt+Del to display the Windows Security dialog box, then click the Task Manager command button. Click the Applications tab, select the problem application, and click the End Task button.

A *file* is a set of instructions or data that has been given a name and stored on disk. There are two basic types of files, *program files* and *data files*. Microsoft Word and Microsoft Excel are examples of program files. The documents and workbooks created by these programs are examples of data files.

A *program file* is an executable file because it contains instructions that tell the computer what to do. A *data file* is not executable and can be used only in conjunction with a specific program. As a typical student, you execute (run) program files, then you use those programs to create and/or modify the associated data files.

Every file has a *file name* that identifies it to the operating system. The file name may contain up to 255 characters and may include spaces. (File names cannot contain the following characters: \, /, :, *, ?, ", <, >, or |. We suggest that you try to keep file names simple and restrict yourself to the use of letters, numbers, and spaces.) Long file names permit descriptive entries such as *Term Paper for Western Civilization* (as distinct from a more cryptic *TPWCIV* that was required under MS-DOS and Windows 3.1).

Files are stored in *folders* to better organize the hundreds (thousands, or tens of thousands) of files on a hard disk. A Windows folder is similar in concept to a manila folder in a filing cabinet into which you put one or more documents (files) that are somehow related to each other. An office worker stores his or her documents in manila folders. In Windows, you store your files (documents) in electronic folders on disk.

Folders are the keys to the Windows storage system. Some folders are created automatically; for example, the installation of a program such as Microsoft Office automatically creates one or more folders to hold the various program files. Other folders are created by the user to hold the documents he or she creates. You could, for example, create one folder for your word processing documents and a second folder for your spreadsheets. Alternatively, you can create a folder to hold all of your work for a specific class, which may contain a combination of word processing documents and spreadsheets. The choice is entirely up to you, and you can use any system that makes sense to you. Anything at all can go into a folder—program files, data files, even other folders.

Figure 7 displays the contents of a hypothetical Homework folder with six documents. Figure 7a enables Web content, and so we see the colorful logo at the left of the folder, together with links to My Documents, My Network Places, and My Computer. Figure 7b is displayed without the Web content, primarily to gain space within the window. The display or suppression of the Web content is determined by a setting in the Folder Options command.

Figures 7a and 7b are displayed in different views. Figure 7a uses the *Large Icons view*, whereas Figure 7b is displayed in the *Details view*, which shows additional information for each file. (Other possible views include Small Icons, List, and Thumbnail.) The file icon, whether large or small, indicates the *file type* or application that was used to create the file. The History of Computers file, for example, is a Microsoft Word document. The Grade Book is a Microsoft Excel workbook.

Regardless of the view and options in effect, the name of the folder (Homework) appears in the title bar next to the icon of an open folder. The minimize, maximize, and Close buttons appear at the right of the title bar. A menu bar with six pull-down menus appears below the title bar. The Standard Buttons toolbar appears below the menu, and the Address Bar (indicating the drive and folder) appears below the toolbar. A status bar appears at the bottom of both windows, indicating that the Homework folder contains six objects (documents) and that the total file size is 525KB.

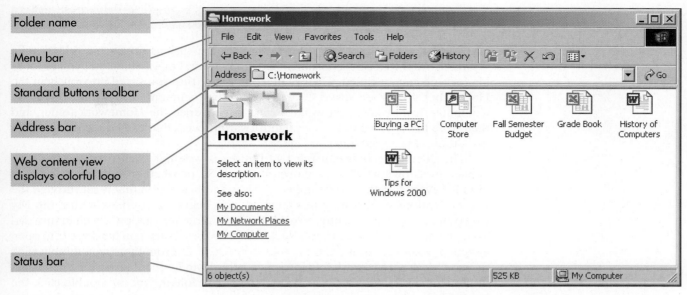

Folder name

Menu bar

Standard Buttons toolbar

Address bar

Web content view
displays colorful logo

Status bar

(a) Large Icons View with Web Content Enabled

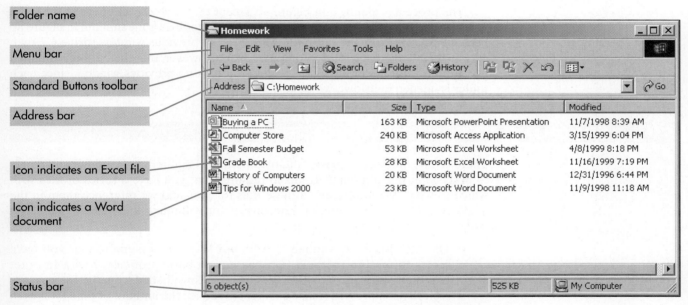

Folder name

Menu bar

Standard Buttons toolbar

Address bar

Icon indicates an Excel file

Icon indicates a Word
document

Status bar

(b) Details View without Web Content

FIGURE 7   *The Homework Folder*

CHANGE THE VIEW

Look closely at the address bar in Figures 7a and 7b to see that both figures
display the Homework folder on drive C, although the figures are very different in appearance. Figure 7a displays Web content to provide direct links to
three other folders, and the contents of the Homework folder are displayed in
the Large Icons view to save space. Figure 7b suppresses the Web content and
uses the Details view to provide the maximum amount of information for each
file in the Homework folder. You are free to choose whichever options you
prefer.

My Computer enables you to browse through the various drives and folders on a system in order to locate a document and go to work. Let's assume that you're looking for a document called "History of Computers" that you saved previously in the Homework folder on drive C. To get to this document, you would open My Computer, from where you would open drive C, open the Homework folder, and then open the document. It's a straightforward process that can be accomplished in two different ways, as shown in Figure 8.

The difference between the two figures is whether each drive or folder is opened in its own window, as shown in Figure 8a, or whether the same window is used for every folder, as in Figure 8b. (This is another option that is set through the Folder Options command.) In Figure 8a you begin by double clicking the My Computer icon on the desktop to open the My Computer window, which in turn displays the devices on your system. Next, you double click the icon for drive C to open a second window that displays the folders on drive C. From there, you double click the icon for the Homework folder to open a third window containing the documents in the Homework folder. Once in the Homework folder, you can double click the icon of an existing document, which starts the associated application and opens the document.

The process is identical in Figure 8b except that each object opens in the same window. The Back arrow on the Standard Buttons toolbar is meaningful in Figure 8b because you can click the button to return to the previous window (drive C), then click it again to go back to My Computer. Note, however, that the button is dimmed in all three windows in Figure 8a because there is no previous window, since each folder is opened in its own window.

THE EXPLORING OFFICE PRACTICE FILES

There is only one way to master the file operations inherent in Windows and that is to practice at the computer. To do so requires that you have a series of files with which to work. We have created these files for you, and we reference them in the next several hands-on exercises. Your instructor will make these files available to you in a variety of ways:

- The files can be downloaded from our Web site, assuming that you have access to the Internet and that you have a basic proficiency with Internet Explorer. Software and other files that are downloaded from the Internet are typically compressed (made smaller) to reduce the amount of time it takes to transmit the file. In essence, you will download a *compressed file* (which may contain multiple individual files) from our Web site and then uncompress the file onto a local drive as described in the next hands-on exercise.
- The files might be on a network drive, in which case you can use My Computer (or Windows Explorer, which is discussed later in the chapter) to copy the files from the network drive to a floppy disk. The procedure to do this is described in the third hands-on exercise.
- There may be an actual "data disk" in the computer lab. Go to the lab with a floppy disk, then use the Copy Disk command (on the File menu of My Computer) to duplicate the data disk and create a copy for yourself.

It doesn't matter how you obtain the practice files, only that you are able to do so. Indeed, you may want to try different techniques in order to gain additional practice with Windows.

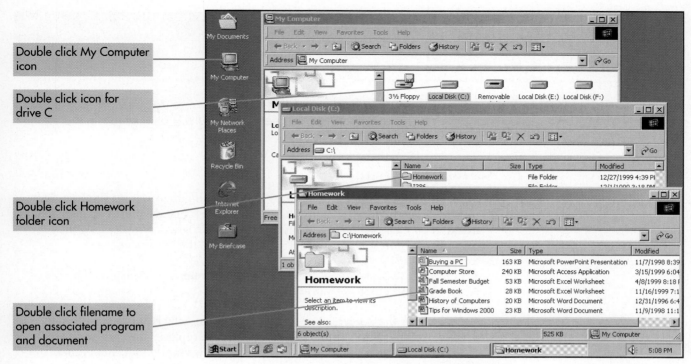

Double click My Computer
icon

Double click icon for
drive C

Double click Homework
folder icon

Double click filename to
open associated program
and document

(a) Multiple Windows

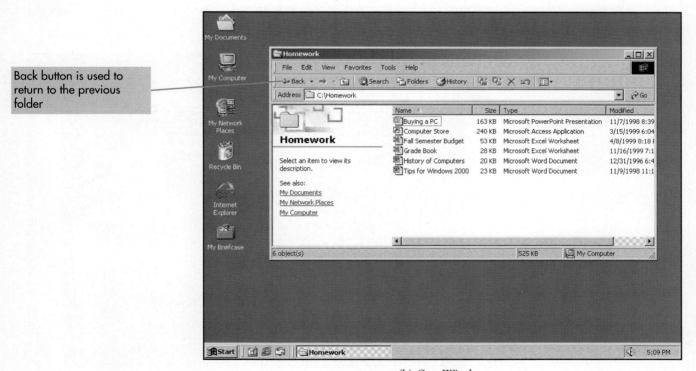

Back button is used to
return to the previous
folder

(b) One Window

FIGURE 8   *Browsing My Computer*

THE PRACTICE FILES VIA THE WEB

Objective   To download a file from the Web. The exercise requires a formatted floppy disk and access to the Internet. Use Figure 9 as a guide in the exercise.

Step 1:   **Start Internet Explorer**

➤ Start Internet Explorer, perhaps by double clicking the **Internet Explorer icon** on the desktop, or by clicking the **Start button**, clicking the **Programs command**, then locating the command to start the program. If necessary, click the **maximize button** so that Internet Explorer takes the entire desktop.

➤ Enter the address of the site you want to visit:

• Pull down the **File menu**, click the **Open command** to display the Open dialog box, and enter **www.prenhall.com/grauer** (the http:// is assumed). Click **OK**.

• *Or,* click in the **Address bar** below the toolbar, which automatically selects the current address (so that whatever you type replaces the current address). Enter the address of the site you want to visit, **www.prenhall.com/grauer** (the http:// is assumed). Press **enter**.

➤ You should see the *Exploring Office Series* home page as shown in Figure 9a. Click the book for **Office XP**, which takes you to the Office XP home page.

➤ Click the **Student Resources link** (at the top of the window) to go to the Student Resources page.

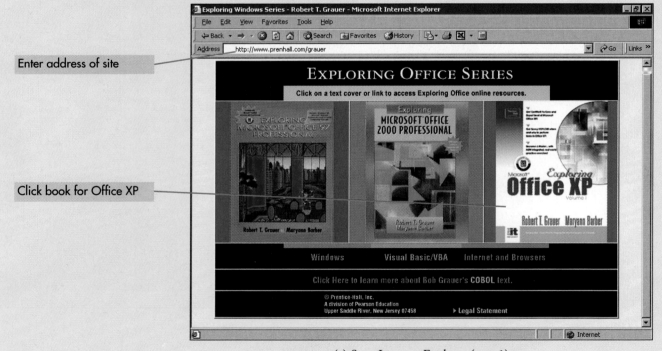

Enter address of site

Click book for Office XP

(a) Start Internet Explorer (step 1)

FIGURE 9   *Hands-on Exercise 2*

Step 2: **Download the Practice Files**

➤ Click the link to **Student Data Disk** (in the left frame), then scroll down the page until you can see **Essentials of Microsoft Windows**.

➤ Click the indicated link to download the practice files. The Save As dialog box is not yet visible.

➤ You will see the File Download dialog box asking what you want to do. The option button to save this program to disk is selected. Click **OK**. The Save As dialog box appears as shown in Figure 9b.

➤ Place a formatted floppy disk in drive A, click the **drop-down arrow** on the Save in list box, and select (click) **drive A**. Click **Save** to begin downloading the file.

➤ The File Download window will reappear on your screen and show you the status of the downloading operation. If necessary, click **OK** when you see the dialog box indicating that the download is complete.

➤ Close Internet Explorer.

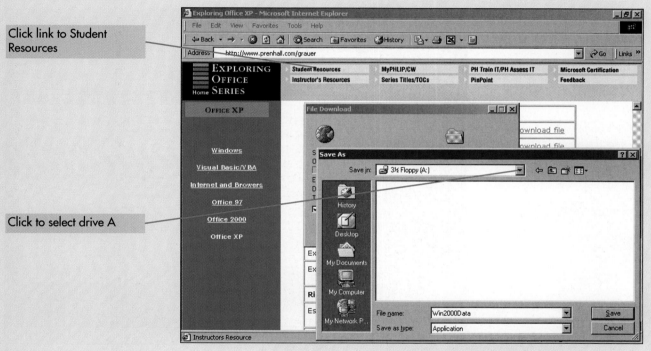

Click link to Student Resources

Click to select drive A

(b) Download the Practice Files (step 2)

FIGURE 9   *Hands-on Exercise 2 (continued)*

REMEMBER THE LOCATION

It's easy to download a file from the Web. The only tricky part, if any, is remembering where you have saved the file. This exercise is written for a laboratory setting, and thus we specified drive A as the destination, so that you will have the file on a floppy disk at the end of the exercise. If you have your own computer, however, it's faster to save the file to the desktop or in a temporary folder on drive C. Just remember where you save the file so that you can access it after it has been downloaded.

Step 3: **Open My Computer**

➤ Double click the My Computer icon on the desktop to open My Computer. If necessary, customize My Computer to match Figure 9c.

• Pull down the **View menu** and change to the **Details view**.

• Pull down the **View menu** a second time, click (or point to) the **Toolbars command**, then check the **Standard buttons** and **Address Bar** toolbars.

➤ Pull down the **Tools menu** and click the **Folder Options command** to verify the settings in effect so that your window matches ours. Be sure to **Enable Web content in folders** (in the Web View area), to **Open each folder in the same window** (in the Browse Folders area), and **Double Click to open an item** (in the Click Items area).

➤ Click the icon for **drive A** to select it. The description of drive A appears at the left of the window.

➤ Double click the icon for **drive A** to open this drive. The contents of the My Computer window are replaced by the contents of drive A.

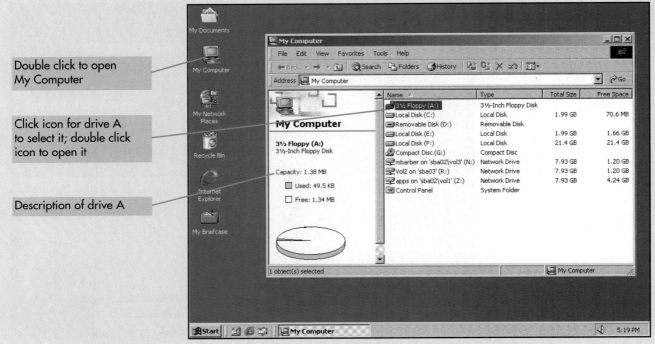

Double click to open
My Computer

Click icon for drive A
to select it; double click
icon to open it

Description of drive A

(c) Open My Computer (step 3)

FIGURE 9   *Hands-on Exercise 2 (continued)*

THE RIGHT MOUSE BUTTON

Point to any object on the Windows desktop or within an application window, then click the right mouse button to see a context-sensitive menu with commands pertaining to that object. You could, for example, right click the icon for drive A, then select the Open command from the resulting menu. The right mouse button is one of the most powerful Windows shortcuts and one of its best-kept secrets. Use it!

Step 4: **Install the Practice Files**

➤ You should see the contents of drive A as shown in Figure 9d. (If your desktop displays two windows rather than one, it is because you did not set the folder options correctly. Pull down the **Tools menu**, click the **Folder Options command**, and choose the option to **Open each folder in the same window**.)

➤ Double click the **Win2000data file** to install the data disk. You will see a dialog box thanking you for selecting the *Exploring Windows* series. Click **OK**.

• Check that the Unzip To Folder text box specifies **A:** to extract the files to the floppy disk. (You may enter a different drive and/or folder.)

• Click the **Unzip button** to extract the practice files and copy them onto the designated drive. Click **OK** after you see the message indicating that the files have been unzipped successfully. Close the WinZip dialog box.

➤ The practice files have been extracted to drive A and should appear in the Drive A window. If you do not see the files, pull down the **View menu** and click the **Refresh command.**

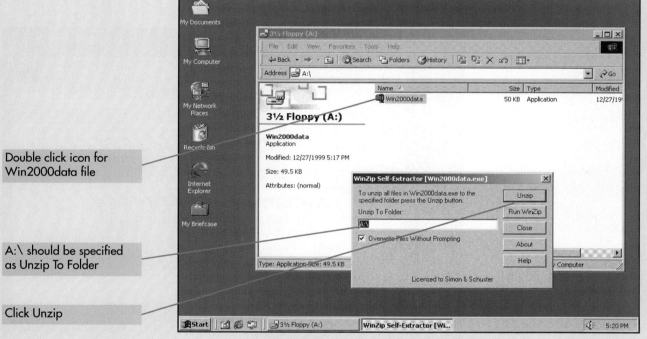

(d) Install the Practice Files (step 4)

FIGURE 9   *Hands-on Exercise 2 (continued)*

DOWNLOADING A FILE

Software and other files are typically compressed to reduce the amount of storage space the files require on disk and/or the time it takes to download the files. In essence, you download a compressed file (which may contain multiple individual files), then you uncompress (expand) the file on your local drive in order to access the individual files. After the file has been expanded, it is no longer needed and can be deleted.

Step 5: **Delete the Compressed File**

➤ If necessary, pull down the **View menu** and click **Details** to change to the Details view in Figure 9e. (If you do not see the descriptive information about drive A at the left of the window, pull down the **Tools menu**, click the **Folder Options command**, and click the option button to **Enable Web content in folders**.)

➤ You should see a total of six files in the Drive A window. Five of these are the practice files on the data disk. The sixth file is the original file that you downloaded earlier. This file is no longer necessary, since it has been already been expanded.

➤ Select (click) the **Win2000data file**. Pull down the **File menu** and click the **Delete command**, or click the **Delete button** on the toolbar. Pause for a moment to be sure you want to delete this file, then click **Yes** when asked to confirm the deletion as shown in Figure 9e.

➤ The Win2000Data file is permanently deleted from drive A. (Items deleted from a floppy disk or network drive are not sent to the Recycle Bin, and cannot be recovered.)

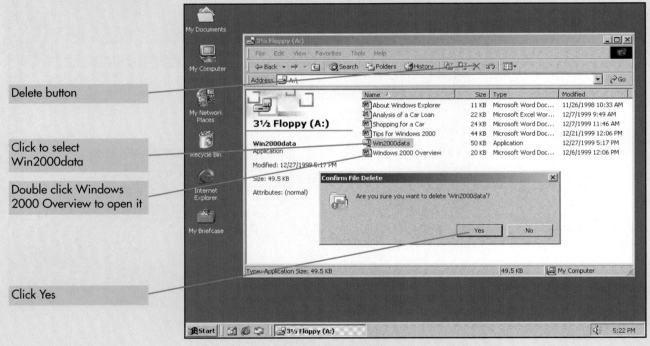

(e) Delete the Compressed File (step 5)

FIGURE 9   *Hands-on Exercise 2 (continued)*

SORT BY NAME, DATE, FILE TYPE, OR SIZE

Files can be displayed in ascending or descending sequence by name, date modified, file type, or size by clicking the appropriate column heading. Click Size, for example, to display files in the order of their size. Click the column heading a second time to reverse the sequence; that is, to switch from ascending to descending, and vice versa.

Step 6: **Modify a Document**

➤ Double click the **Windows 2000 Overview** document from within My Computer to open the document as shown in Figure 9f. (The document will open in the WordPad accessory if Microsoft Word is not installed on your machine.) If necessary, maximize the window for Microsoft Word.

➤ If necessary, click inside the document window, then press **Ctrl+End** to move to the end of the document. Add the sentence shown in Figure 9h followed by your name.

➤ Pull down the **File menu**, click **Print**, then click **OK** to print the document and prove to your instructor that you did the exercise.

➤ Pull down the **File menu** and click **Exit** to close the application. Click **Yes** when prompted to save the file.

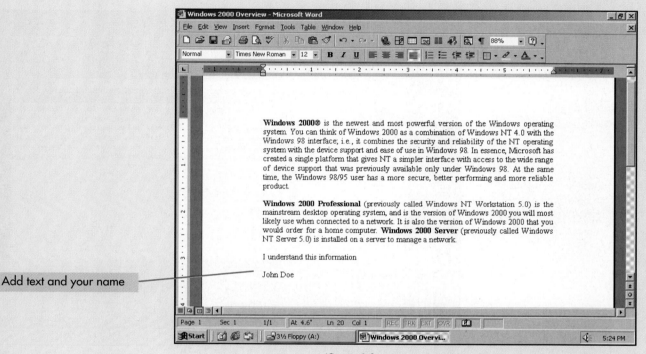

Add text and your name

(f) Modify a Document (step 6)

FIGURE 9 *Hands-on Exercise 2 (continued)*

THE DOCUMENT, NOT THE APPLICATION

All versions of Windows are document oriented, meaning that you are able to think in terms of the document rather than the application that created it. You can still open a document in traditional fashion by starting the application that created the document, then using the File Open command in that program to retrieve the document. It's often easier, however, to open the document from within My Computer (or Windows Explorer) by double clicking its icon. Windows then starts the application and opens the data file. In other words, you can open a document without explicitly starting the application.

Step 7: **Check Your Work**

➤ You should be back in the My Computer window as shown in Figure 9g. If necessary, click the **Views button** to change to the Details view.
➤ Look closely at the date and time that is displayed next to the Windows 2000 Overview document. It should show today's date and the current time (give or take a minute) since that is when the document was last modified.
➤ Look closely and see that Figure 9g also contains a sixth document, called "Backup of Windows 2000 Overview". This is a backup copy of the original document that will be created automatically by Microsoft Word if the appropriate options are in effect. (See the boxed tip below.)
➤ Exit Windows or, alternatively, continue with steps 8 and 9 to return to our Web site and explore additional resources.

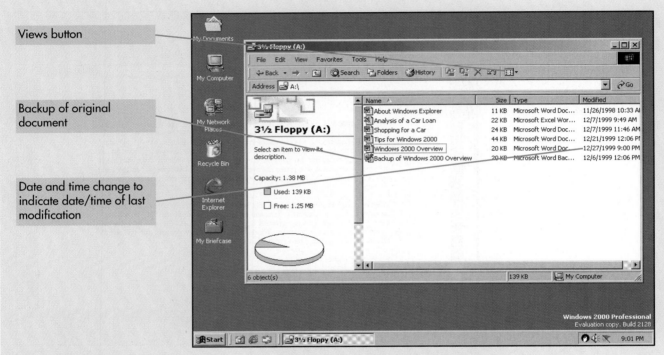

Views button

Backup of original document

Date and time change to indicate date/time of last modification

(g) Check Your Work (step 7)

FIGURE 9 *Hands-on Exercise 2 (continued)*

USE WORD TO CREATE A BACKUP COPY

Microsoft Word enables you to automatically create a backup copy of a document in conjunction with the Save command. The next time you are in Microsoft Word, pull down the Tools menu, click the Options command, click the Save tab, then check the box to always create a backup copy. Every time you save a file from this point on, the previously saved version is renamed "Backup of document," and the document in memory is saved as the current version. The disk will contain the two most recent versions of the document, enabling you to retrieve the previous version if necessary.

Step 8: **Download the PowerPoint Lecture**

➤ Restart Internet Explorer and connect to **www.prenhall.com/grauer**. Click the book for **Office XP**, click the link to **Student Resources**, then choose **PowerPoint Lectures** to display the screen in Figure 9h.

➤ Click the down arrow until you can click the link to the PowerPoint slides for **Essentials of Windows**. The File Download dialog box will appear with the option to save the file to disk selected by default. Click **OK**.

➤ Click the **drop-down arrow** on the Save in list box, and select **drive A**. Be sure that the floppy disk is still in drive A, then click **Save** to begin downloading the file. Click **OK** when you see the dialog box indicating that the download is complete.

➤ Click the taskbar button to return to the **My Computer window** for drive A. You should see all of the files that were previously on the floppy disk plus the file you just downloaded.

➤ Double click the **Win2000ppt file**, then follow the onscreen instructions to unzip the file to drive A.

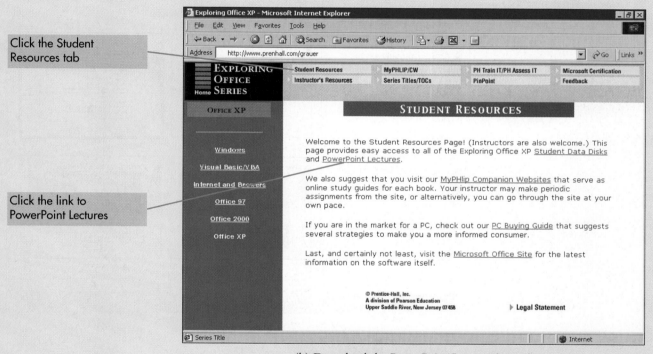

Click the Student Resources tab

Click the link to PowerPoint Lectures

(h) Download the PowerPoint Lecture (step 8)

FIGURE 9 *Hands-on Exercise 2 (continued)*

THE MyPHLIP WEB SITE

The MyPHLIP (Prentice Hall Learning on the Internet Partnership) Web site is another resource that is available for the Exploring Office series. Click the MyPHLIP tab at the top of the screen, which takes you to www.prenhall.com/myphlip, where you will register and select the text you are using. See exercise 3 at the end of the chapter.

Step 9: **Show Time**

➤ Drive A should now contain a PowerPoint file in addition to the self-extracting file. (Pull down the **View menu** and click the **Refresh command** if you do not see the PowerPoint file.)

➤ Double click the PowerPoint file to open the presentation, then click the button to Enable Macros (if prompted). You should see the PowerPoint presentation in Figure 9i. (You must have PowerPoint installed on your computer in order to view the presentation.)

➤ Pull down the **View menu** and click **Slide Show** to begin the presentation, which is intended to review the material in this supplement. Click the left mouse button (or press the **PgDn key**) to move to the next slide.

➤ Click the left mouse button continually to move from one slide to the next. Close PowerPoint at the end of the presentation.

➤ Exit Windows if you do not want to continue with the next exercise at this time.

Pull down the View menu and click the Slide Show command

The presentation reviews the material on Windows

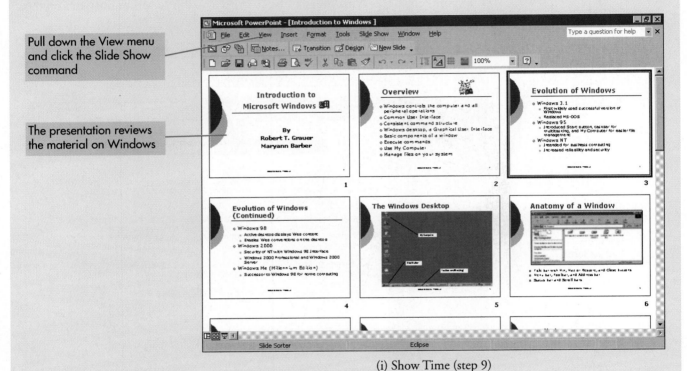

(i) Show Time (step 9)

FIGURE 9 *Hands-on Exercise 2 (continued)*

MISSING POWERPOINT—WHICH VERSION OF OFFICE DO YOU HAVE?

You may have installed Microsoft Office on your computer, but you may not have PowerPoint. That is because Microsoft has created several different versions of Microsoft Office, each with a different set of applications. Unfortunately, PowerPoint is not included in every configuration and may be missing from the suite that is shipped most frequently with new computers.

Windows has two different programs to manage the files and folders on a system, My Computer and Windows Explorer. My Computer is intuitive, but less efficient, as you have to open each folder in succession. Windows Explorer is more sophisticated, as it provides a hierarchical view of the entire system in a single window. A beginner might prefer My Computer, whereas a more experienced user will most likely opt for Windows Explorer.

Assume, for example, that you are taking four classes this semester, and that you are using the computer in each course. You've created a separate folder to hold the work for each class and have stored the contents of all four folders on a single floppy disk. Assume further that you need to retrieve your third English assignment so that you can modify the assignment, then submit the revised version to your instructor. Figure 10 illustrates how Windows Explorer could be used to locate your assignment.

The Explorer window in Figure 10a is divided into two panes. The left pane contains a tree diagram (or hierarchical view) of the entire system showing all drives and, optionally, the folders in each drive. The right pane shows the contents of the active drive or folder. Only one object (a drive or folder) can be active in the left pane, and its contents are displayed automatically in the right pane.

Look carefully at the icon for the English folder in the left pane of Figure 10a. The folder is open, whereas the icon for every other folder is closed. The open folder indicates that the English folder is the active folder. (The name of the active folder also appears in the title bar of Windows Explorer and in the Address bar.) The contents of the active folder (three Word documents in this example) are displayed in the right pane. The right pane is displayed in Details view, but could just as easily have been displayed in another view (e.g., Large Icons).

As indicated, only one folder can be open (active) at a time in the left pane. Thus, to see the contents of a different folder such as Accounting, you would open (click on) the Accounting folder, which automatically closes the English folder. The contents of the Accounting folder would then appear in the right pane. You should organize your folders in ways that make sense to you, such as a separate folder for every class you are taking. You can also create folders within folders; for example, a correspondence folder may contain two folders of its own, one for business correspondence and one for personal letters.

Windows Explorer can also be used to display a Web page, as shown in Figure 10b. All you do is click the icon for Internet Explorer in the left pane to start the program and display its default home page. Alternatively, you can click in the Address bar and enter the address of any Web page directly; for example, click in the Address bar and type www.microsoft.com to display the home page for Microsoft. Once you are browsing pages on the Web, it's convenient to close the left pane so that the page takes the complete window. You can reopen the Folders window by pulling down the View menu, clicking the Explorer Bar command, and toggling Folders on.

THE SMART TOOLBAR

The toolbar in Windows Explorer recognizes whether you are viewing a Web page or a set of files and folders, and changes accordingly. The icons that are displayed when viewing a Web page are identical to those in Internet Explorer and include the Search, Favorites, and History buttons. The buttons that are displayed when viewing a file or folder include the Undo, Delete, and Views buttons that are used in file management.

Name of active folder

Minus indicates object is expanded

Active folder

Plus sign indicates object is collapsed

Contents of active folder

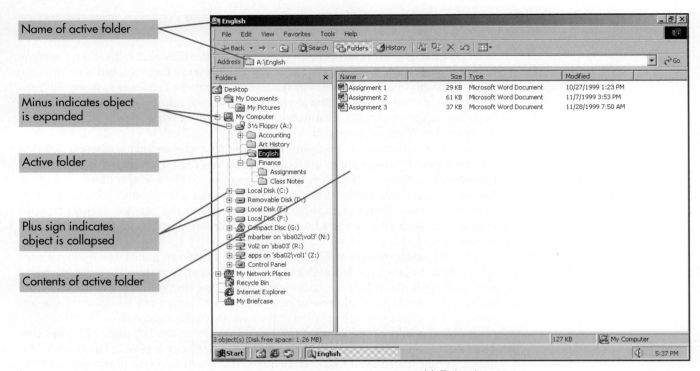

(a) Drive A

Enter address of desired site

Click to close left pane

Click icon for Internet Explorer

Web page is displayed

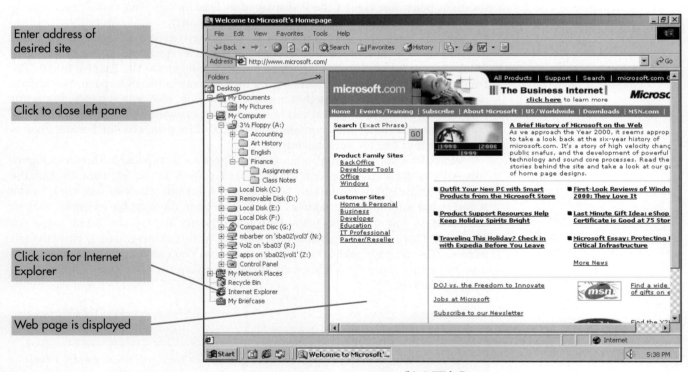

(b) A Web Page

FIGURE 10   *Windows Explorer*

Expanding and Collapsing a Drive or Folder

The tree diagram in Windows Explorer displays the devices on your system in hierarchical fashion. The desktop is always at the top of the hierarchy, and it contains icons such as My Computer, the Recycle Bin, Internet Explorer, and My Network Places. My Computer in turn contains the various drives that are accessible from your system, each of which contains folders, which in turn contain documents and/or additional folders. Each object may be expanded or collapsed by clicking the plus or minus sign, respectively. Click either sign to toggle to the other. Clicking a plus sign, for example, expands the drive, then displays a minus sign next to the drive to indicate that its subordinates are visible.

Look closely at the icon next to My Computer in either Figure 10a or 10b. It is a minus sign (as opposed to a plus sign) and it indicates that My Computer has been expanded to show the devices on the system. There is also a minus sign next to the icon for drive A to indicate that it too has been expanded to show the folders on the disk. Note, however, the plus sign next to drives C and D, indicating that these parts of the tree are currently collapsed and thus their subordinates (in this case, folders) are not visible.

Any folder may contain additional folders, and thus individual folders may also be expanded or collapsed. The minus sign next to the Finance folder, for example, indicates that the folder has been expanded and contains two additional folders, for Assignments and Class Notes, respectively. The plus sign next to the Accounting folder, however, indicates the opposite; that is, the folder is collapsed and its subordinate folders are not currently visible. A folder with neither a plus nor a minus sign, such as Art History, does not contain additional folders and cannot be expanded or collapsed.

The hierarchical view within Windows Explorer, and the ability to expand and collapse the various folders on a system, enables you to quickly locate a specific file or folder. If, for example, you want to see the contents of the Art History folder, you click its icon in the left pane, which automatically changes the display in the right pane to show the documents in that folder. Thus, Windows Explorer is ideal for moving or copying files from one folder or drive to another. You simply select (open) the folder that contains the files, use the scroll bar in the left pane (if necessary) so that the destination folder is visible, then click and drag the files from the right pane to the destination folder.

The Folder Options command functions identically in Windows Explorer and in My Computer. You can decide whether you want to single or double click the icons and/or whether to display Web content within a folder. You can also use the View menu to select the most appropriate view. Our preferences are to double click the icons, to omit Web content, and to use the Details view.

CONVERGENCE OF THE EXPLORERS

Windows Explorer and Internet Explorer are separate programs, but each includes some functionality of the other. You can use Windows Explorer to display a Web page by clicking the Internet Explorer icon within the tree structure in the left pane. Conversely, you can use Internet Explorer to display a local drive, document, or folder. Start Internet Explorer in the usual fashion, click in the Address bar, then enter the appropriate address, such as C:\ to display the contents of drive C.

THE PRACTICE FILES VIA A LOCAL AREA NETWORK

Objective   To use Windows Explorer to copy the practice files from a network drive to a floppy disk. The exercise requires a formatted floppy disk and access to a local area network. Use Figure 11 as a guide in the exercise.

Step 1:   **Start Windows Explorer**

➤ Click the **Start Button**, click **Programs**, click **Accessories**, then click **Windows Explorer**. Click the **maximize button** so that Windows Explorer takes the entire desktop as shown in Figure 11a. Do not be concerned if your desktop is different from ours.

➤ Make or verify the following selections using the **View menu**. You have to pull down the View menu each time you choose a different command.
  • The **Standard buttons** and **Address bar** toolbars should be selected.
  • The **Status Bar command** should be checked.
  • The **Details view** should be selected.

➤ Click (select) the **Desktop icon** in the left pane to display the contents of the desktop in the right pane. Your desktop may have different icons from ours, but your screen should almost match Figure 11a. We set additional options in the next step.

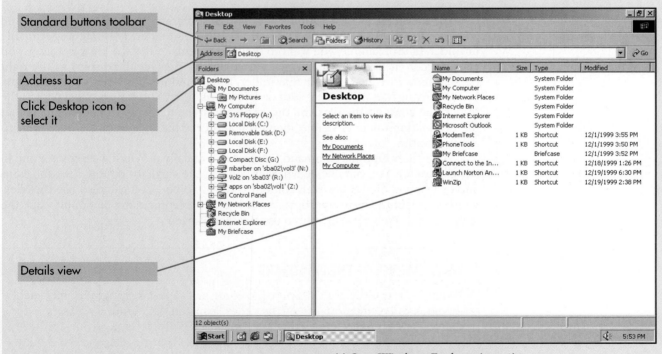

(a) Start Windows Explorer (step 1)

FIGURE 11   *Hands-on Exercise 3*

Step 2: **Change the Folder Options**

➤ Click the **minus** (or the **plus**) **sign** next to My Computer to collapse (or expand) My Computer and hide (or display) the objects it contains. Toggle the signs back and forth a few times for practice. End with a minus sign next to My Computer as shown in Figure 11b.

➤ Place a newly formatted floppy disk in drive A. Click the drive icon next to drive A to select the drive and display its contents in the right pane. The disk does not contain any files since zero bytes are used.

➤ Displaying Web content at the left of a folder (as is done in Figure 11b) is fine when a drive or folder does not contain a large number of files. It is generally a waste of space, however, and so we want to change the folder options.

➤ Pull down the **Tools menu** and click the **Folder Options command** to display the Folder Options dialog box in Figure 11a. Click the option to **Use Windows classic folders**. Click **OK**.

Select Use Windows classic folders

Click minus and plus to practice; end with minus sign

Click to select drive A

Click plus sign next to network drive containing files to be copied

Floppy disk is empty

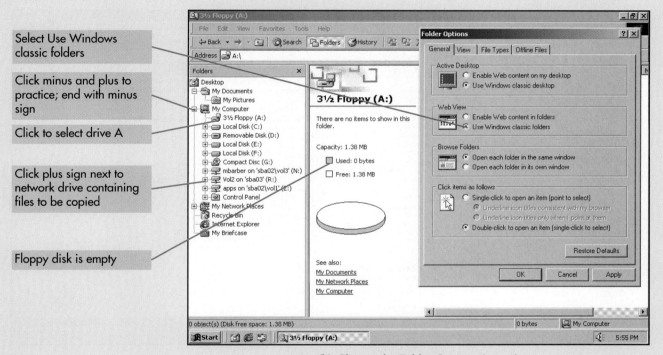

(b) Change the Folder Options (step 2)

FIGURE 11   *Hands-on Exercise 3 (continued)*

THE PLUS AND MINUS SIGN

Any drive, be it local or on the network, may be expanded or collapsed to display or hide its folders. A minus sign indicates that the drive has been expanded and that its folders are visible. A plus sign indicates the reverse; that is, the device is collapsed and its folders are not visible. Click either sign to toggle to the other. Clicking a plus sign, for example, expands the drive, then displays a minus sign next to the drive to indicate that the folders are visible. Clicking a minus sign has the reverse effect.

Step 3:   **Select the Network Drive**

➤ Click the **plus sign** for the network drive that contains the files you are to copy (e.g., drive **R** in Figure 11c). Select (click) the **Exploring Windows 2000 folder** to open this folder.

➤ You may need to expand other folders on the network drive (such as the Datadisk folder on our network) as per instructions from your professor. Note the following:

   • The Exploring Windows 2000 folder is highlighted in the left pane, its icon is an open folder, and its contents are displayed in the right pane.

   • The status bar indicates that the folder contains five objects and the total file size is 119KB.

➤ Click the icon next to any other folder to select the folder, which in turn deselects the Exploring Windows 2000 folder. (Only one folder in the left pane is active at a time.) Reselect (click) the **Exploring Windows 2000 folder**.

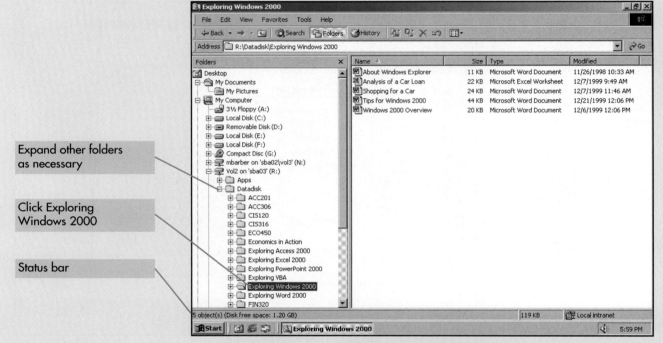

Expand other folders as necessary

Click Exploring Windows 2000

Status bar

(c) Select the Network Drive (step 3)

FIGURE 11   *Hands-on Exercise 3 (continued)*

CUSTOMIZE WINDOWS EXPLORER

Increase or decrease the size of the left pane within Windows Explorer by dragging the vertical line separating the left and right panes in the appropriate direction. You can also drag the right border of the various column headings (Name, Size, Type, and Modified) in the right pane to increase or decrease the width of the column. And best of all, you can click any column heading to display the contents of the selected folder in sequence by that column. Click the heading a second time and the sequence changes from ascending to descending and vice versa.

Step 4: **Copy the Individual Files**

➤ Select (click) the file called **About Windows Explorer**, which highlights the file as shown in Figure 11d. Click and drag the selected file in the right pane to the **drive A icon** in the left pane:

- You will see the ⊘ symbol as you drag the file until you reach a suitable destination (e.g., until you point to the icon for drive A). The ⊘ symbol will change to a plus sign when the icon for drive A is highlighted, indicating that the file can be copied successfully.
- Release the mouse to complete the copy operation. You will see a pop-up window, which indicates the status of the copy operation.

➤ Select (click) the file **Tips for Windows 2000**, which automatically deselects the previously selected file. Copy the selected file to drive A by dragging its icon from the right pane to the drive A icon in the left pane.

➤ Copy the three remaining files to drive A as well. Select (click) drive **A** in the left pane, which in turn displays the contents of the floppy disk in the right pane. You should see the five files you have copied to drive A.

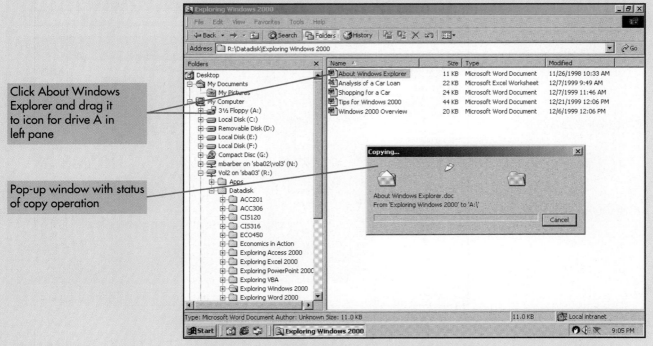

Click About Windows Explorer and drag it to icon for drive A in left pane

Pop-up window with status of copy operation

(d) Copy the Individual Files (step 4)

FIGURE 11   *Hands-on Exercise 3 (continued)*

SELECT MULTIPLE FILES

Selecting one file automatically deselects the previously selected file. You can, however, select multiple files by clicking the first file, then pressing and holding the Ctrl key as you click each additional file. Use the Shift key to select multiple files that are adjacent to one another by clicking the first file, then pressing and holding the Shift key as you click the last file.

Step 5: **Display a Web Page**

➤ This step requires an Internet connection. Click the **minus sign** next to the network drive to collapse that drive. Click the **minus sign** next to any other expanded drive so that the left pane is similar to Figure 11e.

➤ Click the **Internet Explorer icon** to start Internet Explorer and display the starting page for your configuration. The page you see will be different from ours, but you can click in the Address bar near the top of the window to enter the address of any Web site.

➤ Look closely at the icons on the toolbar, which have changed to reflect the tools associated with viewing a Web page. Click the **Back button** to return to drive A, the previously displayed item in Windows Explorer. The icons on the toolbar return to those associated with a folder.

➤ Close Windows Explorer. Shut down the computer if you do not want to continue with the next exercise at this time.

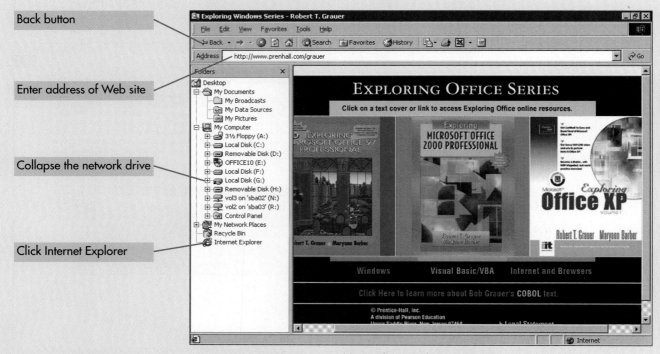

(e) Display a Web Page (step 5)

FIGURE 11   *Hands-on Exercise 3 (continued)*

SERVER NOT RESPONDING

Two things have to occur in order for Internet Explorer to display the requested document—it must locate the server on which the document is stored, and it must be able to connect to that computer. If you see a message similar to "Server too busy or not responding", it implies that Internet Explorer has located the server but was unable to connect because the site is busy or is temporarily down. Try to connect again, in a minute or so, or later in the day.

As you grow to depend on the computer, you will create a variety of files using applications such as Microsoft Word or Excel. Learning how to manage those files is one of the most important skills you can acquire. The previous hands-on exercises provided you with a set of files with which to practice. That way, when you have your own files you will be comfortable executing the various file management commands you will need on a daily basis. This section describes the basic file operations you will need, then presents another hands-on exercise in which you apply those commands.

Moving and Copying a File

The essence of file management is to move and copy a file or folder from one location to another. This can be done in different ways, most easily by clicking and dragging the file icon from the source drive or folder to the destination drive or folder, within Windows Explorer. There is one subtlety, however, in that the result of dragging a file (i.e., whether the file is moved or copied) depends on whether the source and destination are on the same or different drives. Dragging a file from one folder to another folder on the same drive moves the file. Dragging a file to a folder on a different drive copies the file. The same rules apply to dragging a folder, where the folder and every file in it are moved or copied as per the rules for an individual file.

This process is not as arbitrary as it may seem. Windows assumes that if you drag an object (a file or folder) to a different drive (e.g., from drive C to drive A), you want the object to appear in both places. Hence, the default action when you click and drag an object to a different drive is to copy the object. You can, however, override the default and move the object by pressing and holding the Shift key as you drag.

Windows also assumes that you do not want two copies of an object on the same drive, as that would result in wasted disk space. Thus, the default action when you click and drag an object to a different folder on the same drive is to move the object. You can override the default and copy the object by pressing and holding the Ctrl key as you drag. It's not as complicated as it sounds, and you get a chance to practice in the hands-on exercise, which follows shortly.

Deleting a File

The *Delete command* deletes (erases) a file from a disk. The command can be executed in different ways, most easily by selecting a file, then pressing the Del key. It's also comforting to know that you can usually recover a deleted file, because the file is not (initially) removed from the disk, but moved instead to the Recycle Bin, from where it can be restored to its original location. Unfortunately, files deleted from a floppy disk are not put in the Recycle Bin and hence cannot be recovered.

The *Recycle Bin* is a special folder that contains all files that were previously deleted from any hard disk on your system. Think of the Recycle Bin as similar to the wastebasket in your room. You throw out (delete) a report by tossing it into a wastebasket. The report is gone (deleted) from your desk, but you can still get it back by taking it out of the wastebasket as long as the basket wasn't emptied. The Recycle Bin works the same way. Files are not deleted from the hard disk per se, but moved instead to the Recycle Bin from where they can be restored to their original location.

The Recycle Bin will eventually run out of space, in which case the files that have been in the Recycle Bin the longest are permanently deleted to make room for additional files. Accordingly, once a file is removed from the Recycle Bin it can no longer be restored, as it has been physically deleted from the hard disk. Note, too, that the protection afforded by the Recycle Bin does not extend to files deleted from a floppy disk. Such files can be recovered, but only through utility programs outside of Windows 2000.

Renaming a File

Every file or folder is assigned a name at the time it is created, but you may want to change that name at some point in the future. Point to a file or a folder, click the right mouse button to display a menu with commands pertaining to the object, then click the **Rename command**. The name of the file or folder will be highlighted with the insertion point (a flashing vertical line) positioned at the end of the name. Enter a new name to replace the selected name, or click anywhere within the name to change the insertion point and edit the name.

Backup

It's not a question of if it will happen, but when—hard disks die, files are lost, or viruses may infect a system. It has happened to us and it will happen to you, but you can prepare for the inevitable by creating adequate backup *before* the problem occurs. The essence of a **backup strategy** is to decide which files to back up, how often to do the backup, and where to keep the backup. Once you decide on a strategy, follow it, and follow it faithfully!

Our strategy is very simple—back up what you can't afford to lose, do so on a daily basis, and store the backup away from your computer. You need not copy every file, every day. Instead, copy just the files that changed during the current session. Realize, too, that it is much more important to back up your data files than your program files. You can always reinstall the application from the original disks or CD, or if necessary, go to the vendor for another copy of an application. You, however, are the only one who has a copy of your term paper.

Write Protection

A floppy disk is normally **write-enabled** (the square hole is covered with the movable tab) so that you can change the contents of the disk. Thus, you can create (save) new files to a write-enabled disk and/or edit or delete existing files. Occasionally, however, you may want to **write-protect** a floppy disk (by sliding the tab to expose the square hole) so that its contents cannot be modified. This is typically done with a backup disk where you want to prevent the accidental deletion of a file and/or the threat of virus infection.

Our Next Exercise

Our next exercise begins with the floppy disk containing the five practice files in drive A. We ask you to create two folders on drive A (step 1) and to move the various files into these folders (step 2). Next, you copy a folder from drive A to the My Documents folder (step 3), modify one of the files in the My Documents folder (step 4), then copy the modified file back to drive A (step 5). We ask you to delete a file in step 6, then recover it from the Recycle Bin in step 7. We also show you how to write-protect a floppy disk in step 8. Let's get started.

FILE MANAGEMENT

Objective   Use Windows Explorer to move, copy, and delete a file; recover a deleted file from the Recycle Bin; write-protect a floppy disk. Use Figure 12 as a guide in the exercise.

Step 1:   **Create a New Folder**

➤ Start Windows Explorer, maximize its window, and if necessary, change to **Details view**. Place the floppy disk from Exercise 2 or 3 in drive A.

➤ Select (click) the icon for **drive A** in the left pane of the Explorer window. Drive A should contain the files shown in Figure 12a.

➤ You will create two folders on drive A, using two different techniques:

• Point to a blank area anywhere in the **right pane**, click the **right mouse button** to display a context-sensitive menu, click (or point to) the **New command**, then click **Folder** as the type of object to create.

• The icon for a new folder will appear with the name of the folder (New Folder) highlighted. Type **John Doe's Documents** (use your own name) to change the name of the folder. Press **Enter**.

• Click the icon for **drive A** in the left pane. Pull down the **File menu**, click (or point to) the **New command**, and click **Folder** as the type of object to create. Type **Automobile** to change the name of the folder. Press **Enter**. The right pane should now contain five documents and two folders.

➤ Pull down the **View menu**. Click the **Arrange icons command**, then click the **By Name command** to display the folders in alphabetical order.

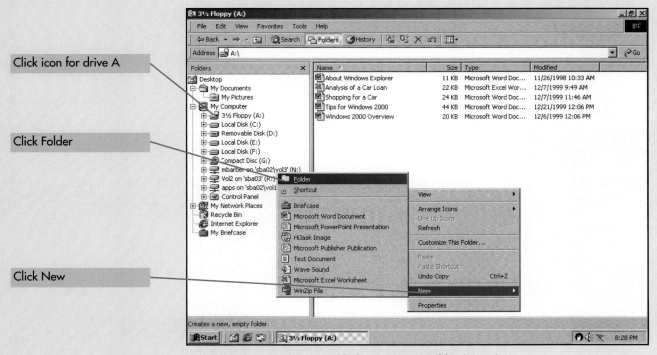

Click icon for drive A

Click Folder

Click New

(a) Create a New Folder (step 1)

FIGURE 12   *Hands-on Exercise 4*

Step 2:   **Move a File**

➤ Click the **plus sign** next to drive A to expand the drive as shown in Figure 12b. Note the following:
  • The left pane shows that drive A is selected. The right pane displays the contents of drive A (the selected object in the left pane).
  • There is a minus sign next to the icon for drive A in the left pane, indicating that it has been expanded and that its folders are visible. Thus, the folder names also appear under drive A in the left pane.

➤ Click and drag the icon for the file **About Windows Explorer** from the right pane, to the **John Doe's Documents folder** in the left pane, to move the file into that folder.

➤ Click and drag the **Tips for Windows 2000** and **Windows 2000 Overview** documents to the **John Doe's Documents folder** in similar fashion.

➤ Click the **John Doe's Documents folder** in the left pane to select the folder and display its contents in the right pane. You should see the three files that were just moved.

➤ Click the icon for **Drive A** in the left pane, then click and drag the remaining files, **Analysis of a Car** and **Shopping for a Car**, to the **Automobile folder**.

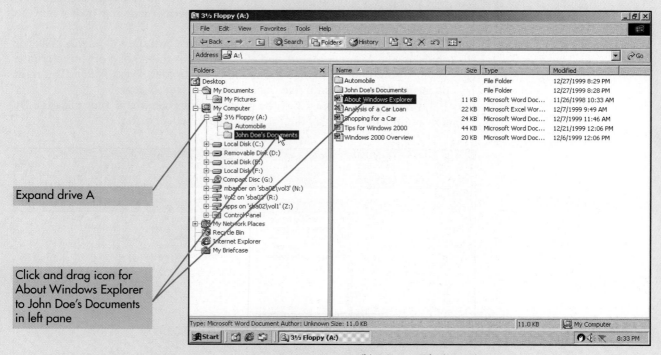

(b) Move a File (step 2)

FIGURE 12   *Hands-on Exercise 4*

RIGHT CLICK AND DRAG

Click and drag with the right mouse button to display a shortcut menu asking whether you want to copy or move the file. This simple tip can save you from making a careless (and potentially serious) error. Use it!

Step 3:   **Copy a Folder**

➤ Point to **John Doe's Documents folder** in either pane, click the **right mouse button**, and drag the folder to the **My Documents folder** in the left pane, then release the mouse to display a shortcut menu. Click the **Copy Here command**.
  • You may see a Copy files message box as the individual files within John Doe's folder are copied to the My Documents folder.
  • If you see the Confirm Folder Replace dialog box, it means that you already copied the files or a previous student used the same folder when he or she did this exercise. Click the **Yes to All button** so that your files replace the previous versions in the My Documents folder.

➤ Click the **My Documents folder** in the left pane. Pull down the **View menu** and click the **Refresh command** (or press the **F5 key**) so that the tree structure shows the newly copied folder. (Please remember to delete John Doe's Documents folder at the end of the exercise.)

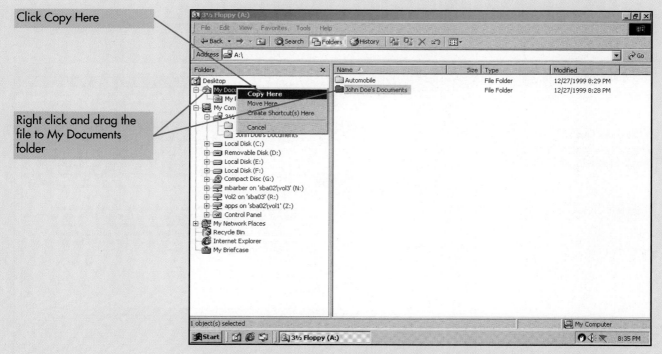

Click Copy Here

Right click and drag the file to My Documents folder

(c) Copy a Folder (step 3)

FIGURE 12   *Hands-on Exercise 4 (continued)*

THE MY DOCUMENTS FOLDER

The My Documents folder is created by default with the installation of Microsoft Windows. There is no requirement that you store your documents in this folder, but it is convenient, especially for beginners who may lack the confidence to create their own folders. The My Documents folder is also helpful in a laboratory environment where the network administrator may prevent you from modifying the desktop and/or from creating your own folders on drive C, in which case you will have to use the My Documents folder.

Step 4: **Modify a Document**

➤ Click **John Doe's Documents folder** within the My Documents folder to make it the active folder and to display its contents in the right pane. Change to the **Details view**.

➤ Double click the **About Windows Explorer** document to start Word and open the document. Do not be concerned if the size and/or position of the Microsoft Word window are different from ours.

➤ If necessary, click inside the document window, then press **Ctrl+End** to move to the end of the document. Add the sentence shown in Figure 12d.

➤ Pull down the **File menu** and click **Save** to save the modified file (or click the **Save button** on the Standard toolbar). Pull down the **File menu** and click **Exit**.

➤ Pull down the **View menu** in Windows Explorer and click **Refresh** (or press the **F5 key**) to update the contents of the right pane. The date and time associated with the About Windows Explorer file has been changed to indicate that the file has just been modified.

Double click About Windows Explorer to open it

Click John Doe's Documents folder within My Documents folder

Add text and your name

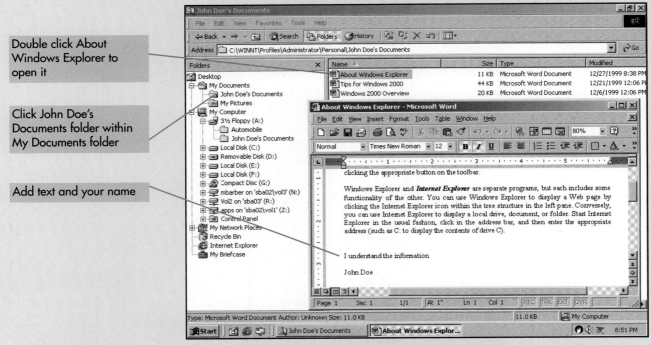

(d) Modify a Document (step 4)

FIGURE 12   *Hands-on Exercise 4 (continued)*

KEYBOARD SHORTCUTS

Ctrl+B, Ctrl+I, and Ctrl+U are shortcuts to boldface, italicize, and underline, respectively. Ctrl+X (the X is supposed to remind you of a pair of scissors), Ctrl+C, and Ctrl+V correspond to Cut, Copy, and Paste, respectively. Ctrl+Home and Ctrl+End move to the beginning or end of a document. These shortcuts are not unique to Microsoft Word, but are recognized in virtually every Windows application. See practice exercise 11 at the end of the chapter.

Step 5: **Copy (Back Up) a File**

➤ Verify that **John Doe's folder** within My Documents is the active folder, as denoted by the open folder icon. Click and drag the icon for the **About Windows Explorer** file from the right pane to John Doe's Documents folder on **Drive A** in the left pane.

➤ You will see the message in Figure 12e, indicating that the folder (on drive A) already contains a file called About Windows Explorer and asking whether you want to replace the existing file. Click **Yes** because you want to replace the previous version of the file on drive A with the updated version from the My Documents folder.

➤ You have just backed up the file; in other words, you have created a copy of the file on the disk in drive A. Thus, you can use the floppy disk to restore the file in the My Documents folder should anything happen to it.

John Doe's Documents folder within My Documents is active

Click and drag About Windows Explorer to the John Doe's Documents folder on drive A

Click Yes

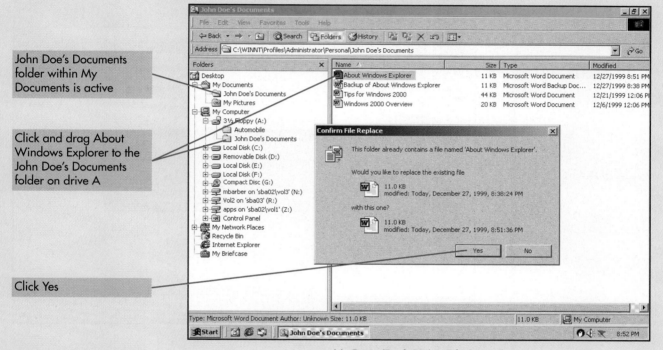

(e) Copy (Back Up) a File (step 5)

FIGURE 12 *Hands-on Exercise 4 (continued)*

FILE EXTENSIONS

Long-time DOS users remember a three-character extension at the end of a file name to indicate the file type; for example, DOC or XLS to indicate a Word document or Excel workbook, respectively. The extensions are displayed or hidden according to a setting in the Folder Options command. Pull down the Tools menu, click the Folder Options command to display the Folder Options dialog box, click the View tab, then check (or clear) the box to hide (or show) file extensions for known file types. Click OK to accept the setting and exit the dialog box.

Step 6: **Delete a Folder**

➤ Select (click) **John Doe's Documents folder** within the My Documents folder in the left pane. Pull down the **File menu** and click **Delete** (or press the **Del key**).

➤ You will see the dialog box in Figure 12f asking whether you are sure you want to delete the folder (i.e., send the folder and its contents to the Recycle Bin). Note the recycle logo within the box, which implies that you will be able to restore the file.

➤ Click **Yes** to delete the folder. The folder disappears from drive C. Pull down the **Edit menu**. Click **Undo Delete**. The deletion is cancelled and the folder reappears in the left pane. If you don't see the folder, pull down the **View menu** and click the **Refresh command**.

Click John Doe's Documents folder within My Documents to select it

Recycle logo

Click Yes

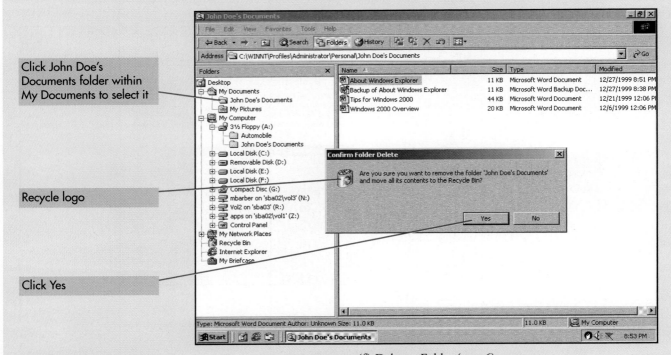

(f) Delete a Folder (step 6)

FIGURE 12   *Hands-on Exercise 4 (continued)*

THE UNDO COMMAND

The Undo command is present not only in application programs such as Word or Excel, but in Windows Explorer as well. You can use the Undo command to undelete a file provided you execute the command immediately (within a few commands) after the Delete command. To execute the Undo command, right-click anywhere in the right pane to display a shortcut menu, then select the Undo action. You can also pull down the Edit menu and click Undo to reverse (undo) the last command. Some operations cannot be undone (in which case the command will be dimmed), but Undo is always worth a try.

Step 7:   **The Recycle Bin**

➤ Select John Doe's Documents folder within the My Documents folder in the left pane. Select (click) the **About Windows Explorer** file in the right pane. Press the **Del key**, then click **Yes**.

➤ Click the **Down arrow** in the vertical scroll bar in the left pane until you see the icon for the **Recycle Bin**. Click the icon to make the Recycle Bin the active folder and display its contents in the right pane.

➤ You will see a different set of files from those displayed in Figure 12g. Pull down the **View menu**, click (or point to) **Arrange icons**, then click **By Delete Date** to display the files in this sequence.

➤ Click in the **right pane**. Press **Ctrl+End** or scroll to the bottom of the window. Point to the **About Windows Explorer** file, click the **right mouse button** to display the shortcut menu in Figure 12g, then click **Restore**.

➤ The file disappears from the Recycle bin because it has been returned to John Doe's Documents folder.

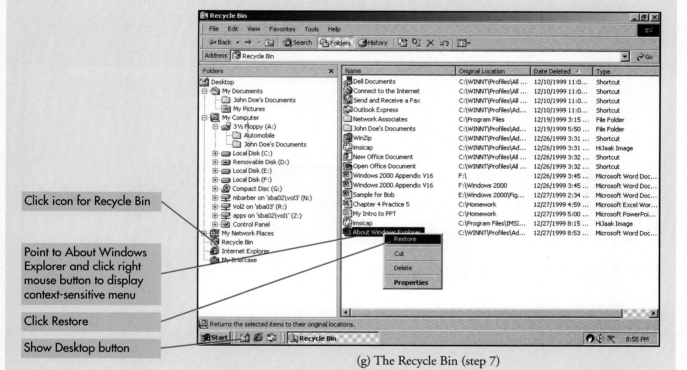

(g) The Recycle Bin (step 7)

FIGURE 12   *Hands-on Exercise 4 (continued)*

THE SHOW DESKTOP BUTTON

The Show Desktop button on the taskbar enables you to minimize all open windows with a single click. The button functions as a toggle switch. Click it once and all windows are minimized. Click it a second time and the open windows are restored to their positions on the desktop. If you do not see the Show Desktop button, right click a blank area of the taskbar to display a context-sensitive menu, click Toolbars, then check the Quick Launch toolbar.

Step 8: **Write-Protect a Floppy Disk**

➤ Remove the floppy disk from drive A, then move the built-in tab on the disk so that the square hole on the disk is open. Return the disk to the drive.

➤ If necessary, expand drive A in the left pane, select the **Automobile folder**, select the **Analysis of a Car Loan document** in the right pane, then press the **Del key**. Click **Yes** when asked whether to delete the file.

➤ You will see the message in Figure 12h indicating that the file cannot be deleted because the disk has been write-protected. Click **OK**. Remove the write-protection by moving the built-in tab to cover the square hole.

➤ Repeat the procedure to delete the **Analysis of a Car Loan document**. Click **Yes** in response to the confirmation message asking whether you want to delete the file.

➤ The file disappears from the right pane, indicating it has been deleted. The **Automobile folder** on drive A should contain only one file.

➤ Delete **John Doe's Documents folder** from My Documents as a courtesy to the next student. Exit Windows Explorer. Shut down the computer.

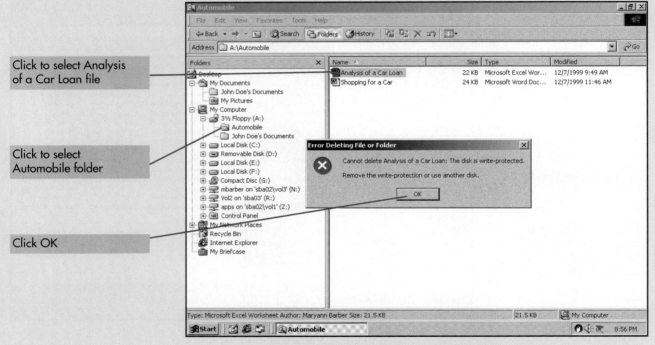

(h) Write-Protect a Floppy Disk (step 8)

FIGURE 12 *Hands-on Exercise 4 (continued)*

BACK UP IMPORTANT FILES

We cannot overemphasize the importance of adequate backup and urge you to copy your data files to floppy disks and store those disks away from your computer. You might also want to write-protect your backup disks so that you cannot accidentally erase a file. It takes only a few minutes, but you will thank us, when (not if) you lose an important file and don't have to wish you had another copy.

Microsoft Windows controls the operation of a computer and its peripherals. Windows 98 and its successor, Windows Me, are geared for the home user and provide extensive support for games and peripheral devices. Windows NT and its successor, Windows 2000, are aimed at the business user and provide increased security and reliability. Windows XP replaces all current versions of Windows. All versions of Windows follow the same conventions and have the same basic interface.

All Windows operations take place on the desktop. Every window on the desktop contains the same basic elements, which include a title bar, a control-menu box, a minimize button, a maximize or restore button, and a close button. Other elements that may be present include a menu bar, vertical and/or horizontal scroll bars, a status bar, and various toolbars. All windows may be moved and sized. The Help command in the Start menu provides access to detailed information.

Multitasking is a major benefit of the Windows environment as it enables you to run several programs at the same time. The taskbar contains a button for each open program and enables you to switch back and forth between those programs by clicking the appropriate button.

A dialog box supplies information needed to execute a command. Option buttons indicate mutually exclusive choices, one of which must be chosen. Check boxes are used if the choices are not mutually exclusive or if an option is not required. A text box supplies descriptive information. A (drop-down or open) list box displays multiple choices, any of which may be selected. A tabbed dialog box provides access to multiple sets of options.

A floppy disk must be formatted before it can store data. Formatting is accomplished through the Format command within the My Computer window. My Computer enables you to browse the disk drives and other devices attached to your system. The contents of My Computer depend on the specific configuration.

A file is a set of data or set of instructions that has been given a name and stored on disk. There are two basic types of files, program files and data files. A program file is an executable file, whereas a data file can be used only in conjunction with a specific program. Every file has a file name and a file type. The file name can be up to 255 characters in length and may include spaces.

Files are stored in folders to better organize the hundreds (or thousands) of files on a disk. A folder may contain program files, data files, and/or other folders. There are two basic ways to search through the folders on your system, My Computer and Windows Explorer. My Computer is intuitive but less efficient than Windows Explorer, as you have to open each folder in succession. Windows Explorer is more sophisticated, as it provides a hierarchical view of the entire system.

Windows Explorer is divided into two panes. The left pane displays all of the devices and, optionally, the folders on each device. The right pane shows the contents of the active (open) drive or folder. Only one drive or folder can be active in the left pane. Any device, be it local or on the network, may be expanded or collapsed to display or hide its folders. A minus sign indicates that the drive has been expanded and that its folders are visible. A plus sign indicates that the device is collapsed and its folders are not visible.

The result of dragging a file (or folder) from one location to another depends on whether the source and destination folders are on the same or different drives. Dragging the file to a folder on the same drive moves the file. Dragging the file to a folder on a different drive copies the file. It's easier, therefore, to click and drag with the right mouse button to display a context-sensitive menu from which you can select the desired operation.

The Delete command deletes (removes) a file from a disk. If, however, the file was deleted from a local (fixed or hard) disk, it is not really gone, but moved instead to the Recycle Bin from where it can be subsequently recovered.

Backup strategy (p. 42)
Check box (p. 8)
Close button (p. 5)
Command button (p. 10)
Common user interface (p. 5)
Compressed file (p. 22)
Contents tab (p. 11)
Copy a file (p. 47)
Data file (p. 20)
Delete a file (p. 41)
Desktop (p. 2)
Details view (p. 20)
Dialog box (p. 8)
Favorites tab (p. 18)
File (p. 20)
Filename (p. 20)
File type (p. 20)
Folder (p. 20)
Folder Options command (p. 14)
Format command (p. 17)
Help command (p. 18)

Index tab (p. 14)
Internet Explorer (p. 40)
List box (p. 8)
Maximize button (p. 5)
Menu bar (p. 5)
Minimize button (p. 5)
Mouse operations (p. 10)
Move a file (p. 44)
Move a window (p. 15)
Multitasking (p. 4)
My Computer (p. 22)
My Documents folder (p. 45)
My Network Places (p. 5)
New command (p. 43)
Option button (p. 8)
Program file (p. 20)
Pull-down menu (p. 7)
Radio button (p. 8)
Recycle Bin (p. 49)
Rename command (p. 42)
Restore a file (p. 5)

Restore button (p. 5)
Scroll bar (p. 5)
Size a window (p. 15)
Spin button (p. 8)
Start button (p. 4)
Status bar (p. 5)
Taskbar (p. 4)
Text box (p. 8)
Task Manager (p. 19)
Title bar (p. 5)
Toolbar (p. 5)
Undo command (p. 48)
Windows 2000 (p. 2)
Windows 95 (p. 2)
Windows 98 (p. 2)
Windows Explorer (p. 33)
Windows Me (p. 2)
Windows NT (p. 2)
Windows XP (p. 2)
Write-enabled (p. 42)
Write-protected (p. 42)

MULTIPLE CHOICE

1. Which versions of the Windows operating system were intended for the home computer?
   (a) Windows NT and Windows 98
   (b) Windows NT and Windows XP
   (c) Windows NT and Windows 2000
   (d) Windows 98 and Windows Me

2. What happens if you click and drag a file from drive C to drive A?
   (a) The file is copied to drive A
   (b) The file is moved to drive A
   (c) A menu appears that allows you to choose between moving and copying
   (d) The file is sent to the recycle bin

3. Which of the following is *not* controlled by the Folder Options command?
   (a) Single or double clicking to open a desktop icon
   (b) The presence or absence of Web content within a folder
   (c) The view (e.g., using large or small icons) within My Computer
   (d) Using one or many windows when browsing My Computer

4. What is the significance of a faded (dimmed) command in a pull-down menu?
   (a) The command is not currently accessible
   (b) A dialog box will appear if the command is selected
   (c) A Help window will appear if the command is selected
   (d) There are no equivalent keystrokes for the particular command

5. Which of the following is true regarding a dialog box?
   (a) Option buttons indicate mutually exclusive choices
   (b) Check boxes imply that multiple options may be selected
   (c) Both (a) and (b)
   (d) Neither (a) nor (b)

6. Which of the following is the first step in sizing a window?
   (a) Point to the title bar
   (b) Pull down the View menu to display the toolbar
   (c) Point to any corner or border
   (d) Pull down the View menu and change to large icons

7. Which of the following is the first step in moving a window?
   (a) Point to the title bar
   (b) Pull down the View menu to display the toolbar
   (c) Point to any corner or border
   (d) Pull down the View menu and change to large icons

8. How do you exit from Windows?
   (a) Click the Start button, then click the Shut Down command
   (b) Right click the Start button, then click the Shut Down command
   (c) Click the End button, then click the Shut Down command
   (d) Right click the End button, then click the Shut Down command

9. Which button appears immediately after a window has been maximized?
   (a) The close button
   (b) The minimize button
   (c) The maximize button
   (d) The restore button

10. What happens to a window that has been minimized?
    (a) The window is still visible but it no longer has a minimize button
    (b) The window shrinks to a button on the taskbar
    (c) The window is closed and the application is removed from memory
    (d) The window is still open but the application is gone from memory

11. What is the significance of three dots next to a command in a pull-down menu?
    (a) The command is not currently accessible
    (b) A dialog box will appear if the command is selected
    (c) A Help window will appear if the command is selected
    (d) There are no equivalent keystrokes for the particular command

12. The Recycle Bin enables you to restore a file that was deleted from:
    (a) Drive A
    (b) Drive C
    (c) Both (a) and (b)
    (d) Neither (a) nor (b)

13. The left pane of Windows Explorer may contain:
    (a) One or more folders with a plus sign
    (b) One or more folders with a minus sign
    (c) Both (a) and (b)
    (d) Neither (a) nor (b)

14. Which of the following was suggested as essential to a backup strategy?
    (a) Back up all program files at the end of every session
    (b) Store backup files at another location
    (c) Both (a) and (b)
    (d) Neither (a) nor (b)

ANSWERS

1. d	**5.** c	**9.** d	**13.** c
2. a	**6.** c	**10.** b	**14.** b
3. c	**7.** a	**11.** b	
4. a	**8.** a	**12.** b	

1. **My Computer:** The document in Figure 13 is an effective way to show your instructor that you understand the My Computer window, and further that you have basic proficiency in Microsoft Word.
   a. Open My Computer to display the contents of your configuration. Pull down the View menu and switch to the Details view. Size the window as necessary. Press Alt + Print Screen to capture the copy of the My Computer window to the Windows clipboard. (The Print Screen key captures the entire screen. Using the Alt key, however, copies just the current window.)
   b. Click the Start menu, click Programs, then click Microsoft Word.
   c. Pull down the Edit menu. Click the Paste command to copy the contents of the clipboard to the document you are about to create. The My Computer window should be pasted into your document.
   d. Press Ctrl+End to move to the end of your document. Press Enter two or three times to leave blank lines as appropriate. Type a modified form of the memo in Figure 13 so that it conforms to your configuration.
   e. Finish the memo and sign your name. Pull down the File menu, click the Print command, then click OK in the dialog box to print the document.

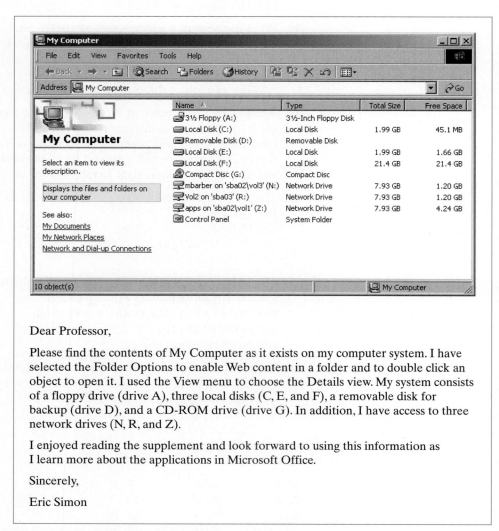

Dear Professor,

Please find the contents of My Computer as it exists on my computer system. I have selected the Folder Options to enable Web content in a folder and to double click an object to open it. I used the View menu to choose the Details view. My system consists of a floppy drive (drive A), three local disks (C, E, and F), a removable disk for backup (drive D), and a CD-ROM drive (drive G). In addition, I have access to three network drives (N, R, and Z).

I enjoyed reading the supplement and look forward to using this information as I learn more about the applications in Microsoft Office.

Sincerely,

Eric Simon

FIGURE 13 *My Computer (exercise 1)*

2. Windows Explorer: Prove to your instructor that you have completed the fourth hands-on exercise by creating a document similar to the one in Figure 14. Use the technique described in the previous problem to capture the screen and paste it into a Word document.

Compare the documents in Figures 13 and 14 that show My Computer and Windows Explorer, respectively. My Computer is intuitive and preferred by beginners, but it is very limited when compared to Windows Explorer. The latter displays a hierarchical view of your system, showing the selected object in the left pane and the contents of the selected object in the right pane. We urge you, therefore, to become comfortable with Windows Explorer, as that will make you more productive.

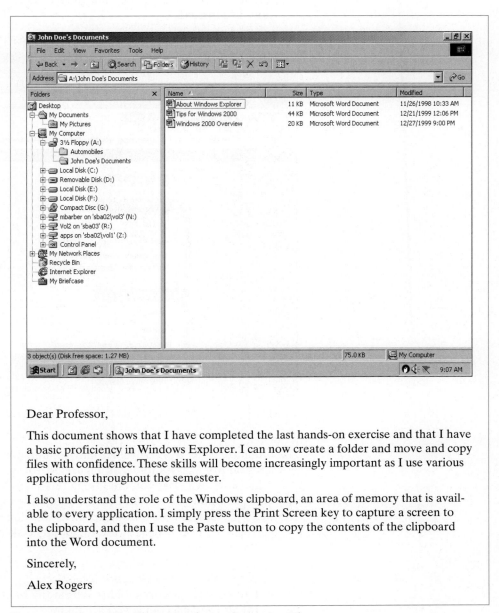

Dear Professor,

This document shows that I have completed the last hands-on exercise and that I have a basic proficiency in Windows Explorer. I can now create a folder and move and copy files with confidence. These skills will become increasingly important as I use various applications throughout the semester.

I also understand the role of the Windows clipboard, an area of memory that is available to every application. I simply press the Print Screen key to capture a screen to the clipboard, and then I use the Paste button to copy the contents of the clipboard into the Word document.

Sincerely,

Alex Rogers

FIGURE 14   *Windows Explorer (exercise 2)*

3. MyPHLIP Web Site: Every text in the *Exploring Office XP* series has a corresponding MyPHLIP (Prentice Hall Learning on the Internet Partnership) Web site, where you will find a variety of student resources as well as online review questions for each chapter. Go to www.prenhall.com/myphlip and follow the instructions. The first time at the site you will be prompted to register by supplying your e-mail address and choosing a password. Next, you choose the discipline (CIS/MIS) and a book (e.g., *Exploring Microsoft Office XP, Volume I*), which in turn will take you to a page similar to Figure 15.

Your professor will tell you whether he or she has created an online syllabus, in which case you should click the link to find your professor after adding the book. Either way, the next time you return to the site, you will be taken directly to your text. Select any chapter, click "Go", then use the review questions as directed.

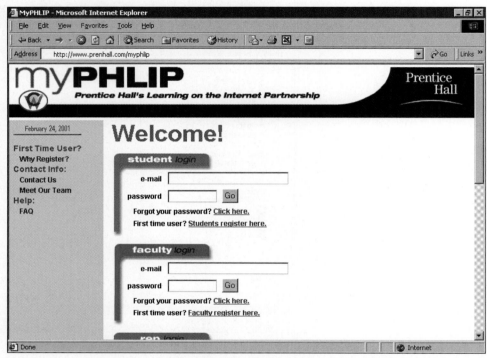

FIGURE 15 *MyPHLIP Web Site (Windows module) (exercise 3)*

4. Organize Your Work: A folder may contain documents, programs, or other folders. The My Classes folder in Figure 16, for example, contains five folders, one folder for each class you are taking this semester. Folders help you to organize your files, and you should become proficient in their use. The best way to practice with folders is on a floppy disk, as was done in Figure 16. Accordingly:
   a. Format a floppy disk or use the floppy disk you have been using throughout the chapter.
   b. Create a Correspondence folder. Create a Business and a Personal folder within the Correspondence folder.
   c. Create a My Courses folder. Within the My Courses folder create a separate folder for each course you are taking.
   d. Use the technique described in problems 1 and 2 to capture the screen in Figure 16 and incorporate it into a document. Add a short paragraph that describes the folders you have created, then submit the document.

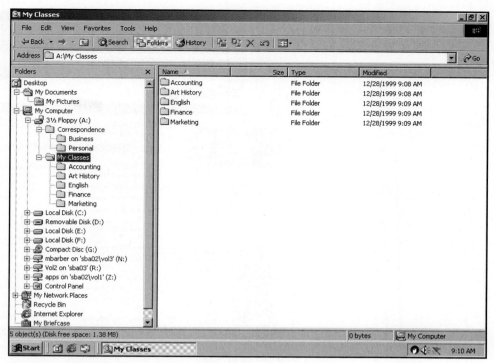

FIGURE 16 *Organize Your Work (exercise 4)*

5. The Windows Web Site: The Web is the best source for information on any application. Go to the Windows home page (www.microsoft.com/windows) as shown in Figure 17, then write a short note to your instructor summarizing the contents of that page and the associated links. Similar pages exist for all Microsoft applications such as www.microsoft.com/office for Microsoft Office.

6. Implement a Screen Saver: A screen saver is a delightful way to personalize your computer and a good way to practice with Microsoft Windows. This is typically not something you can do in a laboratory setting, but it is well worth doing on your own machine. Point to a blank area of the desktop, click the right mouse button to display a context-sensitive menu, then click the Properties command to open the Display Properties dialog box in Figure 18. Click the Screen Saver tab, click the Down arrow in the Screen Saver list box, and select Marquee Display. Click the Settings command button, enter the text and other options for your message, then click OK to close the Options dialog box. Click OK a second time to close the Display Properties dialog box.

7. The Active Desktop: The Active Desktop displays Web content directly on the desktop, then updates the information automatically according to a predefined schedule. You can, for example, display a stock ticker or scoreboard similar to what you see on television. You will need your own machine and an Internet connection to do this exercise, as it is unlikely that the network administrator will let you modify the desktop:
   a. Right click the Windows desktop, click Properties to show the Display Properties dialog box, then click the Web tab. Check the box to show Web content on the Active desktop.
   b. Click the New button, then click the Visit Gallery command button to go to the Active Desktop Gallery in Figure 19 on page 59. Choose any category, then follow the onscreen instructions to display the item on your desktop. We suggest you start with the stock ticker or sports scoreboard.
   c. Summarize your opinion of the active desktop in a short note to your instructor. Did the feature work as advertised? Is the information useful to you?

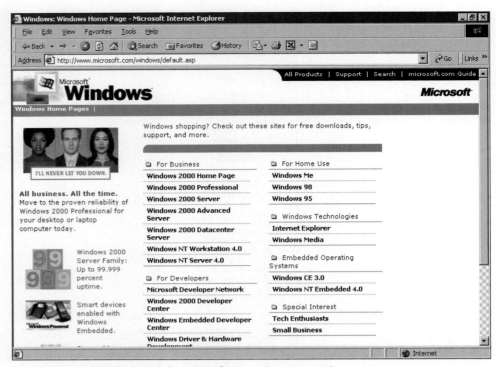

FIGURE 17   *The Windows Web Site (exercise 5)*

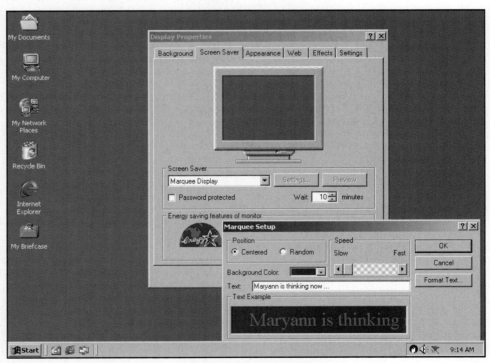

FIGURE 18   *Implement a Screen Saver (exercise 6)*

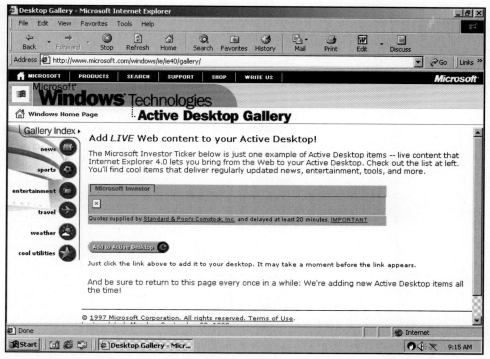

FIGURE 19 *The Active Desktop (exercise 7)*

8. The Control Panel: The Control Panel enables you to change the hardware or software settings on your system. You will not have access to the Control Panel in a lab environment, but you will need it at home if you change your configuration, perhaps by installing a new program. Click the Start button, click Settings, then select Control Panel to display the Control Panel window. Click the down arrow on the Views button to change to the Details view as shown in Figure 20. (The Control Panel can also be opened from My Computer.)

   Write a short report (two or three paragraphs is sufficient) that describes some of the capabilities within Control Panel. *Be careful about making changes, however, and be sure you understand the nature of the new settings before you accept any of the changes.*

9. Users and Passwords: Windows 2000 enables multiple users to log onto the same machine, each with his or her own user name and password. The desktop settings for each user are stored individually, so that all users have their own desktop. The administrator and default user is created when Windows 2000 is first installed, but new users can be added or removed at any time. Once again you will need your own machine:

   a. Click the Start button, click Settings, then click Control Panel to open the Control Panel window as shown in Figure 21. The Control Panel is a special folder that allows you to modify the hardware and/or software settings on your computer.

   b. Double click the Users and Passwords icon to display the dialog box in Figure 20. *Be very careful about removing a user or changing a password, because you might inadvertently deny yourself access to your computer.*

   c. Summarize the capabilities within the users and passwords dialog box in a short note to your instructor. Can you see how these principles apply to the network you use at school or work?

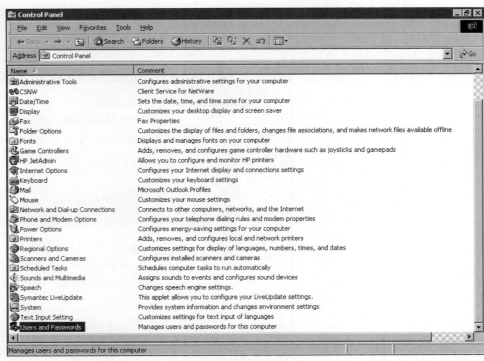

FIGURE 20 *The Control Panel (exercise 8)*

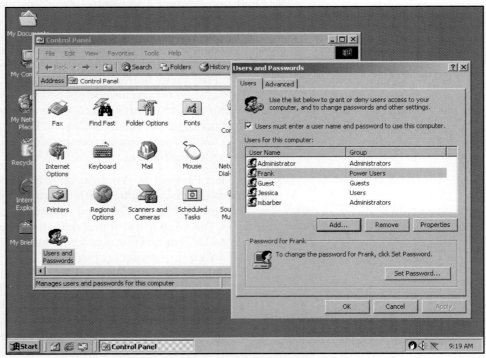

FIGURE 21 *Users and Passwords (exercise 9)*

10. The Fonts Folder: The Fonts folder within the Control Panel displays the names of the fonts available on a system and enables you to obtain a printed sample of any specific font. Click the Start button, click (or point to) the Settings command, click (or point to) Control Panel, then double click the Fonts icon to open the Fonts folder and display the fonts on your system.

   a. Double click any font to open a Fonts window as shown in Figure 22, then click the Print button to print a sample of the selected font.

   b. Open a different font. Print a sample page of this font as well.

   c. Locate the Wingdings font and print this page. Do you see any symbols you recognize? How do you insert these symbols into a document?

   d. How many fonts are there in your fonts Folder? Do some fonts appear to be redundant with others? How much storage space does a typical font require? Write the answers to these questions in a short paragraph.

   e. Start Word. Create a title page containing your name, class, date, and the title of this assignment (My Favorite Fonts). Center the title. Use boldface or italics as you see fit. Be sure to use a suitable type size.

   f. Staple the various pages together (the title page, the three font samples, and the answers to the questions in part d). Submit the assignment to your instructor.

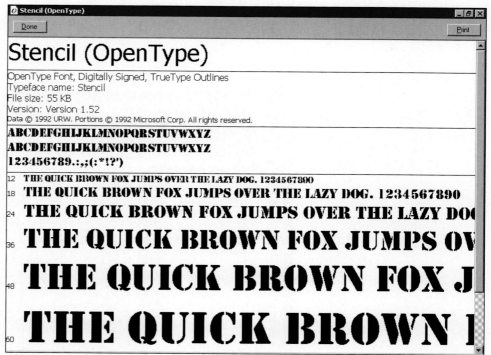

FIGURE 22   *The Fonts Folder (exercise 10)*

11. Keyboard Shortcuts: Microsoft Windows is a graphical user interface in which users "point and click" to execute commands. As you gain proficiency, however, you will find yourself gravitating toward various keyboard shortcuts as shown in Figures 23a and 23b. There is absolutely no need to memorize these shortcuts, nor should you even try. A few, however, have special appeal and everyone has his or her favorite. Use the Help menu to display this information, pick your three favorite shortcuts, and submit them to your instructor. Compare your selections with those of your classmates.

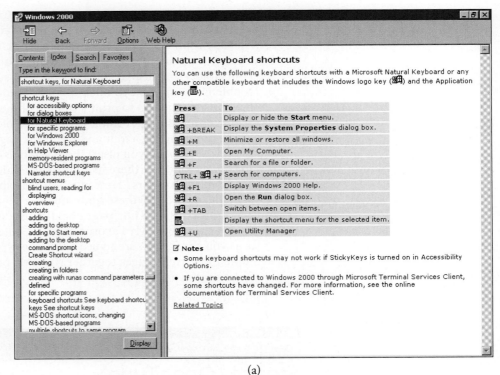

(a)

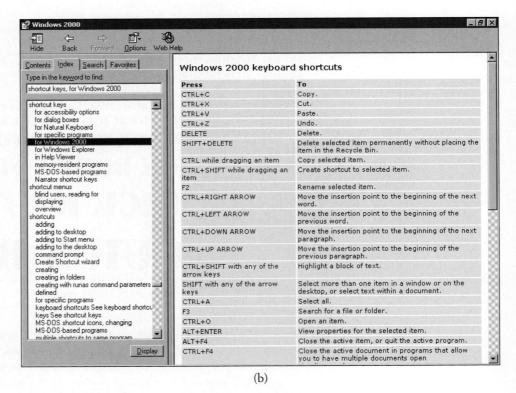

(b)

FIGURE 23   *Shortcut Keys for Natural Keyboard (Exercise 11)*

Planning for Disaster

Do you have a backup strategy? Do you even know what a backup strategy is? You had better learn, because sooner or later you will wish you had one. You will erase a file, be unable to read from a floppy disk, or worse yet suffer a hardware failure in which you are unable to access the hard drive. The problem always seems to occur the night before an assignment is due. The ultimate disaster is the disappearance of your computer, by theft or natural disaster. Describe, in 250 words or less, the backup strategy you plan to implement in conjunction with your work in this class.

Your First Consultant's Job

Go to a real installation such as a doctor's or attorney's office, the company where you work, or the computer lab at school. Determine the backup procedures that are in effect, then write a one-page report indicating whether the policy is adequate and, if necessary, offering suggestions for improvement. Your report should be addressed to the individual in charge of the business, and it should cover all aspects of the backup strategy; that is, which files are backed up and how often, and what software is used for the backup operation. Use appropriate emphasis (for example, bold italics) to identify any potential problems. This is a professional document (it is your first consultant's job), and its appearance should be perfect in every way.

File Compression

You've learned your lesson and have come to appreciate the importance of backing up all of your data files. The problem is that you work with large documents that exceed the 1.44MB capacity of a floppy disk. Accordingly, you might want to consider the acquisition of a file compression program to facilitate copying large documents to a floppy disk in order to transport your documents to and from school, home, or work. (A Zip file is different from a Zip drive. The latter is a hardware device, similar in concept to a large floppy disk, with a capacity of 100MB or 250MB.)

You can download an evaluation copy of the popular WinZip program at www.winzip.com. Investigate the subject of file compression and submit a summary of your findings to your instructor.

The Threat of Virus Infection

A computer virus is an actively infectious program that attaches itself to other programs and alters the way a computer works. Some viruses do nothing more than display an annoying message at an inopportune time. Most, however, are more harmful, and in the worst case, erase all files on the disk. Use your favorite search engine to research the subject of computer viruses in order to answer the following questions. When is a computer subject to infection by a virus? What precautions does your school or university take against the threat of virus infection in its computer lab? What precautions, if any, do you take at home? Can you feel confident that your machine will not be infected if you faithfully use a state-of-the-art antivirus program that was purchased in January 2001?

The Briefcase

It is becoming increasingly common for people to work on more than one machine. Students, for example, may alternate between machines at school and home. In similar fashion, an office worker may use a desktop and a laptop, or have a machine at work and at home. In every instance, you need to transfer files back and forth between the two machines. This can be done using the Copy command from within Windows Explorer. It can also be done via the Briefcase folder. Your instructor has asked you to look into the latter capability and to prepare a brief report describing its use. Do you recommend the Briefcase over a simple Copy command?

Cut, Copy, and Paste

The Cut, Copy, and Paste commands are used in conjunction with one another to move and copy data within a document, or from one Windows document to another. The commands can also be executed from within My Computer or Windows Explorer to move and copy files. You can use the standard Windows shortcuts of Ctrl+X, Ctrl+C, and Ctrl+V to cut, copy, and paste, respectively. You can also click the corresponding icons on the Standard Buttons toolbar within Windows Explorer or My Computer.

Experiment with this technique, then write a short note to your instructor that summarizes the various ways in which files can be moved or copied within Windows 2000.

Register Now

It is good practice to register every program you purchase, so that the vendor can notify you of new releases and/or other pertinent information. Windows provides an online capability whereby you can register via modem. To register your copy of Windows, click the Start button, click Programs, click Accessories, click Welcome to Windows, then click the Registration Wizard. Follow the directions that are displayed on the screen. (Registering a program does carry the risk of having unwanted sales messages sent to you by e-mail. At the Web site, look for a check box in which you choose whether to receive unsolicited e-mail.) You can do this exercise only if you are working on your own computer.

INDEX